Best Practices in Youth Development in Public Park and Recreation Settings

Peter A. Witt
John L. Crompton
Texas A&M University

Published by: Division of Professional Services
National Recreation and Park Association

National Recreation and Park Association

The National Recreation and Park Association is a national 501 (c)(3) organization engaged in education, training, research, technical assistance and public policy analysis — all designed to enhance recreation and park experiences for all people. Association headquarters are 22377 Belmont Ridge Road, Ashburn, VA 20148-4501, (703) 858-0784.

About Authors

Peter A. Witt is the holder of the Elda K. Bradberry Recreation and Youth Development Chair and John Crompton is a Distinguished Professor with the Department of Recreation, Park and Tourism, Texas A&M University.

Acknowledgements

Funding to support development of this book was obtained through a grant to NRPA from the National Recreation Foundation. An endowment at Texas A&M established by the Sequor Foundation also helped support development of the case studies.

ISBN 0-929581-56-3

TABLE OF CONTENTS

Best Practices in Youth Development in Public Park and Recreation Settings

PREFACE

This book is the most recent manifestation of the authors' decade long involvement with NRPA's initiative in youth development. Two major grants from NRPA, with funds provided by the National Recreation Foundation, were used to develop a number of evaluation tools for measuring the impact of recreation programs on youth.[1]

The second of these grants involved developing a consortium of 8 universities and 15 cities which cooperated in a series of studies that reported results from different types of evaluations undertaken in a variety of contexts.[1] The empirical evaluation work reported in these studies was a beginning "to scientifically demonstrate positive outcomes associated with providing recreation programs for at-risk youth" (p 8). The studies represented a coherent effort to move the field beyond simply counting the number of participants, collecting testimonials and anecdotal evidence, or relying on post-program participant satisfaction studies.

In February 1995, the authors coordinated the organization of a Colloquium held in Fort Worth, Texas, "*The Challenge of Shaping the Future: Recreation Programs that Work for At-Risk Youth.*" Sponsors of the Colloquium were the American Academy of Park and Recreation Administration; the National Recreation and Park Association; the Department of Recreation, Park and Tourism Sciences at Texas A&M University; and the Fort Worth Parks and Community Services Department. In the following year, a series of nine regional colloquia were held around North America to disseminate and enhance the information emerging from the National Colloquium.

In 1996, the authors edited a series of case studies describing best practices that emerged from these colloquia. Two versions of the case studies were published. NRPA published executive summaries of 21 of them in a volume titled "Public Recreation in High Risk Environments: Programs that Work".[2] An extended exposition of those cases, together with additional cases, was also published. The expanded version contained a total of 38 cases and was entitled *Programs That work for At-Risk Youth: The Challenge of Shaping the Future.*[3]

The level of support and enthusiasm emanating from these colloquia and the publications emerging from them led the authors to coordinate with NRPA the development of an annual *National Prevention Through Recreation Services School.* Their leadership in this School continued through its first five years from 1998-2002. During this period the School was jointly organized by NRPA, the Department of Recreation, Park and Tourism Sciences at Texas A&M, and the Park and Recreation Department (PARD) agency in the host city in which it was held–either Fort Worth, Phoenix or Austin. Over 1,000 individuals attended the colloquia and the schools. Presentations and informal interactions at these annual gatherings enabled participants to keep abreast of emerging developments in this area of the recreation field.

Most of the 16 case studies included in this text had their genesis in presentations and discussions at the *National Prevention Through Recreation Services School*. The remaining cases were selected by the authors based on responses to an e-mail invitation to PARDs subscribing to NRPAnet to send us materials describing innovative youth development programs for which they were responsible.

The authors developed drafts of the cases and then sent them back for agency managers to review; to provide additional information; and to verify the accuracy of the information. The enthusiasm and support of these managers for this project was central to our ability to bring it to fruition. Thus, we sincerely thank the following PARD managers for their assistance and support:

Kathy Nelson, Aurora, Colorado

Wayne Yee, Richmond, British Columbia

Chuck Wilt, Columbus, Indiana

Manny Tarango, Phoenix, Arizona

Jeff Bass, Virginia Beach, Virginia

Jim Stamborski, North Miami, Florida

Maria Cicciarelli & Carlos Pineda, Austin, Texas

Sheila Russell, Kettering, Ohio

Janice Miller & Barbara Readnower, Chattanooga, Tennessee

Mark Deven, Concord, California

Lyn Kinton & Laura Lizcano-Ortiz, San Antonio, Texas

Lisa Thomas Turpel & Charles Jordan, Portland, Oregon

Nick Duray, Fairfax County, Virginia

Kelli Beavers, Arlington County, Virginia

This NRPA publication is intended to support two of the Association's central initiatives. First, disseminating information about best practices is a key objective of NRPA's *Youth Initiative* whose mission is to extend to the NRPA membership the tools needed to provide positive recreation opportunities to youth, and reinforce their development educationally, culturally, socially and athletically.

Second, NRPA is committed to documenting the knowledge base pertaining to the social and economic contributions made by PARDs to the general commonweal as part of the Association's *Discover the Benefits* mission. To justify existing budgets and the allocation of additional resources, elected officials and the taxpayers they represent, have to be convinced that PARD's deliver collective or "public" benefits. These are defined as benefits that accrue to most people in a community, even though they do not participate in an agency's programs or use its facilities. Youth development, and the alleviation of societal problems created by youth, constitute one of those "public" benefits. Several of the cases in this book offer evidence that can be used by PARD managers to help their elected officials and taxpayers *Discover the Benefits.*

This publication was commissioned by NRPA with funding provided by the National Recreation Foundation. The authors are appreciative of the support from those two organizations especially that given by Dean Tice and Destry Jarvis, the former and current Executive Directors of NRPA; John Webster and Sonia Amir, the former and current leaders of the Urban Youth Initiative; and Reco Bembry of Bembry Consultants who is NRPA's special adviser on the Youth Initiative. The authors also proffer their thanks to Ms. Marguerite Van Dyke in the Department of Recreation, Park and Tourism Sciences at Texas A&M who typed the manuscript drafts of this publication.

Sources:

1. Witt, P.A. & Crompton, J.L. (1996a) *The at-risk youth recreation project. Journal of Park and Recreation Administration* 14(3), 1-9.
2. Witt, P.A. & Crompton, J.L.(1996b) (Editors) *Public recreation in high risk environments. Programs that work.* Arlington, Virginia: National Recreation and Park Association.
3. Witt, P.A. & Crompton, J.L. (1996c) (Editors) *Recreation programs that work for at-risk youth: The challenge of shaping the future.* State College, PA., Venture Publishing.

CHAPTER 1

ORGANIZATION OF THE BOOK

Problems created by youth dropping out of school, using drugs or alcohol, joining gangs, becoming teenage parents, and being involved in anti-social and delinquent acts were widely recognized by the early 1990s. In more recent years, children's educational attainment as measured by their success on state-wide annual achievement tests, also has emerged as a prominent community concern. These concerns led to pressure on the political system to "do something about youth." As a result, a variety of agencies- -educational, social service, law enforcement, recreational, and health- -have responded with youth development programs.

Dealing with these problems offers an opportunity for PARDs to position themselves so they are perceived to be alleviating a problem which is a prevailing political concern of both the public and those policy makers who are responsible for allocating tax funds.[1] The field has a distinguished heritage in this arena. Indeed, public recreation services emerged in response to negative social conditions in major cities. There was a humanistic concern for the welfare of those who found themselves with few resources, places to recreate, and/or skills to undertake recreational activities. Comments made by Jane Addams in 1893 are reminiscent of those made by commentators today:

> *The social organism has broken down through large districts of our great cities. Many of the people living there are very poor, the majority of them without leisure or energy for anything but the gain of subsistence. They move often from one wretched lodging to another. They live for the moment side-by-side, many of them without knowledge of each other, without fellowship, without local tradition or public spirit, without social organization of any kind. Practically nothing is done to remedy this. The people who might do it, who have the social tact and training, the large houses, and the traditions and custom of hospitality, live in other parts of the city. The clubhouses, libraries, galleries, and semipublic conveniences for social life are also blocks away. (p. 4)*[2]

In response to this situation, Addams established Hull House, a settlement house in Chicago, which was in many respects the precursor of the modern recreation center.

Thus, a primary cornerstone upon which public recreation services were founded was the belief that recreation can make a substantive contribution to alleviating the impact of non-productive, personally destructive, and/or anti-social actions by youth.[3] There was no equivocation among early commentators about the "rightness" of providing recreation for this instrumental purpose! These sentiments were especially pervasive in the field's formative years in the first three decades of the 20th century and a sample of them is given in Exhibit 1-1.

Exhibit 1-1

The Role of Recreation in Alleviating Anti-Social Behavior Among Youth: Voices from our Past

The most satisfactory result in establishing public playgrounds has been the decrease of juvenile crime, which is said to be almost 50 percent........For that reason, more public playgrounds should be opened, especially in the congested districts of large cities....It is on the playground that character is formed which is afterward brought into "practical play" by our leaders in thought and action. Every variety of psychological study is open to the resourceful and tactful teacher in the advantages offered by the public playground. (Extracts from a letter by H. Roosevelt Ostrom published in the *New York Times*, June 14, 1902).

Supervised playgrounds, parks, amusements, manual labor classes and boys' clubs have in five years reduced juvenile crime and delinquency 96 per cent in the industrial center of Binghamton in New York State, according to figures recently compiled by the Broome County Humane Society and Relief Association. (William I. Engle (1919). Supervised Amusement Cuts Juvenile Crime by 96 Per Cent. *The American City* 21(6): 515-17.)

Crime Statistics Show Most Offenders Are Under 21 Years and the Figures Drop Whenever Recreation is Provided (New York Times, November 26, 1922.) (The following four paragraphs are extracted from this article).

In his report to the Russell Sage Foundation, Allen T. Burns says, "To provide a probation district with adequate play facilities is coincident with a reduction in delinquency of from 28 percent to 70 percent, or 44 percent as an average."

L.H. Weir, Chief Probation Officer of Cincinnati says: "In 1906 there were 1,748 children legally before the Juvenile Court and 410 were handled unofficially making a total of 2,158 children. Of these, 1,450 were delinquents. In the Fall of that year a beginning was made in opening playgrounds in the down-town portions of the city. In the year just closed there were 993 delinquent children before the court. Each year has noted a marked decrease. While some of the decrease may be due to other causes, the work of the courts for instance, we are perfectly sure that one of the main factors has been the opportunity afforded the thousands of children in the most congested district of the city to play in a natural and spontaneous manner."

Edward C. Hill, President of the Trenton Playground Commission says: "Playgrounds were established in Trenton, N.J., as a municipal undertaking about the middle of 1906. The police records show a decrease of 28 per cent in the number of arrests of boys, while the arrest of men 20 years of age and upward shows an increase of 10 per cent. It is fair to assume that if there had been no playground supervision, the arrests of boys would have shown an increase corresponding to the increase in the arrest of the men."

Mr. Loman, the Special Superintendent of Delinquents in Dallas, Texas, says that the result of establishing Trinity Play Park there has been that the number of juvenile offenders in the cotton mill district has been reduced more than 80 percent during the last year, although the number of children has increased 9 percent.

We find New Orleans today with 13 playgrounds, showing less juvenile delinquency than in 1909, although the city has increased in population over 60,000 in this period. (Playgrounds Cause Child Crime Wane, *New Orleans Item*, New Orleans, LA, February, 4, 1923.)

From Bluefield, West Virginia, which used to send, on an average, approximately 50 boys a year to the state reformatory, came a report that during the last three years, when the city has had under competent direction playgrounds and a boys' club, only two cases have been given over to the reformatory. (Supervised Play Cuts Delinquency, *Christian Science Monitor*, April 17, 1924.)

Exhibit 1-1 Continued

Chief of Police Conlon of Leominster, Mass., says that delinquency cases in Leominster averaged ninety-one a year prior to the organization of Community Service, the local recreation agency. Since its coming, the number decreased to fifty-three in 1923. (Money is Sent for Kiddies' Play, Des Moines, Iowa, *Capital.* April 17, 1924.)

In the communities where there are playgrounds, where healthful sports are encouraged, the morality of boys is high. Not a boy was taken into the juvenile court this year from the neighborhood where there is a playground. (Finds Investment in Youth Pays the Community Well, Prince Albert, Saskatchewan, *Daily Herald,*February 6, 1925.)

Positioning or aligning an agency so it contributes to youth development requires shifting from a "fun and games" orientation that seeks to encourage participation in recreation for its own sake, to a problem-solving orientation requiring that programs contribute to ameliorating what society perceives to be youth problems. Too many community youth programs are limited to "gym and swim" opportunities loosely organized around sports or arts activities, which are intended primarily to "keep youth safe and off the streets."[4] If PARDs elect to go beyond this traditional role and to reposition their youth services by designing them so they contribute to youth development, then they are likely to be viewed more positively by taxpayers and decision-makers as part of the solution to a community's problems.

Substantial progress in repositioning youth services has been made in the past decade. In the early 1990s, some prominent political figures spoke scornfully and derisively of "Midnight Basketball" and similar programs, dismissing them as "wasteful social spending" and "pork." A decade later such comments are no longer heard, which is indicative of a general widespread acceptance of the potential benefits that can emanate from youth programs.

A major shift in the approach to delivering youth services since an earlier volume of cases on this theme was published[5] has been the evolution of rich conceptual underpinnings and frameworks which provide meaningful guidelines for program development. Cases illustrating how these frameworks are being used are grouped in Section 1 which is entitled **Foundational Models.** In contrast to earlier approaches which focused on inputs and/or outputs, these models emphasize the importance of outcomes. In a seminal paper published almost three decades ago Gray and Greben stated: "We should have discovered long ago the nature of the business we are in, but we have not....In the emerging view it is not activities, or facilities, or programs that are central; it is what happens to people" (p. 28). They went on to say: "We must evaluate everything we do in human terms. The critical questions are not, How many were there? Or who won? The critical question is, What happened to Jose, Mary, Sam, and Joan in this experience?" (p. 30).[6]

The Foundational Models that have emerged in recent years embrace Gray and Greben's credo. Two models are pre-eminent. First is the Developmental Assets Model which was created by the Search Institute.[7] It consists of 40 developmental assets that are posited to be important building blocks for helping youth succeed and thrive. The second widely used conceptual framework is the

Protective Factors/Resilience Model.[8] This model was derived from the observation that some youth who are exposed to multiple risk environments avoid the deviant behaviors exhibited by peers who also reside there. Protective factors are those which impinge on an individual's life space and moderate and/or mitigate the impact of risk on subsequent behavior and development. Both of these models identify an array of potential desirable outcomes. The challenge for managers is to select those outcomes that they perceive to be of most value to their targeted groups, and to design and structure youth programs in such a way that there is a high probability the selected desired outcomes will emerge.

A third Foundational Model included in Section 1 is the Youth Involved Process developed in Richmond, British Columbia. The case describes how an agency shifted from its traditional *modus operandi* of the staff being responsible for creating a program, to a revised mode where staff became facilitators and youth took central responsibility for programs. This revised approach places less emphasis on the activity and more on the process. The case describes how the process of having youth centrally involved in developing programs can be used to build desired Developmental Assets.

Section 2, **Creating Spaces and Outreach Programs**, is comprised of two case studies that describe the evolution of two different service delivery vehicles. In Columbus, Indiana, a new $5.9 million, 50,000 square foot youth center was constructed. The center has a wide array of amenities which make it an effective vehicle for delivering services. Its distinctive feature is the multiple partnerships involved both in raising the initial capital funds and in operating the center and delivering services from it. It is illustrative of what can be achieved in a relatively small community (38,000) when a broad powerful vision is supported by inter-organizational trust and a willingness by all partners to forego parochial interests that might impede implementation of the vision.

The use of Roving Leaders can be traced back to the mid-19th century when churchmen and charity workers sought out young delinquents and gangs in the slum areas of American cities. The case presented here offers two contemporary examples of outreach programs operated by PARDs in Austin and San Antonio. The potential and accomplishments of Roving Leader programs are described, together with the challenges of sustaining them over the long term.

Section 3 reports on the **Comprehensive Programs** developed in Phoenix and Virginia Beach. The Phoenix Parks, Recreation and Library Department has been a beacon to which other agencies in this field have long looked for leadership and ideas. The 20 year evolution of the Department's philosophy and organizational response to the challenges of youth development are described, together with a review of a dozen of their most innovative programs.

The focus of Virginia Beach on youth development is more recent. Particular care was taken to identify neighborhoods with the greatest need for prevention programs, so there would be maximum efficacy in the use of the PARD's very limited resources. Despite its relative newness, the PARD's P.L.A.Y. (Promoting Leisure Activities for Youth) unit has developed an impressive range of innovative programs.

Imagination and careful design are characteristics exemplified in the dozen programs described in this case.

The four **Specific Programs** that comprise Section 4 are unusually innovative. Traditionally, PARDs have viewed volunteers as an external resource that enables them to extend, supplement, and enhance their range of services. North Miami's Teens In Action demonstrates that volunteering should also be viewed as a recreation program the PARD offers, since benefits youth receive from it closely resemble those they may receive from traditional programs- -facilitating social interaction; enhancing status in the community, personal growth and self-image; and encouraging tolerance of cultural diversity. This case illustrates how programs can effectively be initiated in multi-racial low-income communities even when only minimal resources are available.

Totally Cool, Totally Art is NRPA's first nationally branded youth development program. The NRPA distributes it to other PARDs and the comprehensive package includes program and staff manuals, publicity materials, powerpoint presentations and evaluation instruments. Six separate four-week sessions are delivered at each of fourteen centers in Austin. They are conducted by artists who have a passion for the art medium they teach. The program is guided by the Protective Factors Model and the creative process is designed to foster participants' creative, self-esteem, and respect for others.

The Kettering S.T.A.N.D. (Students Taking a New Direction) case describes the formative years of the evolution of a youth council, and compares it with a more mature youth council in another community that Kettering aspires to emulate over time.

The Chattanooga/Hamilton County Youth Council (CHYC) was centrally involved in developing Project Choices. This was designed to help the community resolve problems created by large numbers of unsupervised teens congregating on Friday and Saturday nights in Hamilton Place Mall which is the largest mall in Tennessee. Project Choices' goal was to provide alternatives where teens could hang-out with their peers, participate in positive activities, and meet new people.

The final section of the book describes **After-School and Summer Programs** offered in four communities. The Time for Kids Initiative in Portland, Oregon, describes how the Portland PARD partnered with a large number of other organizations in the community to facilitate and coordinate overall service delivery in two of the city's underserved areas. Both areas contained large numbers of ethnic migrant families who had recently moved to the city. The Development Assets Model undergirded the program's mission and goals. The case describes the challenges associated with multi-partnering to achieve the desired ends, and examines the financial challenges inherent in offering outcome-driven youth development programs.

The Concord/Bay Point After-School program involved three lead collaborating agencies and an additional ten agencies that contributed resources and program elements to the effort. A distinctive feature of this program is the establishment of rigorous Performance Indicators, and the development of evaluation measures to report the extent to which the Indicators are achieved.

The San Antonio After-School program discusses issues involved in developing and maintaining a large-scale citywide, after-school program. The program operates on 251 elementary and middle school sites, which are under the jurisdiction of eight different independent school districts within the city of San Antonio. The city allocates $4.2 million from its General Fund to the program; the school districts contribute $1.75 million; USDA grants for food snacks approximate $500,000; and in-kind assistance from the partners is valued at approximately $750,000. Unlike so many after-school programs, the funds in San Antonio are on-going from the city and school districts' general funds and not heavily reliant on grants with a limited longevity.

The next case exemplifies the effectiveness of good evaluation in guiding the evolution and development of youth programs. Fairfax County, Virginia, operates a summer camp program which enrolls over 9,000 youth. It consists of over 100 different camp titles offered at 17 different park locations. The comprehensive evaluation procedures were started ten years ago when it was noted that the camps were failing to retain a large proportion of repeat participants. Continuous feedback from campers, their parents and staff has resulted in consistent improvements to the program and large increases in the number of participants.

The final case illustrates the potential of appropriately used incentives to encourage teen participation. Activities in Motion (AIM) is coordinated by the Arlington County Department of Parks, Recreation and Community Resources. Youth can earn points for their involvement and achievement in educational, leadership and cultural activities. The points are redeemable to reduce trip and activity fees.

Sources

1. Crompton, J. L. (1999). *Measuring the economic impact of visitors to sports tournaments, festivals, and special events.* Ashburn, Virginia: National Recreation and Park Association.
2. Addams, J. [1893] (1960). The subjective necessity for social settlements. In *Philanthropy and Social Progress* pp. 1-26. Freeport, NY: Books for Libraries Press.
3. Crompton, J. L. & Witt, P. A. (1999). Insights from our past. *Trends*, 35(4), 4-9.
4. McLaughlin, M. W. (2000). Community counts. How youth organizations matter for youth development. Available [*www.publiceducation.org/download/PEN23.pdf*] Public Education Network.
5. Witt, P.A. & Crompton, J. L. (1996). (Editors) *Recreation programs that work for at-risk youth: The challenge of shaping the future.* State College, PA: Venture Publishing.
6. Gray, D. E. & Greben, S. (1974). Future perspectives. *Parks and Recreation*, July pp. 26-33, 47-56.
7. Search Institute (1998). *Helping youth thrive: How youth organizations-can and do-build developmental assets.* Minneapolis, MN: Author.
8. Jessor, R. (1992). Risk behavior in adolescence: A psychological framework for understanding and action. In D.E. Rogers and E. Ginzberg (Eds.) *Adolescents at risk: Medical and social perspectives* (pp. 19-33). Boulder, CO: Westview Press.

CHAPTER 2

THEMES EMERGING FROM THE CASE STUDIES

The programs described in the case studies evolved in response to local community circumstances, and each was molded by constraints and opportunities afforded by local administrative practices. Nevertheless, a review of the case studies suggests that there is a reasonably generalizable pattern in the gestation and evolution of youth development services. The pattern is shown in Exhibit 2-1. It offers a framework for the discussion of common themes that emerged across the cases, almost irrespective of local circumstances, which constitutes the content of this chapter.

Exhibit 2-1

A Schemata of the Genesis and Evolution of Youth Development Programs

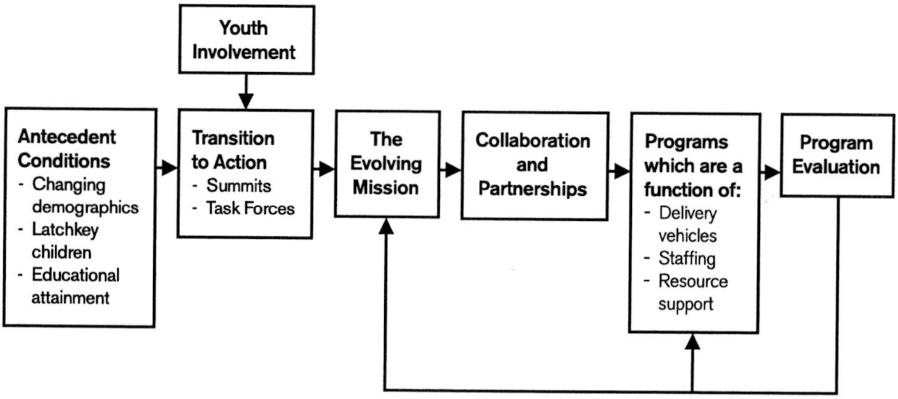

The primary antecedent conditions that move a community both to launch and update programs from inertia are: changing demographics, especially an influx of different ethnic groups; the prevalence of latchkey children; and desires to improve levels of educational attainment. When these antecedent conditions reach a threshold level, elected officials usually act.

Invariably, their initial action is to convene a summit or task force of prominent representatives from the key stakeholder groups to investigate the issues and offer recommendations. There is usually a recognition that youth need to be centrally involved in such forums because (i) without their involvement it is unlikely that youth will "buy-in" to whatever recommendations emerge; and (ii) few adults have a real understanding of what youth perceive to be their needs.

The task force's recommendations are likely to serve as a starting point for initiating programs. At the outset, these are frequently limited to "fun and games" activities designed to keep youth occupied. Over time, as stakeholders acquire a more sophisticated understanding of the goals of youth development, the mission often evolves to become more holistic and to focus on behavior change and desired outcomes.

As the mission evolves, so do both the magnitude of numbers the community seeks to involve and the breadth of programs, which frequently range beyond traditional recreation offerings. PARDs lack the knowledge, monetary, physical plant and personnel resources to meet these expanded expectations. Collaborations and partnerships are the only way to achieve the expanded mission, but PARDs frequently play a leadership role in negotiating and coordinating these partnership efforts.

The quality and quantity of youth development programs which emerge from the joint efforts of the PARD and its collaborators are a function of available delivery vehicles, staff, and resource support.

Evaluation measures assess the success of programs. Exhibit 2-1 shows two feedback loops from program evaluation. First, the success of specific programs is measured by comparing the evaluation results with the outcomes which the program was designed to produce. Second, the overall youth development effort is evaluated by comparing the aggregated outcomes from individual programs with the goals specified in the mission.

Antecedent Conditions

It was noted in chapter 1 that the roots of PARDs' involvement in youth development reside a century or more ago in the formative years of the field's evolution. However, the resurgence in PARDs' contemporary interest in youth services dates back to the late 1980s and early 1990s.[1] Four major stimuli were identified as being particularly prominent in the emergence of this heightened interest. They were: (i) changing demographics; (ii) emergence of negative youth behaviors in smaller communities; (iii) growth in number of latchkey children; and (iv) increased number of high-visibility violent incidents.

A decade later, points (ii) and (iv) of this list appear to be less prominent stimuli as the need for investment in youth development has attained the status of societal and political conventional wisdom. There is now widespread recognition that youth issues are generic across all types of jurisdictions, including smaller communities, and not merely confined to large cities. Similarly, acceptance of the benefits of investing in youth programs has permeated American society to the point that it no longer requires highly visible violent incidents to provoke political action.

However, by the end of the millennium a new stimulus had emerged to prominence- -a desire to increase the educational attainment of the nation's children. Hence, in this section we describe the three stimuli which at this time appear to be most influential in driving increasing amounts of public funding into youth development. They are (i) changing demographics; (ii) latchkey children; and (iii) emphasis on educational attainment.

Changing Demographics

The demographics of many major cities, particularly the inner-city areas, significantly changed during the 1980s and 1990s. The proportion of African Americans, Hispanics, and in some cities, immigrants, frequently increased substantially:

- In 1980 the population of North Miami was 92% white. In 2000, whites constituted 21% of the population while the Hispanic, African-American and Haitian groups comprised 26%, 25% and 21%, respectively.
- In Portland, Oregon, in the 1990s 60,000 Russians and East Europeans and large numbers of Latinos, who traditionally were not a major ethnic group in the city, moved primarily into the Southeast and North Portland areas of the city, respectively.
- Public school data in Virginia Beach showed that in 1991, 74% of students were Caucasian and 19% African American. By 2000, these ratios had changed to 64% and 27%, respectively.

Such extraordinarily rapid shifts in population profiles inevitably create tensions and challenges of assimilation within communities. These tensions added pressure to the insecurity, uncertainty and lack of self-confidence which are characteristic of many adolescents. Hence, there was a desire in some communities to take actions that would facilitate assimilation and enhance tolerance of cultural diversity, and there is an expectation that youth development programs will do this:

- In Richmond, British Columbia, one of the principles guiding formation of the city's youth developments strategy was "The societal pressures facing youth are more intense for recent immigrants." Access to services should take into account these pressures and efforts made to integrate new immigrants. Services and information directed at youth need to be easily accessible and understood by immigrants, particularly those who are new to Richmond.
- One of the four specific goals of the Roving Leader program in San Antonio was to "develop youths' self-esteem and the importance of respect for themselves and others, regardless of neighborhood, skin color, or belonging to a particular group or organization."
- The guiding vision of Portland's Recreation Division is, "We create recreation opportunities that can change people's lives and bring the community together." After-school programs targeted at the economically disadvantaged are perceived to be an operationalization of this vision.
- In North Miami, a primary goal of the Teens in Action program was "to provide a safe place where cultural diversity is respected and encouraged."

The situation is exacerbated by the high rates of unemployment among young people and the relatively large number of families living below the poverty level which often prevail in large cities. During the late 1980s and early 1990s, many cities reported substantial increases in drug use among youth and violent crime committed by and to youth; accelerated school dropout rates, not only amongst high school students, but also among middle school students; and rates of teen pregnancy increased. While declines in these negative trends occurred by the end of the millennium, rates were still unacceptably high. Local residents and political leaders look to youth development programs to be at least part of the solution to these societal problems.

Growth in the Number of Latchkey Children

Problems associated with a lack of adult supervision at home are pervasive across communities because of the number of two wage-earner families and the number of single-parent households. If these children are not directed into constructive activities outside the home, then when they return home from school they are likely either to spend their time watching television or playing video games, or be out on the streets where they may be susceptible to peer pressure to engage in inappropriate or negative activities.

The major changes in federal welfare policy enacted in 1996 required those on welfare to be out of the house "doing something" for at least 30 hours per week. This has contributed to 79% of women with school-age children now being in the workforce, as are 57% of women with infants. This is a transformation from the prevailing culture of a couple of decades ago in which the norm embraced by society was that mothers should stay at home with their children.[2] A consequence has been a burgeoning need for local governments to provide affordable after-school and vacation care for children whose parents are working. Thus, there has been a groundswell among PARDs in the number of after-school and summer camp programs they now offer in response to the need for affordable, supervised out-of-school programs for children. The federal government recognized that many local jurisdictions lack the financial resources to provide such care and responded by enacting the 21st Century After-School Community Learning Centers Fund. Appropriations for this fund increased from $40 million in 1998 to $900 million in 2001:

- San Antonio City Council's goal is to ensure that an after-school program is available at every elementary and middle school in the city. Approximately 27,000 students currently are registered in the program, with an average of 17,000 attending daily, an average of 114 participants per site. One of the goals of the San Antonio program is "to enhance social skills by encouraging children to interact with their peers rather than going home to an empty house."

Emphasis on Educational Attainment

In the 1990s, many states established mandatory standardized tests designed to assess students' abilities in the basic subjects. These legislative initiatives were intended to make schools more accountable for the tax resources invested in them. Results are extensively publicized and debated in the media so educators and education policy makers come under considerable public pressure to demonstrate improvements. While the primary focus is on improving the quality of education within the school day, there has been growing recognition that organizing educational enrichment activities after school can meaningfully contribute to this goal:

- Three of the five goals of the Concord/Bay Point After-School Learning program are:
  - (i) Participating students will increase their reading, writing and math skills to levels consistent with national and district averages.
  - (ii) Participating students will develop critical thinking skills and participate in enriched learning experiences.
  - (iii) The centers will become the focus of community learning and related adult and family services activities for the surrounding communities.
- One of the three goals of San Antonio's after-school program is: "to improve grades through tutoring and enrichment activities."
- In Portland, "the primary goal of The Time For Kids Initiative was to improve academic performance."

Transition to Action: Summits and Task Forces

When community pressures on political leaders "to do something about youth" require them to act, that "something" often is the convening of a youth summit or task force. The typical charge to these forums is to solicit broad community input to (i) identify all dimensions of the problem; (ii) recommend actions to alleviate the problem; and (iii) coordinate and mobilize community resources so the recommendations can be expedited. The case studies suggest that these vehicles have been effective in transitioning communities from the problem identification stage, to creating and organizing institutional entities which implement programs designed to ameliorate the problems:

- In the early 1990s the Mayor's Office in Phoenix, Arizona, sponsored a Summit on Youth, entitled Youth Empowerment in Action. The summit enhanced awareness of the need for comprehensive youth programming and services, and provided momentum for further action. Several city staff committees were formed to discuss youth services in response to the summit's recommendations. Phoenix Parks, Recreation and Library Department convened an internal 29 member Youth-At-Risk Task Force to develop program priorities. Ultimately, this led to creation of the At-Risk Youth Division within the Department and greater involvement of youth in the development of youth programs.
- The Healthy Youth Task Force formed jointly by the City Council and School Board in Kettering furthered its agenda by convening three youth summits comprised of community and student leaders. The summit process resulted in creation of a student youth council and the hiring of a Youth Development Coordinator. They were responsible for identifying youth needs and formulating responses to address them.
- A task force drawn from youth service agencies and city departments in Richmond, British Columbia, was the spark plug which led to the City Council approving a City Strategy for Youth Services. Adoption of that

strategy caused the Richmond Parks, Recreation and Cultural Services Department to formulate its Youth Involved Process which transformed the philosophy and process of delivering youth services in the community.

- The youth summit in Chattanooga and its follow-up agenda were vehicles through which youth and adults developed a set of recommendations and actions to implement them, together with a Charter of Teen Principles.

Youth Involvement

A prerequisite of youth programs being able to deliver the instrumental outcomes that communities seek is that they are sufficiently interesting to young people that they will participate. After joining a recreation program, a former gang member observed, "It's not fun to be a good kid." Those who have been exposed to the "action" and "excitement" of illicit activities require challenging, interesting programs to retain their interest. One PARD director said:

Often, the programs aren't exciting enough because the staff aren't excited enough. They don't know what teenagers want, so the teenagers don't come to our programs...We have to involve teenage leadership or the youth we want to attract won't show up.

Too often youth feel that adults plan for them, rather than with them. Youth empowerment is a central theme that is consistently reaffirmed in these case studies. Empowerment enables youth to take ownership and responsibility for the programs. There has been a shift from centralized top-down decision-making by recreation professionals, to decentralized, youth-centered decision-making:

- In Richmond, British Columbia, the Youth Involved Process (YIP) was created when the agency recognized the need to shift from its traditional top-down program model. The YIP model placed less emphasis on activities and more on processes. It recognized that the process of planning, facilitating, implementing and evaluating was more important than merely participating in a program. Implementation of the YIP was designed to enhance the development of specific internal and external assets from among the Search Institute's 40 Developmental Assets. The shift from a direct delivery to a facilitative role was challenging for staff since it required a change in philosophy, work plans, job expectations and desired outcomes.
- Phoenix has 25 teen councils throughout the city. They meet weekly or bimonthly to plan recreational activities, trips, special events, and social community service programs with the professional recreation staff. Each council elects a member who attends the monthly meeting of the citywide Teen Park and Recreation Board. The Teen Parks and Recreation Board is responsible for development and implementation of the annual teen conference and citywide special events. A member of the citywide Board sits as youths' representative on the city's PARD Advisory Board.
- Kettering's STAND (Students Taking A New Direction) group emerged from a Youth Summit attended by 250 which was convened to address youth issues. STAND members complete a "Pledge to Help" form and their mission is

to provide services to the community, and positive social activities for youth. The group interviewed the full-time Youth Coordinator who was hired to facilitate their initiatives.

- A Chattanooga/Hamilton County Youth Council formed by the Chattanooga Parks, Recreation, Arts and Culture Department played a central role in the evolution of Project Choices, which provided teens with constructive alternatives to hanging-out at a large local mall. The project was developed after teens who were unaccompanied by adults were banned from the mall on Friday and Saturday nights.

The Evolving Mission

In the early years of the contemporary renaissance of youth programs in the late 1980s and early 1990s, the mission in most agencies was defined in terms of targeting programs at at-risk youth which would keep them off the streets and out of trouble by engaging them in "fun and games." It was recognized in most communities that PARDs had the best distribution system available for addressing youth issues, and so could be effective in "keeping youth off the streets." The result of this perspective was that expectations often were limited to opening facilities, and hiring minimum wage, part-time employees to "baby-sit" youth and the facility. This goal of removing the potential for anti-social behavior by diverting them into positive activities elsewhere is of limited value because it is time-bounded. During the large amounts of time when they are not in the diversionary activity, their proclivity for anti-social behavior remains.

As programs have matured, and stakeholders have acquired a more sophisticated understanding of the potential of youth programming, the mission has evolved to become more holistic with a focus on behavior change and desired outcomes. Thus, the emergent view is that the mission of services for youth needs to extend beyond this limited temporal aspiration and aim to remove youths' proclivity for anti-social behavior by increasing their prosocial attitudes and skills. The prevailing paradigm is now "youth development" which has been defined as follows:

- Youth development is a process which prepares young people to meet the challenges of adolescence and adulthood through a coordinated, progressive series of activities and experiences which help them to become socially, morally, emotionally, physically, and cognitively competent. Positive youth development addresses the broader developmental needs of youth, in contrast to deficity-based models which focus solely on youth problems.[3]

While it may be politically useful to label some youth as "at-risk," the term "youth development" recognizes that "all youth are at-risk." This approach does not eliminate the need to target specific high-risk groups or individuals for additional attention, but indicates that efforts should not be restricted to this group. The new paradigm requires development of a "common vision of success at the end of adolescence, in particular, the ability of youth to find rewarding and remunerative employment, form a lasting and quality partnership, and become contributors in their communities".[4]

Several frameworks have been proposed for operationalizing this vision. They help delineate both the role of PARDs in the overall youth development framework and the components that make up quality programs. Among these elements are: (i) a sense of safety; but accompanied by challenging and interesting activities; (ii) a sense of belonging; (iii) supportive relationships with adults; (iv) involvement in decision-making and opportunities for leadership; and (v) involvement in community.[5] Many of these elements are present in the service approaches utilized by programs described in the case studies.

The new paradigm frameworks emphasize the need to design programs to deliver desired attitudinal and behavioral outcomes, rather than to merely keep youth occupied. The TRICS framework suggests effective youth development is dependent on reciprocal relationships of trust, respect, integrity, and consistency between youths and adults, and upon promoting self-esteem.[6] The America's Promise approach articulates a series of five elements which lead to the positive development of young people: (i) creating ongoing relationships with caring adults--parents, mentors, tutors or coaches; (ii) creating safe places with structured activities during the non-school hours; (iii) enabling each child to get a healthy start and have a positive future; (iv) through effective education helping each child to develop marketable skills; and (v) enabling youth to have opportunities to give back through community service.[7]

The two youth development frameworks which have been most widely adopted are the Developmental Assets Model[8] and the Protective Factors/Resiliency Model.[9] The Assets model provides a framework for identifying and building the internal and external supports necessary for youth to grow positively into adulthood, while the protective factors/resiliency framework defines the elements necessary to enable children to overcome risk factors in their lives. Several of the cases in this book use these two frameworks:

- Aurora Library and Recreation Services Department adopted the Developmental Assets Model for conceptualizing delivery of its youth services. Internal surveys were undertaken to determine which assets were being promoted through current programs and additional programs were developed to deliver other desired assets. Staff developed four strategies for enhancing asset development. First, the intentionality of programming and training efforts was increased to enhance asset building. Second, the intensity of programs was increased by working with smaller groups, and terminating or amending drop-in programs in favor of more structured activities. Third, improvements in communication about assets to staff and parents were made in an effort to increase the number of adults who were participating in the asset building process.
- In Austin, the PARD used the Protective Factors Model to develop teen programs as part of the city's Social Fabric Initiative and then used it as the basis for designing program outcome measures. Thus, objectives of the Neighborhood Teen Program include to:
    - provide opportunities for youth to gain help with difficult personal and family issues;

  - increase participants' abilities to make positive choices about issues such as avoiding drug and alcohol usage, gang membership, and pregnancy;
  - teach youth positive means for resolving conflicts.
- Portland required that all funded programs in its Time For Kids Initiative should be designed to contribute to one or more of the 10 Developmental Assets they deemed to be most important to Portland's youth. The focus of most of the programs was on developing three assets:
  - Academic achievement;
  - Developing work and/or life skills; and
  - Community involvement/community service.
- In Richmond, British Columbia, the Youth Involved Process consisted of six basic steps and each step was designed to enhance the development of specific external and internal Developmental Assets.

By their use of these frameworks, the case studies demonstrate the advantages of moving beyond a casual approach to programming, to one that involves "intentionality:" What do we want to have happen and how are we going to make it happen?[10]

> *If created intentionally and strategically, more supports for more youth in more neighborhoods constitute more pathways to success - pathways are diverse, wide and accessible enough for all youth to see, try and ultimately select from. These pathways offer the basic things young people need: people to talk to, places to go, opportunities to explore. [These pathways] build the attitudes, skills, values and knowledge that young people need in a full range of areas from cognitive and vocational to personal and civic (p. 49).*[11]

The broader focus of youth development which seeks to modify youths' behavior, rather than merely keep them occupied with recreation activities, is consistent with society's goals to enhance levels of educational attainment, and to reduce drug abuse, gang membership and juvenile crime. Moving beyond fun and games to focus on these positive outcomes is the core element of NRPA's Benefits Movement which seeks to reshape the way the recreation mission is perceived and presented to decision-makers. PARDs which cling to the fun and games orientation will fail to realize the funding potential that exists in their community for the support of recreation services. They will also fail to position themselves as being relevant to community efforts to develop a system of youth services.

Collaborations and Partnerships

A corollary of the focus on youth development is that it is multi-faceted. Thus, it requires a multi-dimensional response to be successful. Programs described in the case studies illustrate how recreational professionals have been required to adopt different modes of operation, and acquire a new knowledge base and new skills. The former Director of the Phoenix Parks, Recreation, and Library Department observed:

My staff say we are becoming counselors and social workers. That's fine, I believe we should be. We have always done this, but there is much more emphasis on it now than there has been in a couple of decades. My philosophy is that if a young man comes in on drugs or a young woman comes in who is pregnant, we have to help. Young women come to my female staff and say 'I'm pregnant, will you come home with me and help me talk to my mom.' They are scared, so of course we help. We respond as best we can to whatever they need. I would not have a problem with my Department being called a Department of Community Services. Our job is to make young people whole in any way we can, and offering wholesome recreation activities is only one aspect of that. It's a way of reaching them and gives us an opportunity to help them straighten out other parts of their lives (p. 16).[12]

The case studies show that PARDs' programs frequently include after-school tutoring, community service, job training, leadership development, health education, and the development of social skills. Often, existing staff are not equipped to direct such programs. Hence, PARDs are recognizing the need to be an integral part of a larger youth development system viewing their role as part of a system that holistically serves youth, rather than being parochially concerned only with youths' recreational needs:

- There was a long established, pervasive sentiment among leadership of all sectors in Columbus, Indiana, that they should view the community as "one big circle with no boxes." The Director of the PARD explained: "We do not view ourselves as existing in independent silos! We believe there is nothing we cannot do in our community for youth with the resources we have, but it means each organization has to get past the notion of protecting its turf." However, he went on to note, "People have to learn to do that, and in some cases they are reluctant."

In many cases, PARDs have assumed leadership in coordinating community youth services. Hence, they seek to supply services on a residual basis, filling niches not available from other suppliers. PARD personnel invariably have extensive networks that can be mobilized to meet youth needs, so they are able to be effective facilitators in bringing youth development agencies together to develop a community-wide service plan. Perhaps the most frequently cited aphorism in youth development is the African proverb, "It takes a whole village to raise a child." PARDs must be perceived as part of the village. The Director of Portland Parks and Recreation has observed that: "This is the chance for us to demonstrate the full value of who we are and what we can do...society needs help with its youth, and we have a piece of the solution. While retaining our uniqueness and autonomy, we in the field of recreation, who share the same values and goals, can accomplish more by working together than we can on our own"(p. 19):[12]

- The holistic philosophy which undergirds the extensive array of programs coordinated by the At-Risk Youth Division in Phoenix involves the Division in collaborations with such agencies as the City's Youth and Education Office, Human Services Department, Prosecutor's Office, Police Department, Maricopa County Juvenile Court, Vocational Services, Phoenix Mercury/

Phoenix Suns, Arizona Society of Plastic and Reconstructive Surgeons...and many other entities.

- In Columbus, Indiana, the PARD pooled resources for both capital funding of a $5.9 million center for youth and its subsequent operation. Collaborators included the Foundation for Youth, Boys and Girls Club, United Way, business leaders, and philanthropic organizations.
- In Virginia Beach, in addition to the PARD, the Youth Opportunities Team includes the Public School System, Community Services Board, Juvenile Court Services, Public Health, the Volunteer Council, the Department of Agriculture, Housing and Neighborhood Preservation, Police, Public Libraries, and Social Services.
- Portland PARD's Time for Kids Initiative involved collaboration with 17 different partners, all of whom had specific programmatic roles in the Initiative.
- In the Concord/Bay Point After School program which was coordinated by the PARD, there were three lead collaborators, but another 10 organizations and agencies were involved in developing the program and committing resources to it.

Service Delivery Vehicles

A PARD's capacity for distributing programs to where they are most needed is a key factor in the success of youth development efforts. Exhibit 2-2 shows a distribution continuum along which a selection of potential delivery vehicles is arrayed. The continuum is anchored by facility-dependent programs at one pole which are sited at discrete points around the community, and facility-independent services at the other pole which have much greater distributional flexibility.

Exhibit 2-2

A Continuum of Service Delivery Vehicles

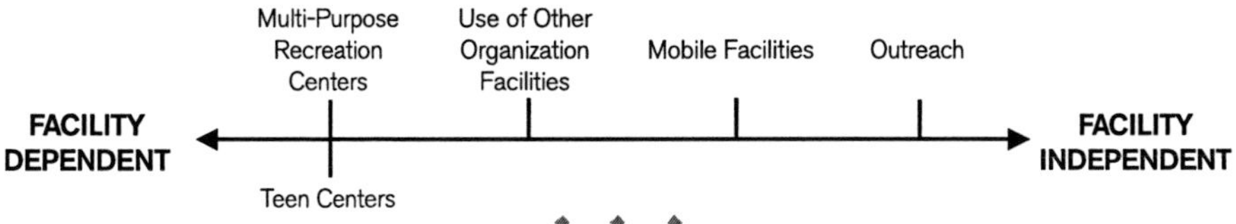

When communities launch a youth development initiative, they are usually based at existing multi-purpose recreation or community centers operated by the PARD. However, when a threshold number of youth are involved in these programs, they frequently agitate to have their own center:

- One of the priority issues identified by the working group task force to examine youth issues in Richmond was youth wanted a place in the community where they had ownership and responsibility, felt welcome and safe, and could socialize, obtain information, and receive services. While community centers catered to a sector of youth, they desired more autonomy and independence from adult-like facilities. Hence, the call for separate dedicated spaces, in which youth could socialize through hanging out.

- The Kettering S.T.A.N.D. program met at the Kettering Recreation Center during its first year, but then lobbied for a teen center. Teenagers wanted a place to call their own. The physical space of a teen center would create a "headquarters" for teenagers, while the symbolism of the center would reaffirm to teens that they were valued by, and important to, the community.

It was noted earlier in this chapter that as programs mature they tend to reach out and involve more youth; the mission tends to evolve to become more holistic; and this involves PARDs' in extensive partnerships and collaborations. From the perspective of service delivery vehicles, these developments result in PARDs expanding their distribution system to deliver programs at facilities operated by other agencies, especially schools. Schools usually are more intensively distributed than community and recreation centers. In addition, in the case of after-school programs, youth are already on site so there is a high level of convenience. Thus, linkage with schools generally leads to a quantum increase in the number of youth served:

- There are 27 community recreation centers in San Antonio, but there are 251 elementary and middle schools. Thus, when the PARD joined with the Independent School District to deliver the After-School Challenge Program, the potential reach was quantumly increased. Approximately 28,600 youth were registered in the program, with an average of 17,700 attending daily.

This broadened approach to distribution of services is often accompanied by PARD's roles shifting from being direct providers to becoming facilitators. Adoption of the facilitator role requires the agency to serve as an enabling agent and take on the tasks of coordination, referral and technical assistance:

- Portland Parks and Recreation (PP&R) viewed the Time For Kids Initiative as an opportunity to serve as a broker of services, rather than as a direct provider. The intent was to partner with other organizations to shape a common mission which would best leverage the limited available resources. Interested potential collaborators submitted proposals to PP&R requesting part of the $200,000 budget. During the three years of the pilot program, 17 partners, representing 32 programs, serving 21 sites were funded.

Recreation does not stop at the center door! Outreach services extend the reach of youth development programs beyond youth who go to agency facilities, to those who do not feel comfortable in institutional settings. Outreach has been defined as "the effort that takes place when an agency reaches out and assists through personal contacts those citizens systematically excluded from, unaware of, or unreceptive to an agency's service or those of related agencies" (xiii).[13] The notion of outreach services incorporating recreation activities can be traced back to the mid-19th century.

In the case studies reported here, outreach is manifested through two different, but related, service delivery vehicles. First, is the mobile recreation center which provides a flexible and adaptable medium for delivering services. The mobile centers can be scheduled in the evening or daytime, for long or short periods of time, on a continuous or one-off basis, and can carry equipment for a wide range of programs. The concept springs from the century long tradition of motorized public libraries providing service to areas of a community that are beyond the recognized service zones of branch libraries:

- The Mobile Activity Center tours the City of Virginia Beach providing programs to youth who lack transportation to access the PARD's fixed facilities. The unit is parked in apartment village play areas, cul-de-sacs, neighborhood parks, or on grassy parts of townhouse complexes. Activities offered include arts and crafts, sports, and special events.
- The Phoenix At-Risk Youth Division views itself as an outreach service providing recreational, educational, social, and cultural programs for teens at sites such as malls, schools, and parks at which there is no regular programming. The Mobile Unit Partnership developed in collaboration with the Girl Scouts is a manifestation of this philosophy. Each week a renovated "bookmobile" serves approximately 1,000 youth with recreation services.

The second form of outreach described in the cases is Roving Leader programs, which are even less facility dependent than mobile facilities. The premise undergirding these programs is that youth workers who "roam" a neighborhood in which they are based will be able to find and connect with disaffected youth. Often, workers live in the areas where they work, which gives them credibility with, and a better understanding of, these youth.

Four elements of Roving Leader programs have been identified which differentiate them from other service vehicles.[14] First, services are based on problems in young people's lives as opposed to a specific program activity. Therefore, services are available to youth who have the greatest need rather than those who have paid a fee or become members of a particular group. Second, programs are heavily dependent on the relationship between youth and staff. Third, contact occurs in the community, not in an institutional setting. This is important since most institutions have formal standards that guide youth leaders in client selection and service, which may eliminate some youth from participating. Finally, the services provided by roving leaders are not initially requested by youth. The leader is required to reach out and take steps to alleviate any fear, suspicion or hostility that might exist. All of these outreach principles stress the importance of the personal relationship between staff and youth.[15]

- Roving leader programs operated in a few big city PARDs in the 1960s, but were victims of funding cutbacks during the 1970s and 1980s. In the 1990s, there was something of a renaissance of these programs: Austin and San Antonio PARDs have extensive Roving Leader programs. Staff make contact with youth not currently affiliated with city or non-profit youth services and attempt to draw youth into constructive activities who would otherwise be on the streets and potentially involved in risk behaviors. To be successful, staff must be sensitive to an understanding of local community circumstances as well as savvy and street-smart.

Staffing

Adults supply the scaffolding necessary to enable youth to navigate from childhood to adulthood. Youth, like an emerging building, need support during "construction or development." Eventually when ready to stand on their own, the scaffolding can be reduced and eventually withdrawn.[11] Throughout the case studies, the key role of adults is consistently recognized both in facilitating and guiding youth input into planning, organizing and leading programs, and in mentoring. A diversified staff (race, gender, age and education) is desirable. An ethnically diverse staff, that includes individuals from a number of different service backgrounds (recreation, arts, education, social work, criminal justice, psychology), is likely to be a more comprehensive and responsive in their approach to youth development. Adults are most effective who "work in partnership with young people, who see themselves as supportive friends and advocates in contrast to adults motivated to save, reform, or rescue young people from their circumstances."[16] The caring adults may be parents or volunteers from the community, but the central responsibility is likely to reside with PARD staff:

- Sensitive and informed leadership is critical to the effective implementation of the Youth Involved process (YIP) in Richmond. The YIP is process rather than activity based, which means adult leaders must possess the skills needed to facilitate youth acquiring the internal and external assets that the process is designed to deliver.
- Roving Leader programs in Austin and San Antonio, emphasize that it is the leadership not the program content that is important. Roving Leaders have to gain and retain the trust of youth, their parents, and the institutions which cooperate with them; they have to be able to organize and teach recreational activities; and to know the array of referral services that are available to support youth. Thus, when hiring for these positions, managers are inclined to be more concerned about Roving Leaders' understanding of the neighborhood and chemistry with these youth, than with formal academic credentials.

Recognizing that the single most important factor in reaching adulthood is a positive relationship with a caring adult, many PARDs are replacing part-time jobs with full-time adult leadership positions. Full-time positions (i) enable staff to develop a stronger rapport with youth; (ii) result in reduced staff turnover which avoids the fission this causes to mentoring relationships; and (iii) provide time for relationships to be established with complementary youth serving organizations.

Training of staff remains a challenge to most agencies since there is frequently no provision for this in budgets. Nevertheless, the cases show that PARDs strive to provide training in such areas as mentoring skills and group facilitation; community development; youth development principles; understanding the broader youth development system; financing and acquiring resources; and marketing.

Training should take place both before a service is initiated and regularly on an ongoing basis so the knowledge base is consistently enhanced.

- In Aurora, before the Assets Model was introduced, 12 key staff were trained to be "asset presenters." The presenters subsequently provided training for other department staff and external groups.
- In Concord, there was a decrease in academic performance among youth in the second year of the After-School Learning Program. This was a surprise, given the increases which had been accomplished in the first year. External evaluators concluded it was attributable to the lack of a uniformly well-trained, enthusiastic staff. A key recommendation in the consultants' report was: "Ensure that recreation specialists and teacher-leaders have ongoing training in how to provide enriched learning experiences to develop the critical thinking skills of participating students. Such experiences should include classes in science, social studies, computing, art, and music, and field trips in an effort to increase academic achievement and appreciation for learning." The existing part-time recreation staff were being expected to fulfill this role without being equipped to do so.
- San Antonio relies for training primarily on other agencies in the city with expertise relevant to their after-school program staffs' needs. Much of the training is given by the city's Department of Community Initiatives. The training covers such topics as conflict resolution, nutrition, safety, curriculum planning, customer service, risk management, recognition of child abuse, neglect and sexual abuse, cultural diversity, CPR and First Aid, life skills and age appropriate activities.

Many of the after-school programs employ teachers since they contain an educational enrichment component and have academic attainment goals. This creates a reimbursement conundrum because teachers typically are compensated at their professional salary rate for these additional duties, while recreation leaders doing similar work typically receive \$6 to \$8 per hour. This disparity, combined with the emotional intensity of the work and the difficult nature of the clientele, often results in high staff turnover and a disruption of mentoring relationships. Low levels of remuneration are endemic in youth development work. Thus, even when high quality staff are recruited who enjoy the job, retaining them for an extended period of time can be difficult.

- The Austin and San Antonio Roving Leaders' case reports that burn-out by staff is frequent. Outreach programs, especially, have highly dedicated individuals who work longer than an eight-hour day and are called to deal with difficult situations as they arise, irrespective of whether they are officially at work. This leaves little time for recovery, personal time, and family or other obligations. While the Roving Leaders may not perceive the long hours to be detrimental immediately, in the long-term there is a high probability these conditions will lead to burn-out. Salaries are lower than other jobs the Roving Leaders could pursue and substantially lower than those received by teachers. The situation is exacerbated by some of them not receiving full benefits as part of their compensation package because of budget constraints. Given these conditions, this work is more than a profession, it is a calling.

Resource Support

Because many youth development programs target clientele in economically distressed areas, services invariably need to be offered either free of charge or at a nominal fee. These programs need substantial resource support which may come either from local government sources or external sources, such as state, federal or foundation grant programs, or from private entities.

In order to be competitive for these grant funds, some agencies have invested in staff specialists. For example, the Phoenix At-Risk Youth Division hired a full-time grants researcher and coordinator. In the first full year, the Division submitted 25 applications for funds, of which 15 were successful, yielding almost $1 million in additional resources. To support this grant application work, a resource library of data and statistical findings related to youth was developed.

External funds are usually short-term, relatively unstable, and often designated for tightly defined programs. Thus, they should be regarded as temporary resources that provide an opportunity to pilot test programs and to demonstrate to elected officials that they have positive outcomes which make them worthy of support from the city's general fund. In some cases this has occurred and they have become a line-item in the general fund:

- In San Antonio, over $6 million of general fund money from the City and School Districts is allocated to the PARD's After-School Program. When budget cuts had to be implemented recently and programs were reviewed for this purpose, the After-School Program was ranked in the "most protected" category.
- In Phoenix, the At-Risk Youth Division increased from 11 to 52 FTEs in the past decade and its general fund budget grew from $400,000 to over $2 million. In addition, a surcharge of 25 cents imposed on each round of golf played at city courses goes into a dedicated fund (approximately $150,000 per year) to support paid youth internships at the recreation centers, youth golf clinics, and staff training.

However, too often this evolution of funding from temporary to permanent sources has not occurred even where effective outcomes have been demonstrated and where strikingly favorable benefit-cost analyses could be shown. The impact of lack of continuity on youth is likely to be traumatic. It reinforces prevailing cynicism with "the system," and engenders a distrust that may preclude any future involvement with mentors and programs. The withdrawal of funding when trust and a mentoring relationship have been established becomes another broken promise in their lives. The limitations and danger of this strategy were pointed out by the former Executive Director of the Minneapolis Park and Recreation Board. He suggested that agencies might actually be contributing to the problems of youth by building expectations through short-term, one-shot recreation programs, then failing to follow-through with long-term ongoing services:

We will undertake a disservice to our clients, who already are beset by part-time parents and part-time education, by offering part-time programs. To be effective, programs must be consistent, constant, and sustainable. Otherwise I believe we simply feed the loop of failing to fulfill our promises (p. 24).[12]

The Portland case study offers detailed insights into this problem. The Time For Kids Initiative (TKIF) was launched by the City Council as a three year pilot project. Comprehensive evaluations of it by outside consultants showed it to be successful in meeting its goals. Hence, it was reasonable to expect that it would be continued and expanded, but that did not occur because of the substantial costs involved. The annual cost per student was around $1,500 per year. There were over 20,000 students in Portland ISD who met the criteria used to define the target population in the pilot study. To extend it to all of them would cost $30 million per year. Given that Portland Park and Recreation's (PP&R) total annual operating budget was approximately $30 million, the political reality was that this scale of investment could not be supported from the city's general fund.

The problem is exacerbated by disconnects between (i) the short and long-term payers and beneficiaries, and (ii) the geographical jurisdictions which pay for, and benefit from, such programs as TFKI.

The short-term actions of many elected officials are guided by their desire to be re-elected. The tax increases needed to fully fund TFKI are likely to be politically unpopular. The general public's decision horizon and perspective is notoriously short term, and elected officials have to be responsive to this. "Pay now or pay later" is not a convincing mantra to either group. Thus, elected officials perceive it to be advantageous to keep taxes low in the short term, recognizing that the societal, financial and political consequences of not providing youth with assets through TFKI will become the problem of their successors in the future. There appear to be few political advantages for those in elected positions to be proactive rather than reactive in the context of youth development. The political pressures are conducive to encouraging short-term rather than long-term action horizons.

A second disconnect discouraging local investment in youth development is that the primary economic beneficiary of such programs is often perceived to be state government. The costs associated with unemployment, welfare, incarceration, courts and other negative consequences emanating from ill-prepared young people emerging into society are primarily borne by state agencies. Thus, local jurisdictions who invest in youth development programs see that most of the long-term economic savings that accrue from investing in them are captured by the state jurisdiction, which further reduces the incentive for local elected officials to accept the negative consequences likely to be associated with their support of a tax increase.

The Director of PP&R believes the funding problem is exacerbated because the targeted populations who would benefit from these programs have no political influence. He notes that the SAMs (shakers and movers!) in a community can make a call and get something done, but calls from those benefiting from programs like TFKI are likely to have relatively little impact on legislators even if the constituents had the confidence and knowledge to make them. Business associations downtown meet on a regular basis. They are organized, they have money, and they give major contributions and in-kind assistance to political campaigns, so they have influence. The TFKI clientele can offer an emotional appeal, but they are likely to receive only a pittance compared to what the business community is likely to receive for its favored projects. Even within the confines of PP&R's primary constituencies, the sports and athletic associations--soccer, Little League and so on- - are typically middle class groups, which can organize and be relatively effective, but potential TFKI constituents are not organized. Thus, in the opinion of the PP&R Director, the long term prognosis for permanent on-going funding for such programs in Portland is not encouraging.

Outreach programs tend to be especially vulnerable to budget cutbacks because at such times there is a tendency for cities to give priority to operating programs emanating from physical facilities. There is a sunk capital cost which the residents have invested in facilities and their return on this very visible investment is not forthcoming if funds for operating them are not made available. In contrast, there are no tangible facility assets which are not being used if the outreach programs are cut. Hence, from a political perspective, this is frequently viewed as a more palatable and expedient solution to budget cuts than reducing staff levels at facilities.

- When we started developing the Roving Leader case in Austin, there were 21 RLs, including 8 full-time RL supervisors, 6 full-time assistant RLs, and 7 part-time RL assistants. Six months later, 9 RLs had left the program (a supervisor, a full-time assistant and 7 part-time assistants). They left because of stress associated with the job, long hours and low pay. Only three of these positions were filled because of departmental budgets being frozen. The high attrition makes it hard to maintain program momentum, continuity and quality. In addition the ongoing advertising, hiring, rehiring, recruiting and training processes are both expensive and time consuming. These ongoing processes make it hard to maintain program momentum, continuity and quality.

It is also more challenging for an agency to demonstrate accountability for the effectiveness of outreach programs than for regular facility-based programs. A corollary is that elected officials have more difficulty collecting political kudos for supporting resources for such a program since results cannot easily be quantified. Without being able to show that the program has been effective, it is difficult for an agency to convince elected officials that it is using its limited resources responsibly. Again, this contributes to the vulnerability of outreach programs being cut in times of economic down turns. Ironically, it is during these times when the need for them is greatest!

There are three sources from which general funds may be acquired to allocate permanent government funding to youth development programs: (i) redirecting resources from other recreational programs; (ii) additional appropriations from legislative bodies, or (iii) additional reliance on collaborators and partners. The first option is likely to be resisted by the users of existing programs, and perhaps also by staff who may perceive a loss of personal power. Lowering service standards for existing client groups frequently leads to political protest. Opposition from staff to changes in emphases may occur since the changes may threaten an individual's status, area of expertise, or self-confidence. Reallocation of resources is likely to occur only when a program's life cycle nears its end and when turnover of staff occurs. This is likely to be a gradual process.

Reluctance to raise tax rates means that if any additional appropriations are made, they are likely to be small, especially in major cities where the tax base is declining. In order to justify tax increases for youth development services to their constituents, legislators have to be provided with evidence that these programs are effective. Hence the importance of undertaking evaluations of outcomes which provide this evidence.

Evaluation of Program Outcomes

One of the major shifts in the past decade has been an increase in the proportion of agencies engaging in evaluation procedures and the greater sophistication of those evaluations. Exhibit 2-1 indicated that evaluations measure the extent to which both individual program outcomes and overall mission goals are attained. Evaluation is key to both continued funding and to guiding managers' continuous improvement efforts. Elected officials are likely to require evidence of a program's success before appropriating public tax dollars for its continuation.

At the beginning of the 1990s, evaluation efforts focused almost exclusively on measuring attendance, service quality and user satisfaction. However, the forces driving the funding support from youth programs are concerned with outcomes. It was noted in chapter 1 that the critical questions are not "How many were there?" or "How efficiently was the program delivered?" The critical questions are "What happened to Jose, Mary, Sam, and Juanita as a result of this experience?" and "What return did the community receive on its investment of resources in this program?"[17]

The authors have evaluated dozens of youth development programs in the past decade. At the beginning of the work, the effort was directed exclusively towards measuring outcomes. Two points quickly became apparent that caused a review of this *modus operandi*. First, improvements in desired outcomes were dependent upon the design and structure of the program. Second, the extent to which desired outcomes were attained could only be measured if they had been specified in measurable terms when the program was launched:

- The early statements of objectives for the programs evaluated in Austin were not expressed in terms that could easily be translated into expected outcomes. Further, program content was not always aligned with the stated objectives. Thus, the evaluators and program staff revisited the objectives and program content for each of programs. This goals explication process helped program staff to think more clearly about the relationship between a program's objectives and the components needed to achieve them, and facilitated the developmental measures for use in the evaluation process.

The design and structure of programs constitutes real repositioning. This has to precede psychological repositioning. That is, communicating positive outcomes to stakeholders is unlikely to be possible, unless the programs have been designed to produce those desired benefits. It may be misleading for agencies to cite benefits documented elsewhere as evidence that their own programs will automatically produce similar benefits. Evidence of benefits in one context is indicative only of a program's *potential* in a different context. That potential will not be realized if the program is not consciously structured to produce the desired outcomes.

Properly formulated objectives serve as guidelines for designing a program. Structured, attainable objectives offer an incentive for improvement, if they are effectively communicated and understood by staff. A good example of specific objectives are those used by Concord Leisure Services Department which established goals and objectives for each program and evaluated the outcomes against these measurable outcomes. Examples of the specific Performance Indicators used are:

- In one year's time, participants will increase their reading, writing and math proficiency to at least grade level or by at least 1.25 academic years.
- In one year's time, school attendance among participants will improve at least 20%.

The outcome measures selected related to students' academic performance and changes in student behavior and attitudes.

The cases offer multiple examples of approaches to evaluation. In some cases, the evaluation instruments are reproduced in the case. In addition, a selection of evaluation reports undertaken by the authors can be viewed at http://rptswebs.tamu.edu/faculty/witt.htm. These reports contain the evaluation instruments and describe the methods that the authors have used.

- Fairfax County Park Authority (FCPA) has a Market Research and Planning Section with the capacity to conduct research in-house. The agency's summer camp program enrolls over 9,000 and grosses nearly $1.8 million. FCPA's Deputy Director stated, "The camp program is driven by what we hear from our clients." The FCPA case offers a good illustration of how a continuous improvement process uses evaluation to revise, expand and improve program delivery.
- With the help of personnel from Texas A&M University, Austin PARD has used the Protective Factors/Resiliency Model to guide outcome studies of its Social Fabric Initiative programs. Annual evaluations have shown that programs such as Totally Cool, Totally Art and the Neighborhood Teen Program have led to a strengthening of protective factors for program participants. Annual evaluations have also been conducted for the Roving Leader program. The focus has been on evaluating the extent to which participants show declines in negative school, family and community related behaviors, and increases in the probability of finishing school, not becoming teen parents, and staying clean from drugs.
- The Phoenix At-Risk Youth Division has commissioned university faculty to undertake evaluations of its programs.
- In Portland, evaluations of the Time For Kids Initiative were comprised of four main elements: attendance and registration analysis; student attitude surveys; family assessments; and collaborating partner assessments.

Concluding Comments

Exhibit 2-1 at the beginning of the chapter offered a framework that appeared to reflect the genesis and evolution of youth development programs in the cases reported in the subsequent chapters of this book. In the afore discussion a number of shifts in the characteristics of youth development programs that have evolved in the past decade were identified. An attempt has been made to summarize these shifts in Exhibit 2-3.

The 1980s and 1990s laid the groundwork for full realization of the positive potential of PARD services. The New Millenium provides the opportunity to build on that base and realize the potential that advocates for the park and recreation field have long recognized it offers for establishing exemplary youth development programs.

Exhibit 2-3

The Shifting Paradigm in Youth Development Programs

Theme	From:	To:
Antecedent Conditions	Resources stimulated by high-visibility violent incidents	Resources stimulated by desires for enhanced cultural assimilation and educational attainment
	Political skepticism towards investing in youth programs	Conventional wisdom that youth programs are good investments
Youth Involvement	Programs initiated and planned by professional leaders	Programs planned and initiated by youth, with support from professionals and other adults
The Evolving Mission	Keep children safe, off the streets, and out of trouble through fun activities	Use programs to build individual and community assets; reduce risk behaviors; promote resiliency
	Services limited to targeted groups of "at risk youth"	Comprehensive, recognizing that youth development programs offer potential benefits to all young people
	Focus on the activity	Focus on "intentionality" and instrumentality emanating from engaging in the activities
	Short-term one-shot programming	Commitment to ongoing programs
Collaborations and Partnerships	Myopic focus on recreation activities	Adoption of an holistic perspective integrating an array of services
	PARD as an independent, compartmentalized provider of services	PARD as a component of youth development systems involved with multiple collaborations and partnerships
	PARD as a direct provider of services	PARD as a leverager of resources: facilitator, coordinator, refiner, and residual supplier when there are no other viable delivery alternatives
Service Delivery Vehicles	Youth activities in multi-purpose centers	Youth activities in teen centers
	Youth come to programs: Programs are building and center-based	Services reach out to contact and attract uninvolved youth
Staffing	Part time staff fulfilling a "minder" role	Full-time staff fulfilling a "mentor" role
Resource Support	Short term funding from grants and special city funds	Base funding from a city's general fund
Evaluation	Focus on attendance, service quality, and satisfaction measures	Focus on outcomes (increased protective factors or developmental assets, or reductions in risk behaviors)

Sources

1. Espericueta-Schultz, L., Crompton, J.L., & Witt, P.A. (1995). A national profile of the status of public recreation services for at-risk children and youth. *Journal of Park and Recreation Administration*, 13(3), 1-26.
2. Goodman, E. (2002). Motherhood at center of culture wars. *The Bryan-College Station Eagle*, May 28, p. A4.
3. National Collaboration for Youth (1998). Youth development definition cited from http://www.nydic.org/nydic/devdef.html#youth
4. Furstenberg, F.E. (1999). *Managing to make it: Urban families and adolescent success.* Chicago, IL: University of Chicago Press.
5. Gambone, M.A., & Arbreton, A.J.A. (1997). *Safe havens: The contributions of youth organizations to healthy adolescent development.* Philadelphia, PA: Public/Private Ventures.
6. Bembry, R. (1998). A youth development strategy: principles to practice in re-creation for the 21st century. *Journal of Park and Recreation Administration*, 17(2), 15-34
7. America's Promise (2002). Source: http://www.americaspromise.org/
8. Search Institute (1998). *Helping youth thrive: How youth organizations-can and do-build developmental assets.* Minneapolis, MN: Author.
9. Jessor, R. (1992). Risk behavior in adolescence: A psychological framework for understanding and action. In D.E. Rogers and E. Ginzberg (Eds.) *Adolescents at risk: Medical and social perspectives* (pp. 19-33). Boulder, CO: Westview Press.
10. McLaughlin, M.W. (2000). Community counts. How youth organizations matter for youth development. Available [www.publiceduation.org/downloadPEN23.pdf] Public Education Network.
11. Pittman, P., Irby. M., Ferber, T. (2000). Unfinished business. In *Youth development: Issues, challenges and directions.* Philadelphia: Public Private Ventures. http://www.ppv.org/indexfiles/yd-index.html
12. Witt, P.A. & Crompton, J.L. (1996). (Eds.) *Recreation programs that work for at-risk youth: The challenge of shaping the future.* State College, PA: Venture Publishing.
13. Bannon, J.J. (1972). The Roving Leader: A new look. *Parks and Recreation*, 7(2), 22-24.
14. Austin, D.M. (1957). Goals for the gang worker. *Social Work*, 2(4), 43-50.
15. Bocarro, J.N. (2002). Reaching out / reaching in: The long-term challenges and issues of outreach programs. *Journal of Park and Recreation Administration* (in press).
16. Walker, J. & White, L. (1998). Caring adults support the healthy development of youth. The Center, pp. 14-19. http://www.fourh.umn.edu/educators/research/Center/Center1998.html
17. Gray, D.E. & Greben, S. (1974). Future perspectives. *Parks and Recreation*, July pp. 26-33, 47-56.

Section 1

FOUNDATIONAL MODELS

CHAPTER 3

ASSET BUILDING IN AURORA

The mission of the Office of Youth Development in the Aurora, Colorado Library and Recreation Services Department (LRSD) is to create a community in which everyone helps build positive life-enhancing skills, attitudes and behavior in youth. These qualities have been termed "developmental assets." Four strategies are used in pursuit of this mission:

i) Asset building is woven into City of Aurora youth programs;

ii) The community is educated on asset building to encourage everyday acts of asset building;

iii) Collaborations with community groups are formed to encourage a unified effort toward community change; and

iv) Collaborative grant projects are undertaken that provide asset development opportunities for Aurora's youth.

This case study demonstrates the utility of the Development Assets Model, created by the Search Institute and widely used by PARDs in youth development programs. In Aurora, the assets model is infused into all aspects of youth development: initial needs identification, program conceptualization, planning, staff training, and program evaluation. Efforts have been made to imbed the approach into departmental practices through highlighting asset building already occurring in department programs and services; offering specialized training to orient staff to asset building practices; developing new programs and services designed to fill those asset gaps; and linking with other community agencies so the asset building approach is community-wide.

The Search Institute's model is comprised of forty developmental assets that are posited to be important building blocks for helping youth succeed and thrive (Exhibit 3-1). The forty assets are divided into eight categories: support, empowerment, boundaries and expectations, time use, educational commitment, values, social competencies, and positive identity. The first four categories are considered *external assets,* which are qualities in the community environment that influence youth. The second four categories are *internal assets,* which are traits that individuals internalize into their belief systems and behavior patterns. Each contact an individual has with another person has the potential both to strengthen these assets and to weaken them.

Exhibit 3-1

The Search Institute's 40 Developmental Assets Model

	Category	Asset Name and Definition
EXTERNAL ASSETS	Support	1. **Family Support** - Family life provides high levels of love and support.
		2. **Positive Family Communication** - Young person and her or his parent(s) communicate positively, and young person is willing to seek advice and counsel from parents.
		3. **Other Adult Relationships** - Young person receives support from three or more nonparent adults.
		4. **Caring Neighborhood** - Young person experiences caring neighbors.
		5. **Caring School Climate** - School provides a caring, encouraging environment.
		6. **Parent Involvement in Schooling** - Parent(s) are actively involved in helping young person succeed in school.
	Empowerment	7. **Community Values Youth** - Young person perceives that adults in the community value youth.
		8. **Youth as Resources** - Young people are given useful roles in the community.
		9. **Service to Others** - Young person serves in the community one hour or more per week.
		10. **Safety** - Young person feels safe at home, school, and in the neighborhood.
	Boundaries & Expectations	11. **Family Boundaries** - Family has clear rules and consequences and monitors the young person's whereabouts.
		12. **School Boundaries** - School provides clear rules and consequences.
		13. **Neighborhood Boundaries** - Neighbors take responsibility for monitoring young people's behavior.
		14. **Adult Role Models** - Parent(s) and teachers encourage the young person to do well.
		15. **Positive Peer Influence** - Young person's best friends model responsible behavior.
		16. **High Expectations** - Both parent(s) and teachers encourage the young person to do well.
	Constructive Use of Time	17. **Creative Activities** - Young person spends three or more hours per week in lessons or practice in music, theater, or other arts.
		18. **Youth Programs** - Young person spends three or more hours per week in sports, clubs, or organizations at school and/or in the community.
		19. **Religious Community** - Young person spends one or more hours per week in activities in a religious institute.
		20. **Time at Home** - Young person is out with friends "with nothing special to do" two or fewer nights per week.

700 S. Third Street, Suite 210, Minneapolis, MN 55415; 800-888-7828
www.search-institute.org.

Exhibit 3-1 Continued

INTERNAL ASSETS

Category	Asset Name and Definition
Commitment to Learning	21. **Achievement Motivation** - Young person is motivated to do well in school.
	22. **School Engagement** - Young person is actively engaged in learning.
	23. **Homework** - Young person reports doing at least one hour of homework every school day.
	24. **Bonding to School** - Young person cares about her or his school.
	25. **Reading for Pleasure** - Young person reads for pleasure three or more hours per week.
Positive Values	26. **Caring** - Young person places high value on helping other people.
	27. **Equality and Social Justice** - Young person places high value on promoting equality and reducing hunger and poverty.
	28. **Integrity** - Young person acts on convictions and stands up for her or his beliefs.
	29. **Honesty** - Young person "tells the truth even when it is not easy."
	30. **Responsibility** - Young person accepts and takes personal responsibility.
	31. **Restraint** - Young person believes it is important not to be sexually active or to use alcohol or other drugs.
Social Competencies	32. **Planning and Decision Making** - Young person knows how to plan ahead and make choices.
	33. **Interpersonal Competence** - Young person has empathy, sensitivity, and friendship skills.
	34. **Cultural Competence** - Young person has knowledge of and comfort with people of different cultural/racial/ethnic backgrounds.
	35. **Resistance Skills** - Young person can resist negative peer pressure and dangerous situations.
	36. **Peaceful Conflict Resolution** - Young person seeks to resolve conflict nonviolently.
Positive Identity	37. **Personal Power** - Young person feels he or she has control over "things that happen to me."
	38. **Self-Esteem** - Young person reports having a high self-esteem.
	39. **Sense of Power** - Young person reports that "my life has a purpose".
	40. **Positive View of Personal Future** - Young person is optimistic about her or his personal future.

Adoption of the Developmental Assets Model, an assets mission, and a commitment to designing programs to strengthen specified assets, evolved in the LRSD over a six-year period. Initially the Youth Services Administrator explored the potential of the assets model as a foundation for conceptualizing and designing youth programs. Soon after, a Prevention Services Supervisor was hired by the LRSD to be responsible for services funded by existing grants that had been moved from the Community Development Department to LRSD. She had extensive experience in the prevention field, having previously worked at a center for alcohol and drug abuse. She consolidated and greatly extended the asset orientation that the LRSD was adopting as its conceptual foundation for youth programs.

Implementing the Assets Approach

The Prevention Services Supervisor developed and implemented a quality improvement process. Rather than initiating new programs, efforts were made to improve the assets focus through amending the design and implementation of existing programs. Staff responsible for the LRSD youth programs were asked to identify three to five assets that each program was designed to develop (i.e., how will participants be different after the program?), and the specific activities used to reach these objectives. Most staff had not previously framed their goals in asset terms, so the exercise raised their consciousness of what they were seeking to achieve. Staff revisited the most fundamental question faced by all organizations: "What business are we in?"

In addition, they were asked information about program length (hours per session), frequency (daily, weekly, etc.), duration (weeks, months), the ratio of adults to youth, and number of program participants (average number per day and number of unduplicated registrants). The Prevention Services Supervisor created a database with this information and used it to develop an intensity index for each activity using the program length, frequency, duration, and adult-to-youth ratio information (Exhibit 3-2).

Scores for each of the four elements in the index ranged from 0 to 100. Decisions on the weighting of the 100 points for each indicator were based on the supervisor's experience in the prevention field. For example, assignment of weights for the duration element reflected prevention research reporting that ongoing programs have more impact than one-time events. Similarly, weightings of the length, frequency and adult-to-youth ratio elements were designed to reflect research findings confirming that more frequent and more intense exposure of youth to adults is key to influencing youth behavior. Index scores could range from 35 to 400, with higher scores indicating a greater amount of contact between adults and youth.

Programs with lower intensity scores (usually those with one-time classes and drop-in programs which serve large numbers, but do not involve sustained participation) were deemed to have lower potential for building assets. The index provided a framework that facilitated discussion of the relative value of programs and oriented staff thinking toward how program impact could be improved.

Exhibit 3-2

The Prevention Intensity Score Chart

	Points	Indicator
Length	100	5 hrs or more
	80	4 hours
	60	3 hours
	40	2 hours
	30	1.5 hours
	20	1 hour
Frequency	100	Daily
	80	4 times/week
	60	3 times/week
	40	2 times/week
	20	1 time/week
	10	1 time
Duration	100	25+ or ongoing
	80	20 times
	60	15 times
	40	10 times
	20	5 times
	16	4 times
	12	3 times
	8	2 times
	4	1 time
Adult-to-Youth-Ratio	100	1:1
	75	1:2
	50	1:5
	25	1:10
	15	1:15
	10	1:20
	5	1:30
	1	1:50

Multiple insights emerged from analyzing the database information.

- Intensity scores ranged from 35 to 320. Scores below 100 were considered low, while scores over 200 were considered high. Choice of these cut-off points was fairly arbitrary. Higher scores usually indicated an ongoing class (such as everyday attendance at after-school, daycare or programs with high adult involvement and continuity). Twenty-one percent (21%) of participation was in low intensity asset strengthening programs, which were either one-time programs, or of brief duration. The data were used as a basis for discussing how to increase program impact by involving more people, providing more ongoing programs, and undertaking fewer "one shot" efforts.

- At least one program was addressing each of twenty-five of the forty assets. For example, responsibility and peaceful conflict resolution were mainly developed through the Youth Ventures program, behavioral restraint through the In Tune program, and positive view of personal future through the girls' group. Adult role models and relationships and planning and decision-making were addressed by multiple programs. Youth programs, adult role models, interpersonal competence, and self-esteem were the assets which were most frequently cited for being appropriate elements for recreation programs to address.
- Specialized programs serving small groups of youth perceived to be especially at-risk were the only programs that focused on the specific prevention assets of behavioral restraint and resistance. For example, after-school programs included activities--like art projects, journals, or discussions--that wove issues of substance abuse, sexuality and healthy choices into their ongoing activities.
- There were no programs targeted at upper level high school students. Existing high school offerings ceased at grade nine. This led to the establishment of a Teen Advisory Group, a Youth Commission and a Teen Library Corps.
- The program perceived by staff to have the highest asset building potential was Youth Ventures, in which youth participated both before and after school three to five days per week. Theater and video productions also had high asset building potential because of the intensity of participation required in the creative process. Subsequently, a middle school leadership program and after-school programs incorporating art and theater were added because of their strong asset building potential.
- Of the 10,000 participants reported as being registered in youth programs, 60.5% were located in two of the city's eleven zip codes, both of which were in central Aurora. Aurora is expanding to the south and east, but there are no recreation centers in these areas, and few other places that can be used to offer programs. This is an issue the LRSD has not yet solved. However, it is collaborating with libraries and schools in areas where there is a dearth of recreation facilities. Transportation from underserved areas to available programs has also been organized.

In one zip code, programs tended to be mainly drop-in. Almost 40% of participants in this zip code were involved in low intensity programs, compared to 21% overall. This zip code had high crime levels. Staff members were reluctant to operate programs there, especially in the evenings. As a result of this identified gap, several middle school after-school grant-funded programs were developed. In addition, the small recreation center in this area initiated several teen leadership groups that plan programs and participate in community service. This was done to involve youth in planning and decision-making, which was a key to more effective programming.

After reviewing these data, staff were guided through a creative exercise to consider how they could increase program asset building intensity without significantly increasing costs. Emphasis was on increasing the number of ongoing programs with relatively small groups, and reducing drop-in type activities.

Training

Approximately 12 key people in the LRSD were trained to be "asset presenters." The training was funded by a $5,000 grant from Aurora Prevention Link, a local coalition that was funded by the Center for Substance Abuse Prevention. Materials provided for the training included a Search Institute video, overheads, and handouts. These could be used by these key staff when doing training for others. Two follow-up "debriefing" sessions were held to provide ongoing support for trainers. These trained asset presenters subsequently provided trainings for other department staff and extended groups such as Parent-Teachers Association, Court Appointed Advocates, and Leadership Aurora. A training outline used in these sessions is shown in Exhibit 3-3.

Exhibit 3-3

Staff Training Sample Schedule

Minutes	
5	Welcome, Introductions
5	Questions: Who works with children? Who sometimes has children come to them? Who has children? Who has neighbors, friends with children: If you could get a 95% guarantee that your children would go through adolescence without drugs, alcohol, crime, pregnancy, would you want to know what that is?
5	Let's brainstorm what kids need to grow up healthy.
10	Explain Search Institute research and graphs.
15	What are these assets? External and Internal Categories What assets were important to you? How does this relate to older adults? How does this relate to younger children? What are you already doing to build assets?
10	Quiz with prizes
10	Break
15	Principles of Asset Building Look at handouts How could you increase asset building without significantly increasing costs. Brainstorm and share more creative ideas (in work groups)
10	Importance of all of us building assets-web activity
5	Closure: One thing you will do in next week to build assets. Say out loud and get asset pin.

Specific means for increasing assets in the community were discussed in these training sessions, including: (a) increasing the number of youth exposed to asset development opportunities; (b) increasing the number of assets available to youth through their involvement in programs; (c) assisting youth to develop each asset more fully; (d) increasing the number of adults involved in building assets in youth; and (e) increasing the ability of youth to build assets in others.

Participants were given examples of how to facilitate asset outcomes from programs and in their communities, and were encouraged to view asset building as part of their everyday interactions with youth. Key questions to help staff implement asset building are contained in Exhibit 3-4. Participants were asked to make a commitment to undertake at least one action to build assets in the next week. This could be as simple as: (a) speaking to neighborhood children or learning their names; (b) looking teenagers in the eye when you pass them; (c) asking young people for their opinions and then listening to the responses without contradicting them; (d) noticing when a youth does something right and commenting on it; (e) becoming a mentor to a young person; and (f) including children in multigenerational activities.

Exhibit 3-4

Key Questions to Stimulate Asset Building Implementation

1. What are you currently doing to build assets?
2. What can you do to increase assets in each of the following five key ways?
   - Increase number of assets focused on in current programs
   - Increase the focus and intensity of a given asset
   - Increase the number of significant adults committed to building assets
   - Increase the ability of youth to build assets in each other
   - Increase the number of youth who are exposed to asset building programs
3. What could you do to build more assets without significantly increasing costs?
4. What can you do to build more assets in each of the eight asset groups? e.g., support, empowerment, boundaries, constructive use of time, commitment to learning, positive values, social competencies, positive identity.
5. Name that Asset: What can you do to build ____________? (name an asset)
6. How can you increase positive intergenerational interactions?

Results

A number of positive outcomes emerged from the asset identification process. For example:

- Youth Ventures incorporated a community service component as part of their activities. Participants became involved in a "Coats for Kids" project, where they collected second-hand coats which were distributed to needy youngsters as part of a larger metro-wide effort called "Coats for Colorado" coordinated by a local television station.
- Youth Ventures began sending home parent newsletters about asset building. These were based on a template provided by the Search Institute. Contents explained the assets, and focused on how parents could impact assets with specific examples, such as improving communication, having family time or game nights, and getting involved in school.
- A brief information sheet, "A Coach's Role," in building assets was developed and distributed to all youth basketball coaches. This provided one more way to educate coaches on "appropriate" behavior. Staff members continually work with coaches to de-emphasize competition and emphasize assets. They stress how important the coach is as a role model.
- A companion information sheet, "A Parent's Role in Youth Sports," was distributed at basketball parents' meetings and was used in other youth programs (e.g., dance and gymnastics).
- The West Jam program, an after-school drop-in gym program, was redesigned to involve students in ongoing small groups with adult leaders, rather than using a drop-in format. This program was scheduled to lose its funding because the drop-in format provided little meaningful contact and impact. When the program was redesigned, funding was increased and the program became sustainable. Positive outcomes were also demonstrated (increased assets, decreased suspensions, improved attendance) with the new small group format.
- Youth Services staff developed plans to conduct a year long, department-wide youth leadership program to foster "leaders in training," "coaches in training," and "junior lifeguards." The intent was to increase youth opportunities for ongoing involvement in contributing to the community and to positive peer and adult influences.

Four general principles for enhancing asset development emerged. First, the intentionality of programming and training efforts was increased to enhance asset building. Second, the intensity of programs was increased by working with smaller groups, and terminating or amending drop-in programs in favor of more structured activities. Third, improvements in communication about assets to staff and parents were made in an effort to increase the number of adults who were consciously building assets.

Fourth, specific focus was directed at enhancing three specific assets: community values youth (#7); youth as resources (#8); and service by youth to others (#9) (Exhibit 3-1). Through the programs described below, youth had multiple opportunities for input into programs designed to facilitate volunteering and contributing to their community in a meaningful way. Five of the eight programs are specifically located in a zip code that was identified as low income and most underserved, and three others, while not located in that area, involved youth from that zip code. These eight programs are described in the following paragraphs.

Aurora's Contributing Teens (ACT) consists of middle school youth who are "hidden leaders" (Exhibit 3-5). The program was developed, using grant funding, specifically to build assets in middle school youth who are not leaders in their schools but who have that potential. Through ACT, youth and their parents are taught about assets. Youth complete 40 hours of training and then volunteer in the community for at least 80 hours of service over a 12-month period. In its second year, the approximately 30 ACT youth (two classes) set a goal of contributing 2000 hours of community service over 12 months and exceeded their target. They volunteered to work at the Senior Center serving meals, to be assistants to an animal groomer; and for a theater group creating scenery, and helped teach swimming and gymnastics classes. Youth are part of the program for a full year and get public recognition and thanks.

Exhibit 3-5

Aurora's Contributing Teens Program

The Aurora Contributing Teens (ACT) program increases youth involvement in community life by providing leadership training and ongoing volunteer opportunities that benefit both youth and the community. Special emphasis is put on recruiting youth, ages 12 to15, who are "hidden leaders;" youth with much potential, but with little opportunity to develop positive connections to the community.

The Volunteer Center provides a vehicle for Aurora residents to locate volunteer opportunities and matches those citizens with a variety of city and non-profit agency projects. Youth were welcome to become involved, but there was no organized effort to recruit or place them in community volunteer positions. Feedback from the community indicated that youth volunteers would be most welcome if they were prepared in job related skills and had ongoing support after placement.

Building and sustaining relationships are critical to the success of this project, as in many other skill building projects involving youth. Significant staff time is spent building relationships with youth and their families, and on fostering similar relationships between youth and volunteers. Youth, especially middle school youth, who are greatly under-served by most communities, need adults and programs that provide structure and stability.

Once youth complete the first year of the project and reach an appropriate age, they receive preference in securing paid positions within the city and the community that utilize their skills. In addition, a connection to the business community has been developed so employers recognize and value the leadership experiences youth have gained when they apply for other types of work.

The first two years' program goals were to train at least 60 youth; train supervisors in asset development; develop a youth advisory committee for the program; enable youth who graduated from or left the project to receive assistance in making connections with other opportunities for volunteering, leadership and/or employment; and ensure that youth received public recognition for their efforts.

Exhibit 3-5 Continued

To ensure the program's continuation after the initial funding period, a loosely formed committee consisting of the project's Advisory Board and Leadership Aurora members, developed a plan for raising continuation funds. The campaign's goal was to find 50 to 60 community partners, who would each donate at least $500 to the project. In the first year seven "official" community partners supported the program with one providing $2000. However, many other businesses donated food, supplies and gifts for the youth. Private foundation funding, and continued in-kind and cash support from the City of Aurora will continue to supplement the campaign.

The main lessons learned during the first two years of the project were how to:

- Recruit and retain middle school youth for a leadership project, from within both urban and suburban schools and neighborhoods.
- Design and deliver an asset-based training series to middle school youth with diverse ethnic, economic and educational backgrounds.
- Provide opportunities for and support middle school youth in volunteer service throughout the community.
- Engage business and community leaders in a youth leadership project.
- Staff and manage a high quality, effective project on a relatively low budget.

The Aurora Youth Commission was created by ordinance of the City Council. After its first full year of activity it was recognized by the Community Development Department for its contributions to the community (Exhibit 3-6). The Commission has 14 youth, aged 14-20 and five adult members who participated in the Adult/Youth Summit, Teen Spree, the Time Capsule, several school/community meetings, and Arbor Day. The Commission also advises the City Council on youth issues.

The Teen Advisory Group consists of eight teens who meet regularly at one of the recreation centers to plan and implement Teen Scene, a weekly drop-in teen program on Wednesday, Friday, and Saturday nights, which includes dances and special events. This group also assists with MVP nights (an evening of swimming, games, basketball, inflatable activities and dancing to a DJ with a prevention related theme), and serves as mentors to the Junior Titans.

Participants in the *Teen Library Corps* (TLC) staff a small library learning center at a neighborhood recreation center in an underserved and low income area which was funded through grant money. This center has four computers, books in English and Spanish, and the ability to locate, reserve and obtain materials from other libraries. TLC members encourage youth to use the library resources after school. The eight teens in this group were trained by library staff to check books in and out, assist users with the computers, and answer questions about the library learning center.

The Junior Titans, Teens In Training for Aurora's Neighbors, is a group of 9-12 year olds (mostly boys), which meets once a week to engage in volunteer projects, e.g., working on assembling packets of information for Original Aurora Renewal. The group was formed after pre-teens saw the TLC group involved in projects at one of recreation centers, and expressed an interest in doing something similar.

Exhibit 3-6

The Aurora Youth Commission

The Aurora Youth Commission (AYC) was created to advise the City Council and the LRSD in matters pertaining to youth interests in the city. The mission of AYC is to create and maintain a positive environment for all youth in the City of Aurora through partnerships that foster community resources for youth involvement, leadership, recognition, and empowerment, where youth and the community are strongly committed to each other's well being. Creation of AYC met a need for creating more opportunities for youth involvement in community life and more programming for older youth.

- The AYC was formed as a direct result of efforts to build assets and convince adults that youth can contribute. The Commission gives youth a voice in city activities, opportunities to develop leadership abilities and undertake service activities. The AYC provides a youth viewpoint on community affairs affecting Aurora's youth. The Commission's goals are to: Make recommendations and advise the City Council and Department of Library and Recreation Services on specific issues, problems, and optional solutions involving youth activities in the community.
- Encourage the initiation of programs of general interest to youth.
- Enlist the cooperation of all segments of the community in being more responsive to the youth community.
- Issue reports regarding its studies, research, examinations and other activities and make annual reports to the City Council Boards, Commissions and Youth Programs Policy Committee and City Council.

To the maximum extent possible, AYC youth members are given responsibility for all aspects of planning activities, running meetings, governance of the group, setting standards of attendance, participation and behavior of youth commission members, and interacting with agencies, boards, committees, schools and elected leaders in the community. The commission is made up of fourteen youth members (14-20 years of age), five adult members and two staff liaisons (in case one cannot attend). Commission members serve two-year terms. Vacancies on the Commission are filled through applications to the City Council. Commission membership is intended to reflect the diversity of Aurora's youth. Adults are considered who express interest in advocating youth positions. Adults may be representatives of school districts, the business community or the general public.

AYC does its work through a series of sub-committees related to:

- leadership, focused on developing youth leadership programs, sponsoring youth employment seminars, etc.;
- community service, focused on identifying opportunities for youth to volunteer services within the community; and
- specific issues of interest to youth.

Go Girls meets weekly. This group of 8-10 girls, aged 11-18, sets their agenda, establishes group norms for positive behavior, explores career options and gets involved in periodic community service projects such as the North Aurora Pumpkinfest.

Make a Difference Day. Working with the Volunteer Center, youth from Downtown Aurora Visual Arts, the Asian Pacific Development Center, Go Girls and TAG joined together and created three portable plexiglas murals on Make a Difference Day. These murals demonstrated cultural inclusion and sensitivity to world issues. The murals have been on display at North Branch Library, Asian Pacific Center, Moorhead Recreation Center, and a local mall.

The LRSD hosts a "Youth Recognition" ceremony to honor 60 youth who have been leaders and who have provided volunteer service through these programs. Each youth is given an award based on one, two or three years of service. The Mayor and several City Council members attend to present awards. This annual event helps communicate that the community values its youth.

Development of Surveys to Evaluate the Assets Model

In a previous position, the Prevention Services Supervisor developed a database consisting of 400 questions (approximately 10 per asset area) that could be used in program evaluations. Program leaders can enter the database and identify the questions relevant to their top five asset impact areas, and then select three to seven questions for each asset. A computer program generates either a post-retrospective survey form, or a pre-test, post-test format. The computer was programmed to alternate items and to print a survey form with a five point Likert-type scale ranging from "Always (5) to Never (1)." (Exhibit 3-7 describes the steps taken to develop the instrument).

In Aurora, Aurora Public Schools use the survey to evaluate their Safe and Drug Free Schools Program, while the LRSD has used it to evaluate both its after-school and the Aurora's Contributing Teens programs. In one after-school program, the evaluation indicated an impact on caring adults and role models, but no impact on attitudes toward school engagement. As a result, further efforts were made to provide connections between the program, school teachers and school day activities. The positive changes in the programs revealed by the evaluations made it more possible to obtain grant funding.

Lessons Learned

- *Train several people from various program areas to be "asset champions."* They may be supervisors or program leaders. The best people are those who have a passion for the usefulness of the asset building approach. Ongoing and updated training is needed to reflect changes in staff and improvements in procedures.
- *Build on what is already being done.* Staff are likely to be resistant if they believe this is just "another program," and that their previous work is being devalued. Developmental Assets is not a program, but an approach to youth development which complements their existing work. When staff are shown how to extend what they are already doing by doing it more effectively, they are more likely to become excited. This builds on people's strengths rather than focusing on the negative, a key principle in the asset-building paradigm.

Exhibit 3-7

Development of Surveys to Evaluate Asset Model Outcomes

To develop questions for the assets survey, the Prevention Services Supervisor took each of the Search Institute's 40 Developmental Assets and asked how would someone "see, hear, know" that this asset is being learned. From this, several different statements were written that demonstrated strength of the selected asset in a variety of ways. At least one statement in each set was stated in the negative form. For example:

Adult Role Models (#14)

- Adults I know volunteer in my community.
- Most adults I know show respect for people and their property.
- I have never seen my parents/guardians drunk.
- My parents/guardians help other people.
- Lots of adults I know break the law if they can get away with it (reverse scored).

After statements for all the assets had been written, three people who worked in the prevention field and were familiar with the asset approach reviewed all the items and provided feedback. Once there was agreement on the statements, they were reviewed by someone at a literacy center to evaluate whether the statements were written at the sixth grade reading level.

The analysis portion of the database was then developed. The mean and standard deviation of each asset was calculated and a t-test for paired comparison scores conducted. In addition to showing the change in each asset level, all scores are translated to a 100-point standard scale so that the relative strength of any given asset can be determined.

As a pilot, a form for five assets was developed for a Multicultural Youth Leadership Program that met weekly from September to May. Group members were surveyed, along with a group of 30 ninth graders in a local study hall class which did not have any designed interventions. The Leadership group showed statistically significant changes on the items, while the control group did not. Indeed, the control group showed a negative change on the item relating to abstaining from drug use, which is consistent with the developmental trends for increased substance use between the freshman and sophomore years in high-school. The results of this procedure gave the developer confidence in the instrument's validity.

Finally, the Executive Director of the Center for Health Policy and Program Evaluation at the University of Wisconsin reviewed the instrument and development processes. The reviewer felt that the methodology was sound, but recommended the development of two separate forms of the post-retrospective test (one form reflecting attitudes or behavior before the program and one form reflecting attitudes after the program) to reduce the likelihood of selection of "desirable responses."

❖ ❖ ❖

- *Seek every opportunity to weave assets into what the department, (or community) is doing.* Raise the subject at staff meetings and teach others in the department and city. In Aurora, the assets approach is periodically presented at brown bags for city staff. Special presentations have been done for police and librarians. Include the asset principles in newsletters, department flyers, and parent handouts. Try to imbed them into existing programs.

- *Be patient and join forces.* Both major school districts in Aurora are now using the asset framework so there is synergy and shared resources, exemplified by such actions as doing presentations for each other and joining together on projects. Asset building is never complete. It takes patience and repetition to begin to see real outcomes.
- *Do not forget adults need assets too!* Recognize staff efforts and new ideas by rewarding adult asset builders. Keep staff from getting burned out. Make the process fun. Point out how staff interactions also build assets for each other. For example, in Aurora, a bimonthly column is written about staff who are "caught" building assets in the department. When someone is highlighted, a copy of the newsletter with an asset pin and a movie pass are sent to the person.

Sources

1. Search Institute, www.search-institute.org
2. Kathy Nelson, Administrator of Special Services, City of Aurora, Colorado

CHAPTER 4

THE YOUTH INVOLVED PROCESS

In the City of Richmond, British Columbia, Canada, a working group was created consisting of people from youth service agencies and city departments to gather information from youth, service providers, parents and others on youth issues. There were three main reasons for creating it: (i) youth issues were becoming more visible and greater concern was being expressed about dealing with them; (ii) the 10- 24 age cohort comprised 20% of Richmond's population and development of a youth strategy would communicate that youth initiatives were as important as other prominent community concerns; and (iii) the City of Richmond and community associations were investing considerable resources in services and programs targeted at youth, but these services had evolved independently of one another and it was recognized that more could be achieved if there was a unified approach to service provision.

The working group identified six priority issues:

- *Youth wanted a strong voice and involvement in decisions.* They wanted to be consulted in decisions that affected them. Suggestions included: incorporating the views of youth when making city/community decisions; and consultation in the design and operation of programs and services targeted at youth.
- *Youth wanted a place in the community where they had ownership and responsibility, felt welcome and safe, and could socialize, obtain information, and receive services.* While community centers catered to a sector of youth, they desired more autonomy and independence from adult-like facilities. Hence, the call for separate dedicated spaces, in which youth could socialize through hanging out. Suggestions included: youth friendly spaces in community centers and youth resource centers/spaces.
- *Youth wanted support for their agenda.* They wanted institutions like City Government, School Board, Health Board, Library Board, community associations, and community groups to be advocates for youth resources. Youth acknowledged the need for support from adults, but wanted this support to emerge from a cooperative effort. Suggestions included: better communications about services and programs; direct access to services; more information and education on health matters; more media coverage of the positive contributions that youth provide to the community; and more youth workers at community centers.
- *Youth wanted to be seen as positive contributors to the community.* They wanted the community to see them as a valuable resource, instead of being influenced only by media images which too often were negative. Acceptance, recognition and fair treatment by adults was as important to them as participating in particular activities. Suggestions included: promotion of youth activities;

working with media to develop positive news stories; annual youth week festivities; and creating opportunities for youth to gain an understanding of their city.

- *Youth wanted to know what programs and services were available to them.* Although multiple programs were offered to youth, many did not have access to the programs or to information telling them what was available. Suggestions included: more structured program delivery; direct information given to students in schools classrooms, youth organizations and clubs; and information presented in a simple, easy to understand, youth-friendly manner.
- *Youth wanted more education/ information about drugs, sex, and health matters.* They believed this education should begin at an earlier age, and that the information should be presented in an uncensored form. Many believed that by grades 11 and 12 youth already have taken action on these issues, so extensive information needed to be made available much sooner. Suggestions included: providing education/information in the public libraries and schools, and providing uncensored information on health issues in grades 5, 6, and 7.

The Adopted Youth Services Strategy

Based on the information gathered by the working group, the City Council approved a City Strategy for Youth Services. The strategy was based on ten principles which provided a framework for coordinating actions by city departments, multiple community groups and youth groups (Exhibit 4-1). For example, it was recognized that working with adolescent youth is different from working with younger age groups because adolescents need to be more involved in decision making. Other principles addressed program structure, program spaces, and the way youth are perceived by the community.

Exhibit 4-1

Principles for Formulating a Youth Development Strategy

1. *The definition of youth is problematic.* Some community organizations define youth as 12 to 19, while others expand the definition to 24 years old. The 20 - 24 year age cohort is often under-serviced at a time when they lack job opportunities and economic self-sufficiency. The 20 - 24 age group has been included in the definition of youth by the U.N. Convention on the Rights for Children, and other entities. While the focus may be on 12 to 19 year olds, the community's broader mandate should be cognizant of the needs of 19 -24 year olds. With limited funds and many still living at home, positive social and recreational opportunities should be made available for this age group.
2. *The goal of all community services for youth should be to empower youth.* This requires that youth must have the opportunity to participate fully in societal decisions. Where youth have input and show responsibility, they should be given shared decision-making. Where they have shared decision-making, they should be given authority to plan, manage, implement and evaluate. The empowerment of youth becomes the output rather than the service.

Exhibit 4-1 Continued

3. *The vehicles for allowing youth input need to be adapted.* To encourage youth involvement, community organizations and agencies responsible for delivering services to a variety of ages will need to adopt mechanisms that are less structured. Having one youth attend a Board meeting of adults, with rules of governance, etc., is not likely to be perceived as meaningful involvement. Youth should be empowered to develop their own procedures, which lead to real decision-making power. Giving youth a budget for their area of influence, and allowing them to control how it is spent and what process they will go through to reach decisions, is advisable. A model of "parallel boards," with independent youth and adult boards working towards the same end, could operate in wide-ranging contexts. Agencies should consider getting youth input via means other than attending meetings.

4. *While youth have a desire to have their own space, every effort should be made for inter-generational opportunities.* Opportunities for youth and seniors to interact through recreation should be explored. Often discussions between youth and seniors show they have a greater understanding of each other than was initially recognized.

5. *Working with youth is different from working with younger age groups.* Youth desire control over decisions that affect them, and are likely to critically examine decisions made for them. Some city agencies and community organizations expect their services to be used and uncritically accepted. Youth often will be critical and demonstrate their disapproval or acceptance.

6. *Less structure is better than more structure.* A key youth activity is "hanging out". Facility space and program design must take this into account. Youth will use services only if they feel comfortable. Consider that the "who" and "where" of activities may be more important than the "what". New facility design and renovations should ensure there is space for "hanging out" as well as organized activities. Developing socialization skills is an important developmental task for youth. It involves independence from parents and establishing effective relationships with peers.

7. *The concept of community service for youth is generic, yet youth are comprised of individuals.* Individual differences and preferences must be accommodated. Generic "Teen Programs" are not effective. Treating youth as individuals and moving the service relationship with them from rapport to trust, and then from trust to relationship building is critical.

8. *The societal pressures facing youth are more intense for recent immigrants.* Access to services should take into account these pressures and efforts made to integrate new immigrants. Services and information directed at youth need to be easily accessible and understood by immigrants, particularly those who are new to Richmond.

9. *The needs of youth in Richmond must be met in a collaborative manner.* Just as the needs of youth will vary, so will the target services of the organizations and agencies serving them. Sharing information and resources is paramount. Since funding sources are likely to be reduced rather than expanded, there should be more joint funding of programs. The planning and implementation of Youth Week can serve as a model for collaborative activities.

10. *The community should invest more effort in promoting the successes of youth.* This strategy both builds youths' self-esteem and helps improve public and political perceptions of youth programs. The focus should be on accomplishments as well as needs. Ongoing press releases about youth successes should be part of every organization's mandate. Efforts to create awareness of what various agencies and committees have accomplished for youth also should be undertaken.

To translate the principles into practice, six core goals were specified and objectives were developed for each (Exhibit 4-2). Thus, for example, the recognition that working with youth requires different approaches from working with younger children, led to the goal of facilitating a voice and involvement for youth in decisions that affect them, and to operationalizing this with an objective to schedule city meetings at times when youth could contribute input.

Exhibit 4-2

Core Goals and Associated Objectives

Core Goals	This means that the City and/or pertinent community organizations will work to
1) Facilitate a strong youth voice and involvement in decisions that affect them	• Schedule meeting times that are convenient to youth. • Seek avenues other than "traditional" meetings to solicit youth input. • Support those youth who wish to make presentations or reports to city and community organizations. • Include input from youth at the beginning stages of city projects, programs and services.
2) Recognize youth as positive contributors to the community	• Promote and coordinate an annual youth week. • Publicize the variety of activities in which youth are involved in the community. • Encourage the media to create positive opportunities for youth to express their views and interests. • Create opportunities for youth to gain an understanding of their city and community. • Invite youth to participate in city and community organizations and activities. • Establish a civic recognition program for Richmond youth.
3) Develop a support base for youth in the City	• Establish full time youth workers at community centers. • Provide an adequate operating budget for the Richmond Youth Advisory Council, subject to approval of their work. • Encourage the Richmond Youth Advisory Council to expand its base to include non-traditional youth members (e.g. those in alternative education programs, street youth, parenting teens, etc.). • Initiate a communication/information program of available services and programs to youth. • Continue to support grants to community organizations providing services to youth. • Encourage the business community to create opportunities for youth involvement. • Focus attention on locations that attract youth to a place (e.g., malls) to involve and inform youth about services, programs and community activities. • Strengthen the presence and involvement of the police and outreach workers with youth in schools, community centers and places with youth activities.

Exhibit 4-2 Continued

Core Goals	This means that the City and/or pertinent community organizations will work to
	• Promote visitations, information and education with the Provincial courts and justice systems. • Provide in-service training for staff to help them better understand youth behavior and attitudes.
4) Develop physical places for youth in the community	• Develop dedicated places and programs for youth. • Enhance existing community centers and services so they are more responsive and friendly to youth (e.g., hours of operation, signage, information, staff training, etc.). • Facilitate the development of a safe shelter or place for youth.
5) Directly deliver programs and services to youth	• Seek youth input/involvement in compiling and distributing the information to youth. • Direct information to students in schools, classrooms, youth organizations and clubs; • Provide information to youth with a teen-friendly, realistic, practical approach. • Develop partnerships between schools, community centers and community agencies involved with youth. • Consider establishment of special teen talk/awareness phone line or electronic communication links for youth services and programs.
6) Provide good access for youth to education/ information about health.	• Expand sex and health education/information in schools, starting at earlier grades. • Familiarize youth with the services of community health nurses and the free clinic for youth. • Relocate the free health clinic to a central, more user-friendly location. • Create a network that better integrates community, parents and youth on health matters. • Improve linkages between school counselors and community health nurses. • Develop linkages with other community agencies involved with youth.

Adoption of the youth strategy required a shift in the working philosophy of youth workers in Richmond's Parks, Recreation and Cultural Services Department from the traditional structured program model to one which emphasized what became known as the "Youth Involved Process" (YIP). Under the traditional model, staff created a program (often with little input from youth), priced it, placed it at a location, promoted it, and hoped that youth would come. Under the YIP model, emphasis was placed less on the activity and more on processes. YIP recognized that the process of planning, facilitating, implementing and evaluating was more important than merely participating in a program. The shift in *modus operandi* was challenging for staff since it required a change in philosophy, work plans, job expectations and desired outcomes.

When the YIP approach was implemented, program and community leaders saw the value of the process as an effective tool for achieving desired youth outcomes. Buy-in was also evident from other key service providers such as the police and schools.

YIP is consistent with youth development practices which suggest that giving youth "voice" in the decisions and processes that impact their daily lives, empowers and helps train them to function more successfully as adults.

The YIP involves six steps: (1) group development, (2) idea generation, (3) facilitation, (4) logistics, (5) implementation, and (6) evaluation. Each of the steps is designed to enhance the development of specific external and internal assets from among the Search Institute's 40 Developmental Assets (Exhibit 4-3). For example, during the initial group development process, youth and leaders come to understand their roles and develop procedures for how the group will function.

Exhibit 4-3

The Youth Involved Process

The city's delivery of services to youth involves forming youth groups to undertake the steps necessary to create recreation and cultural opportunities for them.

External Assets	Steps for Involving Youth in Program Planning and Facilitation	Internal Assets
* Positive Peer Influence * Makes Constructive Use	GROUP DEVELOPMENT Understanding Roles and Functions	* Sense of Belonging * Interpersonal Competence * Cultural Understanding
* Youth Feel Empowered * Are Seen as a Valuable Resource * Community Values Youth	IDEA GENERATION Generated by Youth or Adults or Both	* Promotes Critical Thinking * Opportunity for Conflict Resolution/Consensus Building
* Presence of Adult Role Models * Positive Peer Influence	FACILITATION by Adults or Youth Guides the Process	* Caring * Equality * Integrity * Honesty * Responsibility
* Creates Goals and Expectations	LOGISTICS The Delegation of Tasks	* Achievement and Motivation * Planning and Decision-Making
* Service to Others * Providing Safe Places	IMPLEMENTATION	* Sense of Achievement
* Empowerment * High Expectations * Youth Are Seen As Resources	EVALUATION What Happened? So What? What Now?	* Recognizes Personal Power * Gives Sense of Power * Builds self-esteem

This promotes the external assets of *positive peer influence* and *making constructive use of time*. The internal assets of *sense of belonging, interpersonal competence* and *cultural understanding* may also be enhanced through these processes. Use of the Assets Model has given Richmond's youth programs more credence with professionals in related fields because they can directly see the benefits that are being sought and achieved. The YIP creates a positive culture, which attracts youth because they see that they are respected, and that their ideas and involvement are supported.

Exhibit 4-4 illustrates the use of the YIP with a group of approximately 50 teens who were involved in a group called HYPE (Harnessing Youth Power and Ethics). It describes how the six steps in Exhibit 4-3 were operationalized in the context of the HYPE program. Exhibit 4-5 reports the perspective of a HYPE participant on what was gained through participation in the group and its activities.

Exhibit 4-4

Using the Youth Involved Process with the HYPE Group

1. Group Development

Developing cohesive, functional groups creates the foundation upon which youth can move towards accomplishing projects, events, community service, etc. The focus is on finding ways for youth to create bonds with each other and with the youth workers.

The HYPE (Harnessing Youth Power and Ethics) youth group came together to organize National Youth Week activities. Some of these youth had been part of previous Youth Weeks and formed the core of the group. Get togethers were structured to include some type of icebreaker activity (e.g., Lame Name Games), team building or initiative task exercise. These activities provided a window for exploration of thoughts and critical arguments that could act as bonding agents to further the group's cohesiveness.

2. Idea Generation

Given the opportunity to meet new people and come together as a self-identifying group, young people will express their thoughts and ideas about what is important to them and their peers. Five months after planning a successful Youth Week, many of the youth were brought back together to begin the process of developing a new project. Brainstorming yielded suggestions for addressing common social problems such as bullying, substance abuse, racism, and environmental pollution. Discussion led the group to conclude that a lack of respect within an individual was a significant factor leading to these types of behavior. The discussion then flowed into identifying ways of promoting respect. As a result, the Respect Campaign was launched and supported by a small line of merchandise to support the message, including:

- Lanyards, with "*get up, stand up, be the change*" printed on them.
- Phat shoelaces, with "*respect...what if?*" printed on them
- A line of shampoo was developed and named "*Brainwash – Harnessing Youth Power and Ethics for a better World and Cleaner Hair*". Instructions on the back label read:
  - lather rinse...respect
  - suitable for all colours and ages
  - let it all sink in
  - *helps eliminate "flakes"*

Exhibit 4-4 Continued

3. Facilitation

The role of facilitating the Youth Involved Process usually falls upon the youth worker. Its form is dependent on factors such as the "maturity" of the group, and presence of older youth who have a working knowledge of facilitation. The facilitator is guided by an underlying goal of creating avenues for asset building, as well as accomplishing project goals.

With the Respect Campaign, the facilitator engaged the group in discussions through which youth were able to articulate issues/problems and solutions to address those problems. Discussion enables participants to relate to issues on a personal level, to tell their stories, to share and have their ideas validated by others. Open-ended or front-end loading questions were asked (e.g., Do you think there is a way to take the Respect Campaign into the community) to stimulate conversation.

4. Logistics

Once the project concept was solidified and everyone had a reasonably good understanding of what they were doing, the Respect Campaign moved into production which involved developing the merchandise and a method for taking the message into the community. Merchandising involved sourcing out shampoos, bottles, labeling etc. Taking the message into the community required another round of generating ideas, reaching consensus, identifying roles and steps to implement the plan.

5. Implementation

The Respect Campaign developed a hair washing station to promote the brainwash shampoo concept as well as random acts of kindness by blitzing the public with carnations, chocolate and free smiles. The afternoon started with presentations of the U-ROC (Richmond Outstanding Community)Youth Awards. The campaign put youth before the public and enabled them to express a message to people without fear of reprisal, stereotyping or "ageism". Working as a group helped develop a sense of place and pride within each youth.

6. Evaluating

After the event the group met to celebrate their successes and lay the foundation for future projects. The reflection was a guided process designed to recognize, acknowledge and validate the impacts that occurred relative to intended goals and unintended outcomes. The learning comes from integrating new and past experiences. What did you see? Feel? How did it affect you? How do you think it affected others? HYPE members felt the campaign was well received by those who experienced it. They were excited by the media attention, proud to be able to assert themselves in a pro-active manner, and saw a need to maintain the respect theme in future projects. The experience also created a strong sense of belonging and loyalty to the group. Many continued to meet weekly until the end of the school year, and each week during the summer.

Exhibit 4-5

Thoughts from a Richmond Youth about Her Involvement in Hype

Today is Monday Sept, 24th. As I sit here I can't help but think that it is just 4 days short of the one year anniversary of my first HYPE meeting . I came to the meeting under the impression that because the people there were former youth week planners, this meeting was going to be about that. I was surprised that all of the planning had to get started as early as September. About 10 minutes into the meeting I realized I thought wrong, but was not quite sure what the purpose was. There was all this talk about shoelaces and bracelets and somebody recapping that at the last meeting they decided to focus on promoting respect. We played the Lame Name Game and "if you had any siblings," and after that we were split up into four groups with our own color. Ben (our youth leader) told us to go all over the 8th floor to find our own colored yarn and then tie pieces together to make a long string. Through this we figured out that tying all the coloured strings together demonstrated how much of a team we truly are. Thanks Ben.

I left the meeting knowing that this group was something totally different than I've ever been involved in. I was quite intimidated that there were so many people there and only a couple that I knew, but I vowed to come back the next week. And I did.

I know that I have learned so much, but it is difficult to put it all into words. I'm not scared to go alone because I know that I am comfortable there. But I am also comfortable everywhere. I used to think I always needed to go to new things with a friend so I wouldn't look out of place and have someone to talk to. I have a totally different outlook on that now. I feel that I am more independent, and I know I can start talking to someone whereas before I would not dream of doing something like that. Pretty much since the start of HYPE I have interacted more freely with people, and since then I have joined various groups on my own and made friends there instead of bringing mine with me. I am also not afraid of talking in front of a group as much as I used to be. I admit I'm quiet, but I don't start to get nervous at the idea that my turn will be soon and I will have to talk and everyone will be listening to just me. I think that my friends who have known me from the beginning have probably noticed that.

My favorite part of being in all these different youth groups was knowing that everybody's ideas are always wanted and we can do anything we put our minds to. I have many memories. The trip to Seattle with YIA was fun and interesting. During a HYPE meeting once in March, I remember Ben and others trying to figure out the physical equation of spit travelling off of the 8th floor of the city hall.

....being involved makes me feel complete, going longer than a week without doing anything makes me slowly begin to forget an important part of me. I know that I have grown as a person because I chose to get involved. I know I have changed for the better and I know that when I'm older I want to give others that opportunity as well.

I guess there's really only one thing left to say: See you next Thursday. Same HYPE time, Same HYPE floor, Same HYPE channel.

The YIP can be viewed as one dimension of an overall community development model. The process is consistent with the principles of the City's youth strategy by providing youth with a voice and involvement in decisions that affect them, recognizing youth as positive contributors to the community, and delivering programs and services directly to youth. Transition to the YIP model requires a shift in philosophical approach, changes in youth workers' job expectations, and requires evaluative tools that focus on process as well as outcomes. The coordinator of Youth Services has been responsible for facilitating the shift through providing training, staff workshops, and retreats within the department.

Groups that remain coherent over an extended period of time look for new challenges which may take their activity into realms beyond recreation; such as community service, humanitarian work, or social or political activism. Youth grow up and leave the YIP because they graduate from high school, enter the workforce or in some cases drop out of school. Youth who have been part of this system, sometimes return as mentors to help guide youth who are beginning in the program.

The YIP facilitates youth input into planning processes. This differs from identifying a single youth "representative" to serve on an adult planning committee or task force. This alternative approach respects the role of youth as major stakeholders in the process of identifying both issues and vehicles through which they can be addressed. For example, youth should play significant roles in the development of skateparks, prevention strategies (such as substance abuse, crime prevention and violence prevention), late-night programming initiatives, safe communities projects, public art projects, and transportation systems.

Staff Development and Training

The YIP provides the foundation for staff training and development. In staff meetings, youth workers revisit the central program principles and discuss better ways to implement the YIP process (Exhibits 4-1, 4-2 and 4-3). At annual staff retreats work plans are reviewed which support and further the effectiveness of the YIP. Departmental activities that have been guided by the YIP conceptual framework include:

- developing the YIP/asset building model;developing a youth co-ordinator job analysis;
- developing work plans placing a high emphasis on asset building through involving youth;
- developing tools for evaluating successes and learning;
- ascertaining the value of the YIP through testimonials from youth and parents;
- promoting recognition within the department, city, provincial recreation agencies and the immediate community; and
- advocating support for youth services.

Richmond's eight youth workers (two of whom are outreach workers) are employed on a full-time rather than a part-time basis, which enables them to better develop a rapport with youth, decreases staff turnover, and provides time to create relationships and undertake program advocacy with other youth serving organizations.

Staff attendance at conferences helps to: broaden understanding of youth issues; provide exposure to a variety of youth driven initiatives; obtain information on developing youth friendly communities; and gain information about other safe communities initiatives. Staff are also encouraged to enroll in courses that enhance their skills in topic areas such as group facilitation; communication skills in building relationships with youth; values and beliefs in working with youth; principles of positive peer culture; and conflict resolution.

Evaluation

At this time, a formal evaluation process for the YIP has not been established. However, staff have developed a series of questions that can be used to determine if inputs to the program are being appropriately managed. In addition, the program tracks indicators of program outcomes. These indicators include the extent to which the YIP:

- creates avenues for asset building;
- promotes the intrinsic benefits of recreation and social development through recreation.
- bridges gender, race and other demographic variables, encouraging people to work together;
- creates youth friendly programs and services which lead to higher participation rates overall. Over time, this leads to a change in perception where youth begin to expect a higher level of service;
- develops youth specific services; e.g, skateparks, youth health clinics, and reduced criminal activity and problematic behaviors in parks;
- creates mutual networking between youth and community resources, e.g, youth and police partnerships;
- creates a sense of identity, ownership and community through involvement with the group;
- leads to recognition by other youth serving agencies or government agencies such as police; and
- increases levels of support, financial and moral, from city council, administration and community boards.

Lessons Learned

The Youth Involved Process exemplifies how the City's youth services unit defines its youth development philosophy and practices. Youth involvement and forums for a youth voice are seen as keys to developing a range of opportunities for youth.

A key contribution of the Richmond Parks, Recreation and Cultural Arts Department to youth service delivery has been the agency's responsiveness in developing objectives, processes and programs for meeting the needs that were articulated in the initial city-wide youth strategy. The Department defined what its overall role in youth development should be, and then developed approaches to service delivery that were consistent with their objectives. In many departments, service delivery involves delineating a calendar of events and programs, often with little relationship to understanding the outcomes that these events and programs are intended to accomplish with youth.

Strong, consistent leadership from the Youth Services Coordinator has facilitated the development of a process for working with youth. Leadership by the same coordinator for over seven years has ensured adherence to program goals, refinement of youth development processes, and consistency of staff training. Too often, key leadership staff create program concepts, but then move on to other responsibilities so the conceptualization does not have time to be fully implemented and mature.

Training is essential to help staff develop an understanding of both their program goals and their role in achieving those goals. Training should be geared towards building youth development skills such as conflict resolution, facilitation, adventure based learning and anger management. Training must take place both before a service is initiated and regularly on an ongoing basis so the knowledge base is consistently enhanced. For the YIP to work, leaders must be true to its principles. YIP represents a process that can be used in almost every context of youth service delivery.

Sources

Wayne Yee, Coordinator of Youth Recreation Services, Richmond, British Columbia, Parks, Recreation and Cultural Services.

CHAPTER 5

OPERATIONALIZING AND EVALUATING PROGRAM OUTCOMES IN AUSTIN

USING THE PROTECTIVE FACTORS MODEL

The Social Fabric Initiative (SFI) was launched by the Austin, Texas, City Council to reduce crime by adding police patrols and recreation activities, and adopting new approaches to service delivery in selected low income Austin neighborhoods. To fund its contribution to the initiative, the Austin Parks and Recreation Department (PARD) received $1.4 million for expanded recreation programming and services targeted at teens in these areas. This case describes the role of the Protective Factors model in guiding the recreation programming and evaluation components of the SFI.

Most of the PARD's SFI funding was used to initiate four programs: Neighborhood Teen Program; Roving Leader Program; Totally Cool, Totally Art; and the Summer Teen Academy. Each of these programs focused on a major facet of teen programming.

The Neighborhood Teen Program (NTP) is a teen club program designed to help youth develop life skills, knowledge and attitudes that will enable them to grow into productive adults. While the program is "fun," and uses recreational experiences to attract participants, the overall goal is to aid and enhance the quality of life for youth by providing relevant, diversified, educational and recreational programs and services within a safe and positive learning environment. The program's goals are to (a) increase youths' motivation to stay in school; (b) improve ability to make positive choices and resolve conflicts in a peaceful manner; (c) increase free-time activity skills; (d) increase knowledge about college and other forms of advanced education; and (e) improve job search and application skills. Teen club groups were formed at each of 12 community centers. At each site, teen coordinators facilitate a series of activities to accomplish the goals, and to establish a system that awards points for program participation. Points are tradeable for trips, concert tickets and other items (most of which are donated by businesses or community organizations). In a given year, approximately 400 teens participate in the program, with about 225 participating on a regular basis.

The *Roving Leader (RL)* program recognizes that many children and youth do not take advantage of the structured and drop-in programs available at the city's recreation centers or those offered in their neighborhoods by non-profit agencies. Some youth simply do not feel comfortable or are not inclined to participate in structured programs. In other cases, there are structural barriers to participation since some areas of the city do not have a recreation center. In other areas centers are too small to service all the needs of the community, are too distant for children to walk or bike safely, or access to them involves crossing dangerous intersections or gang territory demarcations. By bringing recreation activities to youth and taking them on a variety of educational and entertaining field trips, Roving Leaders hope to keep them out of trouble and to provide mentoring. While similar programs exist in other cities, Austin's is a relatively large program with a staff of approximately 20. The program leaders interact with approximately 800 youth per year, with 250 of these receiving intensive contact. A more detailed description of this program appears in Chapter 7 of this text.

The *Totally Cool, Totally Art (TCTA)* component emerged from recognition that few programs were offered by PARD which were not sports related. TCTA introduces approximately 400 youth per year to a variety of art media. During each program year, visual arts classes are offered to teens twice a week at 14 PARD recreation centers. Six separate four-week sessions are offered at each site. The program is designed to serve children in grades six through ten. The classes are conducted by artists who have a passion for the art medium they are teaching. The program's goals are to:

- increase teens' sense of belonging and sense that they have safe, positive and creative environments in which to participate during available free time;
- provide opportunities for new experiences in order to increase participants' knowledge, skills and possible interest in art as a career field;
- increase teens' trust and respect for other teens, adult mentors, artists and other authority figures;
- increase teens' ability to work cooperatively with others and communicate effectively in a group; and
- increase teens' ability to make creative and positive choices through self-expression.

The artistic media each year are changed in order to attract teens who have previously participated in the program. Media have included abstract art, illustration, computer animation, claymation, silk screening, bookmaking, 3-D art, movie making, storytelling and photography. This program is described in Chapter 11.

The *Summer Teen Academy (STA)* is the fourth component of the SFI recreation initiative. It was established to serve teens during the out-of-school summer months. It attempts to provide interesting activities in nonthreatening settings that will draw youth off the streets. The program is offered at approximately 10 school sites each year. While basketball remains the favorite activity, efforts are made to involve youth in other sports, the arts, and field trips. Program staff are drawn from school personnel, so youth from the surrounding neighborhood feel a connection to, and are comfortable with the staff. Using school staff also helps retain the support of principals for their school facilities being used during the summer months. Approximately 800 different youth participate in the program each summer.

When the initial SFI funding was authorized, PARD staff committed to conducting annual program evaluations. These evaluations fulfilled two main purposes: (i) The City Council wanted annual reports on program development, and empirical validation of the effectiveness of SFI would provide a strong case for continued funding; and (ii) PARD staff were committed to continuous program improvement and evaluations were key to achieving this. PARD invited faculty from the Department of Recreation, Park and Tourism Sciences, Texas A&M University (TAMU) to be the external evaluators. TAMU used funding from the National Recreation and Park Association and the National Recreation Foundation to undertake the initial evaluations. Over time, however, funding for the evaluations shifted from NRPA to the PARD. The willingness of the PARD to provide funding was tangible recognition of the perceived value of the evaluation process and outcomes.

The Protective Factors Conceptual Framework

The Protective Factors (PF) model was used as the basis for designing programs and it provided a framework for the evaluation of outcomes. The principle underlying the PF model can be illustrated by analogy. In winter, many people live under conditions that lead some of them to get the flu. These individuals may become debilitated from being out in the cold, or from stressful conditions in their lives; may not get enough exercise because of being confined indoors; and perhaps may not follow a nutritious diet. All of these factors stress the immune system. The risk of catching the flu also is increased by the number of people with whom there is contact. Having a flu vaccination often results in avoidance of the illness or in it being less debilitating. Lifestyle, habits and the surrounding environment put people at risk, but the flu vaccination provides a degree of protection that results in avoidance or reduction in risk. Those who have this protection and, thus, are not inflicted by the flu under conditions of exposure to risk, are said to be resilient.

An analogous situation applies to youth who are exposed to multiple risk circumstances in their homes, schools and communities. Some of them avoid the deviant behaviors exhibited by peers who grow up in the same environment. This observation has resulted in growing interest in "protective factors" that are operative in the lives of "resilient" youth, which enable them to avoid the negative consequences of multiple risk environments. Protective factors are those facets which impinge on an individual's life space that moderate and/or mitigate the impact of risk on subsequent behavior and development.[1] Resiliency has been defined as a pattern of successful adaptation following exposure to biological risk factors, and psycho-social risk factors, and/or stressful life events.[2] Protective factors and resilience help children and youth from high risk environments avoid behaviors that compromise health and normal growth, and help them achieve economic self-sufficiency, positive and responsible family and social relationships, and good citizenship.[1, 3] The protective factors approach shifts attention from identifying the risks to which children are exposed, to focusing on the protective mechanisms and processes of negotiating risk situations.[4]

Exhibit 5-1 provides a simplified view of this framework for understanding adolescent risk behavior. Column A identifies risk conditions to which youth may be exposed through their biological background, social environment, personality or behavior. Through exposure to these risk factors, the individual is "at-risk" of undertaking one or more risk behaviors (Column C), which in turn can lead to some of the health or life compromising outcomes listed in Column D.

Exhibit 5-1

Protective Factors Model

(A) Factors	(B) Protective Factors	(C) Risk Behaviors	(D) Health/Life Compromising Outcomes
Poverty Illegitimate Opportunity Models for Deviant Behavior Low Perceived Life Chances Low Self-Esteem Risk Taking Propensity Poor School Work Latchkey Situations	Interested & Caring Adults Neighborhood Resources School and Club Involvement High Control Against Deviant Behavior Models for Conventional Behavior Positive Attitudes toward the Future Value on Achievement Ability to Work with Others Ability to Work Out Conflicts Sense of Belonging Church Attendance Quality Schools Cohesive Family	Illicit Drug Use Drunk Driving Tobacco Use Delinquency Truancy Unprotected Sex	School Failure Legal Trouble Low Work Skills Unemployability Disease/Illness Early Childbearing Social Isolation Depression/Suicide Amotivation

Column B displays the protective factors which play a role in mediating, insulating and buffering "at-risk" individuals against the risk factors. Protective factors include such elements as youth knowing there is at least one adult who supports their positive development; the existence of places for youth to spend free time in a positive, productive environment; opportunities for youth to learn how to work together in a group and how to constructively resolve conflicts; and the opportunity to be around other youth who are demonstrating positive conventional behavior.

Development of the Protective Factors Scale

To evaluate program outcomes, an instrument was needed to measure them. Thus, the Protective Factors Scale was developed.[5] The survey instrument needed to be sufficiently short so that it would not deter staff or program participants from using it. Thus, it was limited to those 10 protective factors that the PARD deemed to be the most important outcomes of the recreation programs. These are listed and defined in Exhibit 5-2.

Exhibit 5-2

The Protective Factors Used in Austin

1) *Neighborhood Resources*: Knowledge of, and interest in, utilizing neighborhood recreation opportunities, including organized and informal programs and opportunities.
2) *Interested and Caring Adults*: The perception that there are adults who care about and are interested in teens, and who are available to help teens when they have problems.
3) *Sense of Acceptance and Belonging*: The perception of being liked and accepted by other teens and/or family members.
4) *High Controls Against Deviant Behavior*: The understanding that it is important and necessary to stay out of trouble and obey the rules.
5) *Models for Conventional Behavior*: Respect for, and appreciation of, teens, adults and institutions who model or reinforce appropriate behavior.
6) *Positive Attitude Toward the Future/Future Expectations*: Perception of oneself as having a positive future including the willingness to set and work to achieve goals, the willingness to be spontaneous and creative, and the understanding that one has some control over the outcome of daily events.
7) *Value on Achievement*: Interest in, and understanding of, the importance of doing well in school. Also includes the general idea of being successful and trying to do one's best in any area of involvement.
8) *Ability to Work with Others*: Understanding the importance of, and having the ability to get along with, other teens, be cooperative and be a good member of a team or group.
9) *Ability to Work Out Conflicts*: The ability to deal in a positive manner with problems that arise with other teens.
10) *Liking/Perceived Competence in Activity:* The degree to which one likes to do a particular activity and perceives oneself to be good at the activity.

A list of 8 to 15 items which described facets of each of the ten protective factors was developed. The list was reduced by a panel of university personnel and PARD professionals who selected the best worded and most divergent items for each factor. A statistical process was then used to identify the most reliable and valid items for each factor. The final instrument along with several different response formats is shown in Exhibit 5-3

Exhibit 5-3

Protective Factors Scale Formats

Pre-Post Version	Post Test Only Version	Retrospective Pre-Post Version
For each statement below, please indicate how much you disagree or agree with each statement.	As a result of participating in X, I have increased:	Two different forms used at end of the program: Form A: Before the program began, Form B: Currently, Note: tense for questions need to be adjusted depending on which form is being used. Wording below is for Form B.
Response Format: 1 = "Strongly Disagree" to 5 = "Strongly Agree"	Response Format: 1 = "Strongly Disagree" to 5 = "Strongly Agree"	Response Format: 1 = "Strongly Disagree" to 5 = "Strongly Agree"
1) I know a lot of activities in my community	My knowledge of a lot of activities in my community	I know a lot of activities in my community
1) There are things for me to do in my neighborhood	Knowledge of things for me to do in my neighborhood	There are things for me to do in my neighborhood
1) I am interested in programs that take place after school	My interest in programs that take place after school	I am interested in programs that that take place after school
1) I am interested in participating in programs in my community	My interest in participating in programs in my community	I am interested in participating in programs in my community
2) Adults are willing to help me with my problems	My understanding that there are adults who are willing to help me with my problems	Adults are willing to help me with my problems
2) I can turn to adults for help	My understanding that I can turn to adults for help	I can turn to adults for help
2) There are a lot of adults who are interested in me	Knowledge that there are a lot of adults who are interested in me	There are a lot of adults who are interested in me
2) There are adults who will look out for me	My understanding that there are adults who will look out for me	There are adults who will look out for me
3) I am an OK person	My understanding that I am an OK person	I am an OK person
3) I am wanted by the people around me	My understanding that I am wanted by the people around me	I am wanted by the people around me
3) There are other children who like me	My understanding that there are other children who like me	There are other children who like me
3) I am able to get along with friends	Ability to get along with friends	I am able to get along with friends
4) I must stay out of trouble	My understanding that I must stay out of trouble	I must stay out of trouble
4) I will be punished if I break the rules	My understanding that I will be punished if I break the rules	I will be punished if I break the rules
4) I must obey the rules	My understanding that I must obey the rules	I must obey the rules
4) I must follow the rules if I want to participate	My understanding that I must follow the rules if I want to participate	I must follow the rules if I want to participate
5) I respect authority figures	My respect for authority figures	I respect authority figures
5) I respect adults	My respect for adults	I respect adults
5) I respect children who stay out of trouble	My respect for children who stay out of trouble	I respect children who stay out of trouble
5) I respect people in charge	My respect for people in charge	I respect people in charge

Exhibit 5-3 Continued

6) I like to try new things	My desire to try new things	I like to try new things
6) I can set goals	My ability to set goals	I can set goals
6) I am creative	My ability to be creative	I am creative
6) I can deal with problems that might come up in the future	My understanding that I can deal with problems that might come up in the future	I can deal with problems that might come up in the future
7) It is important for me to always do my best	My understanding that it is important for me to always do my best	It is important for me to always do my best
7) It is important for me to stay in school	My understanding that it is important for me to stay in school	It is important for me to stay in school
7) It is important for me to do well in school	My understanding that it is important for me to do well in school	It is important for me to do well in school
7) I can succeed in life	My understanding that I can succeed in life	I can succeed in life
8) Cooperation is important	My understanding that cooperation is important	Cooperation is important
8) All players need a chance to play	My understanding that all players need a chance to play	All players need a chance to play
8) I try to treat other children with respect	My ability to treat other children with respect	I try to treat other children with respect
8) Teamwork is important	My understanding that teamwork is important	Teamwork is important
9) I can settle arguments without fighting	My ability to settle arguments without fighting	I can settle arguments without fighting
9) I try to solve problems in a positive manner	My ability to solve problems in a positive manner	I try to solve problems in a positive manner
9) I try to listen to the opinions of others	My ability to listen to the opinions of others	I try to listen to the opinions of others
9) I try to control my anger	My ability to control my anger	I try to control my anger
10) I like (name acitivity)	My liking for (name acitivity)	I like (name activity)
10) I am interested in (name activity)	My interest in (name activity)	I am interested in (name activity)
10) I want to improve my (name activity) skills	My desire to improve my (name activity) skills	I want to improve my (name activity) skills
10) My desire to keep playing/ doing (name activity)	My desire to keep playing/doing (name activity)	My desire to keep playing/doing (name activity)

This completed instrument has been used in evaluations in multiple communities across the United States. The A&M project team, for example, found the scales to be effective for measuring outcomes in studies of after-school programs in Dallas, as well as in the TCTA and NTP programs in Austin. In the Austin studies, the instrument showed positive results on factors where the PARD team anticipated programming would produce them and showed less impact on factors where the team predicted less change would occur because the programs had not been designed and structured to strengthen those particular factors.

The core elements of the overall evaluations undertaken for all SFI programs were similar. In general, they embraced measures of program inputs, outputs and outcomes (Exhibit 5-4). *Inputs* are the resources that are invested in the program, such as its leaders, facilities and equipment. *Outputs* are the types and number of activities offered, the number of youth participating in the program, the number of program hours provided, and the cost per unit of service. *Outcomes* are what happens to participants, parents and the community as a result of children participating in the program.

Exhibit 5-4

Evaluation Model

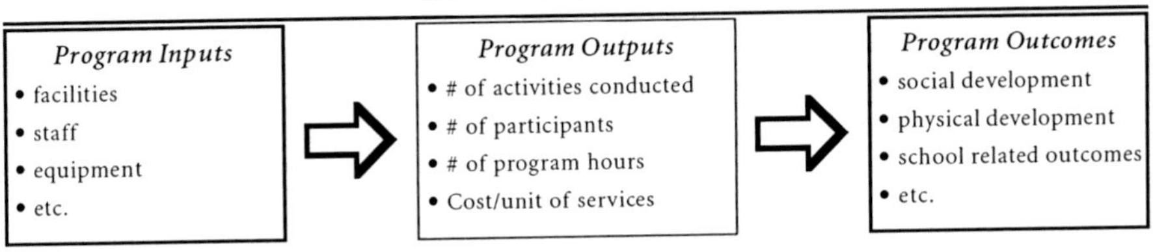

Using the framework shown in Exhibit 5-4 the evaluations consisted of five components: (a) verification of program rationale and need for the program; (b) program participation; program cost per unit of service; (c) ratings of quality of program inputs; (d) program satisfaction ratings; and (e) indicators of program outcomes (Exhibit 5-5). Registration and attendance databases were established for each program. Surveys and interviews with participants, parents, program personnel and, in some cases, other members of the community (e.g., teachers) were used to collect program satisfaction, program quality and outcome data.

Exhibit 5-5

Program Evaluation Components

Category of Evaluation	Means for Determining
Program Rationale Verification	Surveys and interviews with participants and parents regarding program need, what participants would be doing if not in the program.
Program Participation	Registration information including demographic indicators; attendance data.
Program Cost per Unit of Service	Program budget; cost divided by service units (e.g., number of program hours or number of participant hours).
Ratings of Quality of Program Inputs	Surveys of participants and parents. Format: Program X has "staff who care about me."
Program Satisfaction Ratings	Surveys of participants and parents regarding interest in signing up again for the program, and whether they would recommend the program to others.
Indicators of Program Outcomes	Surveys and interviews of participants, parents (and in some cases, teachers) regarding changes in knowledge, attitudes, skills, and behavior associated with program participation; data from school records.

An Example: Use of the Protective Factors Scale to Evaluate Austin's Neighborhood Teen Program (NTP)

The Protective Factors Model was used to evaluate the NTP outcomes. As an initial step for each program, program objectives were examined to ensure they clearly identified desired outcomes that were consistent with the model. A matrix was established which showed the relationships among program objectives, programming components necessary to achieve the stated objectives (program design), and measures used to determine whether the objectives had been met (evaluation). Exhibit 5-6 shows the matrix for the NTP.

Exhibit 5-6

Neighborhood Teen Program: Program Objectives and Means to Achieve and Measure Objectives

Objective	Means for Achieving Objective	Means for Measuring Objectives
To motivate youth to stay in school and maintain passing grades.	a) provide tutoring. b) show interest and discuss advantages of youth staying in school. c) provide points for getting good grades and being in school.	Protective Factor Items Value on Achievement Positive Attitude Toward the Future Other Measures: Improved school attendance Improved grades Attend tutoring sessions on a regular basis
To provide a setting where youth can feel a sense of belonging, be off the streets and in a positive, supportive environment.	a) create a positive, supportive club environment. b) provide mentoring and interaction with other teens. c) provide opportunities for teens to be responsible and make positive choices through leadership of the teen club.	Protective Factor Items: Neighborhood Resources Sense of Acceptance and Belonging Other Measures: Repeat attendance Efforts to recruit other teens to join the program
To increase participants' abilities to make positive choices about issues such as avoiding drug and alcohol usage, avoiding gang membership, avoiding pregnancy, and sex education.	a) utilize services of outside organizations to provide information about drug and alcohol abuse, and safe sex/ abstinence practices. b) provide alternatives to feeling a sense of belonging without having to join a gang.	Protective Factor Item: Models for Conventional Behavior Other Measures: Express negative attitudes toward use of alcohol/drugs Amount of time spent with youth undertaking conventional behavior Membership in gang Increased participation in teen programs
To contribute to participants' personal growth and job readiness.	a) teach job related skills. b) provide opportunities for teens to hold jobs and learn appropriate job-related skills.	Protective Factor Items: Neighborhood Resources Value on Achievement Positive Attitude toward the Future Other Measures: Ability to fill out a job application Knowledge of where to look for a job Successful pursuit of job opportunity when available

Exhibit 5-6 Continued

Objective	Means for Achieving Objective	Means for Measuring Objectives
To teach youth positive means for resolving conflicts	a) provide opportunities to discuss and find positive alternatives for resolving conflict situations.	Protective Factor Items: Ability to Work with Others Ability to Work out Conflicts
To increase trust and respect for other teens, adult mentors, and other authority figures.	a) provide opportunities for youth to interact with positive adult role models (e.g., center staff and other adult community leaders). b) provide opportunities for youth to interact with fellow teens in an environment that encourages respect and trust.	Protective Factor Items: Interested and Caring Adults Ability to Work with Others Ability to Work out Conflicts High Controls Against Deviant Behavior Other Measures: Teen rating of knowledge, teaching ability and preparation of teen leader
To provide opportunities for new experiences in order to increase participants' recreation and job choice repertoires.	a) provide opportunities for youth to experience new recreation activities. b) provide volunteer and other community service opportunities.	Protective Factor Items: Neighborhood Resources Value on Achievement Positive Attitude Toward the Future Other Measures: Participation of teens in new recreation activities, volunteer and other community service activities
To provide opportunities for youth to gain help with difficult personal and family issues.	a) provide adult mentors to talk with teens about difficult issues. b) when issues are beyond staff capacity to provide guidance, provide referral to appropriate organizations and agencies that can provide youth with assistance.	Protective Factor Items: Interested and Caring Adults Other Measures: Attendance at self/self-awareness programs Asks staff for help or where to go for assistance
To encourage cultural diversity awareness.	a) provide opportunities to interact with teens from other recreation centers/ethnic and cultural backgrounds.	Protective Factor Items: Other Measures: Willingness to interact with teens from various neighborhoods Positive statements about the value and importance of diversity

❖ ❖ ❖

The early statements of objectives for each of the four programs in the SFI were not expressed in terms that could easily be translated into expected outcomes. Further, program content was not always aligned with the stated objectives. Thus, the evaluators and program staff revisited the objectives and program content for each of the SFI programs. This goals explication process helped program staff to think more clearly about the relationship between a program's objectives and the components needed to achieve them, and facilitated the evaluation process.

This explication process also defined the way in which evaluators and program staff interacted. The evaluators were recognized as team members with responsibilities for helping shape the programs, as well as for providing feedback on how well the programs were meeting their stated objectives. At the same time, program personnel played a key role in providing input and feedback regarding the evaluation processes since the PARD needed evaluations that produced information which was relevant to program improvement.

Results from surveys using the Protective Factors Scale indicated that participants showed increases in several of the protective factor sub-scale areas as a result of participating in the NTP program (Exhibit 5-7). These scales have been used for several years in evaluating this program and results have consistently shown increases in ability to develop a positive outlook about the future, ability to work well with others, understanding that there are adults who are interested and care, and understanding that it is important to stay out of trouble.

Exhibit 5-7

NTP Program Protective Factor Scale Results From a Typical Annual Evaluation

As a result of participating in the NTP program, I increased:	Mean	Standard Deviation
my understanding that it is important to stay out of trouble	4.43	.76
my respect for teens and adults who are positive role models	4.39	.68
my understanding that there are adults who are interested in and care about me	4.38	.69
my ability to work well with others	4.35	.64
my ability to develop a positive outlook about the future	4.35	.65
my understanding that I am accepted by others	4.30	.75
the value I place on doing things well	4.29	.62
my ability to work out conflicts in a positive manner	4.18	.78
my knowledge of neighborhood resources	4.05	.71

* Response categories were from 1= Strongly Disagree to 5= Strongly Agree

Questionnaires have been administered over a number of program years. Different question and response formats have been used in an effort to derive the most meaningful and understandable results. In the early years, a stem of "As a result of participating in the TCTA program, I increased/decreased my..." was used for each item and responses were scored from -5 = Decreased a Great Deal to +5 = Increased a Great Deal. However, this format was found to be cumbersome for participants to fill out, and results were not easily interpretable by practitioners. More recently, the stem for questions has been modified to read, "As a result of participating in the NTP program, I increased my:" with responses ranging from 1 = Strongly Disagree to 5 = Strongly Agree. In the first instance, the assumption was made that the program could lead to either negative or positive impacts, but results using the initial survey response format showed there was much more likelihood of positive impacts.

For recent NTP evaluations, a reduced list of survey questions was used with single items representing each of the PF dimensions.[6] This was done to further reduce the time participants needed to complete the survey. The results displayed in Exhibit 5-7 suggest that the program was successful in strengthening protective factors for all dimensions. The greatest impact was on participants' understanding that it is important to stay out of trouble, respect for teens and adults who are positive role models, and understanding that there are adults who care about them. High, but lesser, impact was achieved in ability to work out conflicts in a positive manner, and knowledge of neighborhood resources. Program planners use this information to determine if program goals are being attained and sharpen program focus to deal with areas that are receiving lower scores.

Lessons Learned

- *In many cases, PARDs offer activities, without specifically thinking about goals.* The Protective Factors Model assisted Austin PARD personnel to understand the importance of designing programs to achieve desired outcomes. The model guided program conceptualization and planning, staff training, and the evaluation process.
- *Evaluation is of value both to funders and to program personnel.* The annual reports given to Austin City Council for each of the SFI component programs caused the Council to appreciate that PARD programs are more than "fun and games," and encouraged sustained funding for them. Program organizers conscientiously used the findings and recommendations to continuously improve the programs.
- *Meaningful evaluation requires full staff involvement in the development of data collection instruments, data collection, and interpretation of the data.* While it is possible to hire an external evaluator who does all of this work independently without involving staff, this approach will be much less meaningful to staff, and hence less likely to lead to substantive program improvements.
- *Most PARDs do not budget adequately for evaluation.* While it is possible to have evaluations undertaken by student interns from local universities, good quality evaluations usually require the leadership of people who are knowledgeable about evaluation practices and sensitive to working with professionals. Larger initiatives, such as the SFI, should plan to allocate between three and five percent of their budget (in this case $40-$70,000/year) to secure meaningful evaluations. Since there are economies of scale in these procedures, smaller programs are likely to require a larger percentage of overall funds.

- *Evaluation cannot be an after-thought.* If evaluation is considered only at the end of a program cycle, then it is unlikely to be effective because the objectives, program components and outcome measures are likely to be in non-measurable form, inconsistent or incomplete. For example, programs frequently do not specify what they expect to accomplish in measurable terms, which precludes meaningful evaluation.

Sources

1. Jessor, R. (1991). Risk behavior in adolescence: A Psychosocial framework for understanding and action. *Journal of Adolescent Health*, 12, 597-605.
2. Public/Private Ventures. (1994). *Community ecology and youth resilience: A report to the Annie E. Casey Foundation.* Philadelphia: Author.
3. Masten, A. S., & Garmezy, N. (1985). Risk, vulnerability and protective factors in developmental psychopathology. In B. B. Lahey & A. E. Kazkin (Eds.), *Advances in Clinical Child Psychology* (Volume 8, pp. 1-52). New York: Plenum Press.
4. Rutter, M. (1990). Psychosocial resilience and protective mechanisms. In J. Role, A. Masten, D. Cached, K. H. Nuechterlein, & S. Weintraub (Eds.), *Risk and Protective Factors in the Development of Psychopathology* (pp. 181-214). Cambridge, England: Cambridge University Press.
5. Witt, P. A., Baker, D. A., & Scott, D. (1996). *The Protective Factors Scale.* College Station, TX: Texas A&M University. http://rptsweb.tamu.edu/faculty/pubs/wittpub4.htm
6. Witt, P.A. *Non-Traditional Program Evaluation Reports.*
7. http://rptsweb.tamu.edu/faculty/witt/conpubs/ntp2000.PDF

Section 2

CREATING SPACES AND OUTREACH PROGRAMS

CHAPTER 6

THE OPPORTUNITIES AND CHALLENGES OF PARTNERSHIPS

While retaining our uniqueness and autonomy, we in the field of recreation, who share the same values and goals, can accomplish more by working together than we can on our own. This is the chance for us to demonstrate the full value of who we are and what we can do...Society needs help with its youth, and we have a piece of the solution.[1]

This case describes how multiple youth serving organizations in the city of Columbus, Indiana, (population 38,000) pooled their resources to both construct and operate a $5.9 million center for youth. The primary stakeholders included the Columbus Parks and Recreation Department (PARD), Columbus mayor and city council, Foundation for Youth (FFY), Boys and Girls Club, United Way, business leaders, and philanthropic organizations.

Background

The Columbus FFY was formed in 1928. The rationale for its genesis was to serve as an antidote to the growing community problem of juvenile delinquency. For the first 33 years, its main goal was supporting the Columbus Youth Camp facility which operated mainly in the spring and summer months.

In 1961, this was supplemented with a 32,000 square foot indoor facility, which included a gymnasium and indoor swimming pool, located in the low-income area of Columbus. When it opened, both the Boys Club and the Girls Club moved their programs into it. The goal of FFY is to provide an umbrella of support for all youth service organizations in Columbus, and to support the cost of FFY programming. Civic leaders were concerned about the outbreak of lawlessness by juvenile gangs. Thus, the enduring mission statement of FFY was "to promote the physical, mental and moral well-being of youth and to discourage and prevent juvenile delinquency."

The first Executive Director of the Foundation for Youth also became the first director of the Columbus PARD from 1948-1959. Thus, an early working relationship was established between the two organizations. The relationship was institutionalized by the Director of Columbus PARD also being on the FFY Board of Directors. Thus, the current Director has served on the FFY Board for over 20 years.

The FFY financed the operation of the center and its youth camp programs with fees from users, and funds solicited primarily from the United Way and the Arvin Foundation. However, these were inadequate to support long-term maintenance or any renovations to the center. Thus, by the mid-1990s, the heavy use of the center over a 35 year period had resulted in its deterioration and, consequently, a substantial decline in participants.

Momentum for a New Center

Given the facility's need for major renovation and repair, the associated decline in participation, and lack of funds to rectify the situation, serious consideration was given to closing the facility. The city government is a strong Mayor/Council Form and in 1995, following his election, the new mayor organized a series of public meetings throughout the community to listen to what residents believed should be the priority issues for the city council to address. His predecessor had been in office for 12 years, so the change in mayors was an obvious time to reassess the pulse of the community.

The new mayor was a former police officer. He anticipated that the priority concerns would relate to public safety. However, to his surprise, at every meeting the major concern was the FFY center. Repeatedly he was told, "We cannot let this youth facility continue to decline." *The Republic*, Columbus' daily newspaper observed in a lead editorial: "The $5 million that will be needed to rehabilitate and expand the current facility is a pittance compared to what we would have to pay for not doing anything." As this sentiment was repeatedly reiterated, the mayor recognized it should become one of his priority issues. The mayor's commitment to the project was enhanced because he had some personal emotional attachment to it. He stated,

> *The FFY has been a part of my life, or your life or the life of someone in this community for 70 years. Whatever success history might afford me, I will owe it — in no small part — to the FFY. I see the faces of several others in this audience who, like me, owe a debt of gratitude to this institution.*

In response, the mayor established a committee under his leadership to review the available options. It included representatives from the Columbus PARD, FFY, United Way, local corporate foundations, and interested community members. There was a lot of discussion about putting this building elsewhere i.e., it's a rundown part of town. However, the community was outspoken in opposing this plan. Thus, there was general agreement that the facility should remain in that area because that is where the need for it was greatest. The PARD Director commented, "We were confident that the 600-700 kids in the gymnastics program would travel to this facility from other parts of town, but if it wasn't in this location we believed most of the kids in this area wouldn't go to it and wouldn't be involved."

The committee learned that in addition to the FFY's need for a new or completely renovated center, the PARD was considering development of a new facility to house its gymnastics program. This program had 600 female participants and had outgrown the facility which it was currently leasing. Since both facilities were targeted at serving youth, the committee suggested that they be integrated into one center.

They recognized that both the FFY and CPARD facility needs had widespread community support. They believed that partnering to develop a joint facility would lead to cost savings in both construction and operating costs, and enhanced service delivery resulting from the complementary assets and strengths of the two organizations.

Financing the New Center

A study which was commissioned to develop a specification of the facilities needed, and the cost of renovating and expanding the FFY center to accommodate these facilities, projected the cost to be $5.9 million. The committee recognized that in addition to this capital cost, funding sources for the center's daily operation and maintenance, and for periodic major renovations also needed to be identified.

The Cummins Engine Foundation agreed to fund the architectural fees. Cummins funds the hiring of outstanding architects to design all public buildings in Columbus. The foundation provided the committee with a list of top-class architects and the committee selected one of them.

The Mayor and City Council agreed to issue $3.9 million in Economic Development Bonds which financed approximately 60% of the capital costs. Essentially, these were Certificates of Participation which meant the Economic Development Board (EDB) served as an intermediary trustee technically holding title to the center which is leased to the FFY. The financial institution which purchased the EDB bonds is reimbursed annually from the lease fees which the city pays FFY which then pays the EDB. Thus, the EDB's role is simply that of a pass-through organization. Using this mechanism meant that a referendum was not required because the lease agreement technically is not backed by the full faith and credit of the city. This also means that it does not count against the city's debt ceiling. At the end of 21 years when the bonds have been fully redeemed, the center title passes to the FFY.

One of the community's largest businesses is Arvin Industries and one of that business' founders helped establish the original FFY youth camp program. Hence, the FFY has always been the main focus of Arvins' charitable interests. The President and Chief Operating Officer of Arvin pledged that the Arvin Foundation would provide $250,000 as part of a $1 million Community Foundation challenge grant which would match other private source amounts that were contributed on a dollar-for-dollar basis.

There were five signatories to the Memorandum of Understanding which represents a 21 year commitment by all parties and identifies the responsibilities of each partner in the collaboration.

- *The FFY Board of Trustees* are the "owners" of FFY and the center. Their primary role is fund-raising. In addition to raising the $2 million of private funds for the center, the Trustees committed to establishing an endowment to be used for future capital improvements and renovations of the center. This will ensure the building will not deteriorate to the level it had fallen in the mid-1990s. Leading business figures in the community are on the Board.
- *The FFY Board of Directors* consists of 20 individuals who supervise the daily operations of the facility. In contrast to the trustees, their focus is on operations.

- *The Columbus PARD* provides the staff, supplies and other resources needed to manage the day-to-day maintenance of the center at no cost to FFY. This amounts to $316,000 a year.
- *The City of Columbus* committed to paying the annual funds required to meet the lease payments to the FFY Board.
- *The United Way of Bartholomew County* (county population is 71,000) agreed to continue financial support of funding requests presented by FFY for all program related expenses.

Exhibit 6-1

Floor Plan of the FFY Center

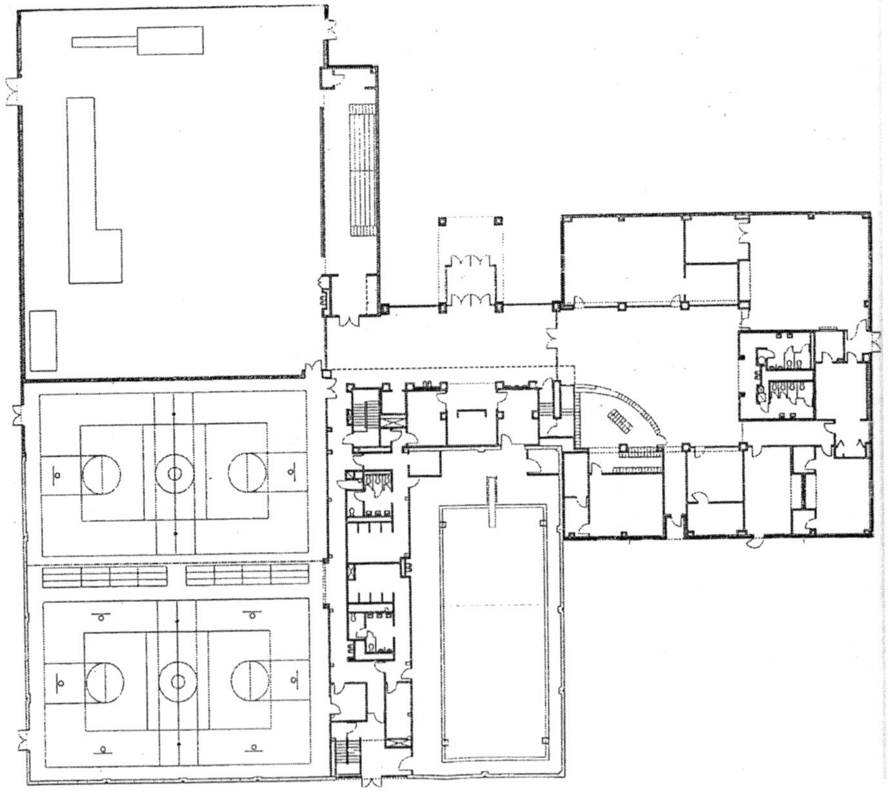

Exhibit 6-2

Entrance to the FFY Center

❖ ❖ ❖

Elements in the facility

Construction was started in early 1997 and the facility opened in stages between November 1998 and June 1999 when it was formally dedicated. A floor plan and photograph of the facility are shown in Exhibit 6-1 and 6-2. It has 50,000 square feet of space compared to 33,000 square feet in the old building. The five main elements are:

- a six-lane, 25 yard swimming pool operated by FFY;
- 2 full size gymnasia, which are the best gyms in the city operated by FFY;
- a 12,000 square feet gymnastics center operated by PARD adjacent to the gyms. By linking with the two gyms, the city is able to host large gymnastics meets with up to 500 competitors.
- Boys and Girls Club area which includes: large game room, teen facility, computer lab, library, and crafts area.

In addition to the main elements, there are offices, a large multi-purpose room and a kitchen which are shared by all three major user groups.

Operating Arrangements

There is a long established, pervasive sentiment among leadership of all sectors in Columbus that they should view the community as "one big circle with no boxes." The Director of the PARD explained: "We do not view ourselves as existing in independent silos! We believe there is nothing we cannot do in our community for youth with the resources we have, but it means each organization has to get past the notion of protecting its turf." Thus, there was a genuine desire at Board and senior executive level in both the FFY and PARD to develop a collaborative team to operate the facility. However, as the PARD Director noted: "People have to learn to do that, and in some cases they are reluctant."

Thus, the challenge was to obtain the full cooperation of the seven or eight staff from each organization who were responsible for the center's day-to-day operation. There was concern among the FFY staff that PARD was moving into "their domain" and taking over. To address these issues, the Directors and staffs of both organizations met regularly in the year preceding the opening of the center. The meetings were directed by an independent facilitator and all the concerns people had about the collaboration were worked through.

The broad principles of the collaboration were established in the original Memorandum of Understanding among the parties that was signed before building construction was authorized. As a result of these regular meetings, those broad principles were operationalized by the staffs so there were clear guidelines as to how the center would operate on a day-to-day basis. The details of this operating agreement are given in Exhibit 6-3.

Exhibit 6-3

Operating Agreement

The following is an operating agreement between the Foundation For Youth (FFY) and the Columbus Park and Recreation Department (P&R) for the operation of the Foundation for Youth facility located at 405 Hope Ave.

I. <u>Maintenance</u>

1. The Park and Recreation Department shall be responsible for the following:
   - Supervise all maintenance staff necessary to maintain the facility.
   - Oversee the custodial requirements which include OSHA, IOSHA, and ADA compliance and preventative maintenance.
   - Provide the daily and long-term managerial requirements of maintenance.
   - Maintain the building as required and be responsible for the general upkeep of the building including the exterior, grounds, HVAC system, security system, electrical, plumbing, roof, glass, doors, etc.
   - Cleaning the pool deck area.
   - Using P&R charge accounts for all maintenance supplies.
   - Pay deductibles on insurance claims regarding the facility only.

2. The Foundation For Youth shall be responsible for the following:
   - FFY Director of Operations shall provide P&R Maintenance Supervisor with information regarding condition of the building. Any necessary repairs shall be submitted to P&R via a work order.
   - The FFY Director of Operations shall conduct a monthly inspection with FFY Maintenance Team Leader.

Exhibit 6-3 Continued

- Maintaining proper chemical levels and cleanliness of pool.
- Pay deductibles on insurance claims regarding the contents of the facility only.

3. A Facility Committee shall be established consisting of:
   - FFY Director of Operations
   - P&R Director of Operations
   - P&R Manager of Operations
   - FFY Maintenance Team Leader
   - P&R Assistant to the Director
   - Aquatics Manager
   - Gymnastics Facility Manager

   This committee shall be responsible for the following:
   - Oversee the general maintenance, renovation, restoration, and refurbishment of the building, facility and grounds.
   - Ensure the cooperative effort between P&R and FFY continues in a highly effective manner.
   - Maintain an equipment inventory and approve all equipment purchases.
   - Plan and publish a capital budget and develop a long range capital improvements plan.
   - Approve all expansions or modifications of the existing building
   - Evaluate maintenance staff needs and determine duties.

II. <u>Scheduling</u>

1. A Scheduling committee shall be established consisting of:
   - Aquatics Manager
   - FFY Office Manager
   - FFY Director of Operations
   - Gymnastics Facility Manager
   - P&R Sports Manager
   - FFY Athletic Director
   - Boys & Girls Club Program Director

   This committee shall be responsible for the following:
   - Determine priorities for each of the following areas of facility use:
     Gymnasium
     Pool
     Gymnastics Center
     Boys & Girls Club
     Administrative Areas
   - Determine security schedule for the entire facility
   - Determine procedures for supervision of users.
   - Recommend rental rates and policies.

2. FFY shall be responsible for the following:
   - Scheduling all rental of the facility.
   - Collecting all fees and contracts from users.
   - Payment to P&R for all Set up and/or Cleaning fees collected from rental activities as outlined in paragraph two (2) of the FFY Facility Rental Request/Agreement.

3. P&R shall be responsible for the following:
   - All scheduling of the Columbus Gymnastics Center.
   - All rental activity within the Columbus Gymnastics Center

III. <u>Registration</u>

1. A Registration Committee shall be established consisting of:
   - Registration Desk Supervisor
   - Aquatics Manager
   - Boys & Girls Club Program Director
   - Gymnastics Facility Manager
   - FFY Business Manager

Exhibit 6-3 Continued

This committee shall be responsible for the following:

- Maintain all registrations of FFY and P&R programs
- Determine job requirements of registration staff.
- Publish materials about all programs offered in the facility and provide public information regarding program changes after said publications.
- Determine costs to FFY and P&R for program publications.
- Oversee all programs jointly operated by FFY and P&R.

2. FFY and P&R shall be responsible for the following:
   - Supervision of the registration staff.

3. Oversight Committee
   The oversight committee consisting of the FFY Executive Director, P&R Director, and one representative from each Board of Directors shall be established in order to resolve conflicts that cannot be resolved by the appropriate committees.

The challenge of building this collaborative team was exacerbated by many of the FFY staff leaving the organization during the construction year, so there was a need to periodically readdress issues in order to secure the buy-in of new staff. By the time the center opened, the FFY had relatively young leadership and staff who were enthusiastic, aggressive, somewhat idealistic, and occasionally naive. In contrast, PARD had a relatively veteran staff. Sometimes these contrasts led to conflicts of ideas, but the operating agreement was designed to ensure these were resolved in committees at the staff level, rather than at the director level. In addition to the standing committees listed in the operating agreement, the directors set up ad hoc committees to deal with particular issues which were outside the scope of the standing committees. After the center opened, the whole group of 15 or so staff working in the center and the directors met regularly each quarter. Committees report on issues they have been working on. The PARD Director commented that the collaboration was working well "because these quarterly meetings typically last less than 30 minutes."

The FFY director who led her staff through this process accepted another leadership position in the community as soon as the center opened, which created a leadership vacuum in FFY. The PARD Director became acting FFY Director because he was so familiar with FFY from being on their Board and was widely accepted by them. This was indicative of the close relationship of the two organizations.

Programming

Daily attendance for the Boys and Girls Club after-school programs increased from 100 to 200 once the new center was opened. Similarly, the PARD gymnastics program also almost doubled its number of participants and through a special scholarship fund it has been able to arrange for interested Boys and Girls Club members to participate in gymnastic classes.

The PARD has an extensive range of youth programs beyond its involvement in the center, but the center serves as a central headquarters for youth development organizations in the city. The PARD views its role as being a catalyst for youth development in Columbus by supporting and empowering youth and other youth organizations, rather than being focused primarily on directly delivering youth services. Thus, other organizations offering services for youth in Columbus have been encouraged to locate their offices and programs in the center. The Home School Partners were given office space in exchange for the School District providing bus transportation to the center from the various elementary schools in the afternoons. Typically, 200 youth take advantage of this service each day. The Child Abuse Prevention Council located their offices there and they provide informative puppet shows for Boys and Girls Club participants to increase awareness of child abuse. The United Way funded and located the Teen Court program in the facility. It meets weekly and processes approximately 100 cases a year with organizational support from the city's probation department.

The Recreation and Enrichment Program for Students (REPS) is an after-school program that occurs between 2:45 p.m. and 5:30 p.m. at eight elementary schools mid-August through May. Activities include games, snack time, homework help and a variety of enrichment activities such as arts and crafts, career exploration, science, cultural studies, and field trips to sites of interest. A Boys and Girls Club Membership plus a monthly fee are required and gives a child the option to participate at the school sites or at the Foundation for Youth. Transportation is available to the Boys and Girls Club where game room activities, athletics, swimming, and classes in computers, cooking, science, arts and crafts and a homework help program are offered.

The Youth Advocate Priority One: Put Kids First Program is an umbrella advocacy group headquartered in the center. The FFY Executive Director, Director of PARD, President of United Way, and other community leaders interviewed 400 high school students to better understand how to respond to their needs. They asked the question, "What is it you want adults in this community to do to make your lives better?" Pervasive across the youths' responses was an insistence that they wanted to be involved in determining additional services that should be delivered to youth and to have their opinions respected. This was the genesis of the Priority One program, which is described in Exhibit 6-4. It incorporates youth councils representing the high and middle schools who have an active role in youth services. For example, they were given responsibility for organizing a summer concert series in the city's amphitheater. They select the bands, raise the funds, and operate the series. They have been doing it for three years and it has resulted in strong attendances at the concerts.

Exhibit 6-4

History, Components, and Milestones of Priority One: Put Kids First
A Collaboration of People and Organizations Committed to Making Bartholomew County the Best Place in America to Raise Kids or to be a Kid

Priority One began its work in late-1998. It was determined that there would be a dual focus – teens and younger children.

The Teen Development Council, formed in January, 1999 is led by teens with a few adult advisers. At any given time, about 20 teens are active in the work of the council. Their mission is driven by the results of focus group meetings. These meetings involved several community leaders meeting with teens in small groups to ask about conditions of being a teen in Bartholomew County. The two most common answers, by far, were, "Nothing to do" and "We are not respected." Priority one has addressed those concerns by organizing many events (concerts, dances, pool parties) heavily attended by their peers and by doing community service work (fund-raisers for charity, work parties for low-cost housing, and events for small children and families).

In preparing to address other needs around youth and families, Priority One initiated a program called 100 Meetings In 100 Days. Two Priority One leaders made themselves available to groups throughout the county to talk about the need for stronger youth development. There was a presentation of the current situation, a description of the need for change, and a discussion period with each group. Meetings were held with service organizations, PTO's, church groups, government offices, school staffs, school classes at high schools and colleges, and more. At the end of the 100 days a community meeting was held to develop actions and recruit champions for each. Those action teams continue to work in various forms today.

A major component of the work was a partnership with the Indiana Division of Family and Children (the welfare department). The state funded a three-year pilot with several components.

- A child care scholarship program to help families above the state imposed cutoff for assistance. About 300 children in 200 families benefit from this effort.
- Expansion of the Child Care Resource and Referral staff to enable the implementation of a mentoring program for child care providers. The intent of this effort was to improve the quality of care provided, and to improve the level of credentials among the provider community (more licensed and accredited professionals). Ten providers took part in the pilot of this work.
- Two additional early intervention case managers to assist in the turnaround of young lives that had gotten slightly off track.
- Two additional paralegals in the prosecutor's office to help work the case load in collecting child support.
- An additional case worker in the Healthy Families program to assist parents of newborns to understand how to care for the needs of their baby.

At the conclusion of the pilot, the United Way of Bartholomew County was committed to continue all of the components with local funding.

Source: Doug Otto, President, United Way of Bartholomew County.

Another program at the facility is Youth as Resources, which is a youth-adult partnership that gives youth responsibility for making decisions on the distribution of grant funds for community service projects developed and implemented by youth. Any youth group may apply that has an adult leader and affiliation with an organization. During the year 2000, 24 project grants were made with 509 youth involved. There were 2,595 volunteer service hours given through this program. The Police Athletic League was allocated program space for youth volleyball and basketball programs. The PARD moved its adult basketball programs to the two FFY gyms and scheduled them after youth programs finished in the evenings. During the daytime, the PARD scheduled adult and senior citizen activities throughout the center. In addition, elements of the facility are rented to outside groups at non-programmed times, and the demand for this exceeded initial expectations. A Senior Citizen Volunteer Coordinator position was established to solicit seniors to assist with the Boys and Girls Club activities, and one outcome of this was a foster grandparents program.

Conclusions

The PARD had previously established its credentials as a trustworthy partner through collaborations with the local hospital on wellness and fitness programs, the school district on facilities, and the Columbus Area Arts Council on programs and facilities. These arrangements demonstrated the PARD's commitment to high quality facility management and programs, and its willingness to forego "turf" in order to reap the synergistic benefits accruing from genuine collaboration. In addition to this track record, the PARD had a long history of demonstrated support for FFY's youth service efforts which included the PARD Director being a member of the FFY Board. Thus, the FFY Board and senior managers were not defensive about concerns that the PARD may "take them over."

The partnership enables the FFY, PARD and Boys and Girls Club to maintain their autonomy and identity, while at the same time being able to collaborate on or co-sponsor activities. The PARD and FFY logos are both on the front doors of the center to subtly remind visitors that it is a joint endeavor. The PARD Director noted "Neither of us are interested in building silos, but we both recognize the importance of having the contributions of each-entity publicly recognized."

By taking responsibility for day-to-day maintenance of the facility, the PARD enabled FFY to focus exclusively on providing high quality youth development programs which is what they do best.

The collaboration permits the sharing of costs which has led to several service improvements which probably would not have been financially feasible if the entities were operating independently. For example, the registration desk can be staffed more efficiently, and the FFY is able to share the PARD's Rec Trac software which enables both the FFY programs and PARD's gymnastics center to offer better customer service. Their joint funding of a professional aquatics manager has enhanced the quality of aquatic programs offered by both the FFY and PARD. FFY utilizes space in PARD brochures to promote their programs. In the light of his experience in Columbus, the PARD Director observed:

> *Whenever I hear that we are trying to go our own way in the Federal Congress on funding bills without partnering with the non-profit groups, I think it is a mistake. The Boys and Girls Club, for example, are good at getting funding, and I believe if we get together with them we will be more effective. They have legislative "pull" that we do not have because we are viewed differently. Legislators' view of us often is, "You are funded by tax dollars, so you have got all the money you need."*

Lessons Learned

The key ingredients in effective partnerships are trust and vision. In this case, trust existed at the policy and executive management levels. It had been nurtured in the prior relationship between the FFY and PARD, and it had been further manifested by the PARD's collaborations with other non-profit organizations in the community. Even so, the staffs responsible for the center's day-to-day working had not necessarily been exposed to this heritage and so tended to be apprehensive towards each other. Thus, to enhance their trust and confidence in each other, in the year before the center opened considerable effort was invested in team building, working through the operational issues, and establishing conflict or issue resolution mechanisms.

A major obstacle to partnerships and collaborations is parochial, departmentalized thinking, and lack of a broad vision among elected officials, senior managers, and community leaders. It is easier for managers and elected officials to develop and operate facilities that are fully under their control without the complexities brought by cooperative ventures. A recreation manager experienced in partnerships observed:

> *The difficult part of getting these partnerships going is there is a lot of hostility because everyone is looking out for their own best interests. It is hard to step back and look at what is best for the community. And what is best for the community, particularly in these times of very difficult funding, is to combine your efforts and work together. (p.38)*[2]

In this case, the partnering groups were able to move beyond these potential obstacles.

They started with a broad vision which was jointly developed by the leaders in each group, and then they developed a strategy to bring it to fruition. Too often, when partnerships are considered a more myopic approach is adopted whereby an agency develops a strategy and seeks to persuade others to embrace it. Without a broad vision developed and enthusiastically embraced by all potential partners at the outset, a collaboration is likely to be sub-optimal.

Sources

Mr. Chuck W. Wilt, Director of Parks and Recreation, City of Columbus.

1. Witt, Peter A. & John L. Crompton (1996). *Recreation programs that work for at-risk youth.* State College, PA: Venture Publications, (p. 19).
2. Schmid, Sue (1995). Partners in recreation. *Athletic Business* 19(10), 38.

CHAPTER 7

TAKING IT TO THE STREETS: ROVING LEADER PROGRAMS

Following the same principle that impelled Mohammed to go to the mountain, the New York City Youth Board soon will assign eleven friendly, experienced persons to seek out children who, for whatever reason, have not visited the play areas recreational facilities provided for them. (p. 61)[1]

The evolution of Roving Leader (RL) program can be traced to the mid-19th century when churchmen and charity workers sought out young delinquents and gangs in the slum areas of the emerging American cities. Many early social workers adapted their traditional methods when working in low-income neighborhoods by developing a "neighborly" as opposed to a professional relationship with individuals they sought to help. Programs were developed in New York City, Chicago, Los Angeles, Boston, San Francisco, Philadelphia, Detroit and Cleveland. Although not specifically run by PARDs, they incorporated recreation activities as central components of their programs.

The basic premise undergirding these efforts was that youth workers who "roamed" in communities would be knowledgeable about the neighborhood in which they worked and, therefore, would be better able to find and interact with disaffected youth. Often workers lived in the areas where they worked, which gave them added insight into the issues their clienteles faced.[2] In the 1930s, Chicago initiated a RL-type program. This was followed by similar efforts in New York and other U.S. cities in the 1950s.[3]

In the context of parks and recreation, street workers were given the designation of Roving Leaders. They are part of the genre of "detached youth workers' who are defined as individuals who works with youth in non-organized, informal settings, usually on the street.[4]

Detached work involves intensive contact with a corner-group where the worker meets the teen-age group in their natural environment. By close association with them and getting to know their needs as a group and as individuals, the worker forms a positive relationship and helps them to engage in socially acceptable activities which they come to choose. The basic goal is helping them to change undesirable attitudes and patterns of behavior (p.87).

It has been suggested that detached youth worker programs are effective only if three elements exist: (i) financial security; (ii) a firm commitment to imagination, flexibility and integrity; and (iii) a readiness to deal with failures and to be prepared for change.[5] These elements require communities to make a long term commitment toward both content and design of the program and the staff (e.g., providing a living wage for youth workers).

There are four characteristics of street worker programs that make them unique.[6] First, services are based on problems in young people's lives as opposed to a specific program activity. Therefore, services are available to youth who have the greatest need rather than those who have paid a fee or become members of a particular group. Second, contact occurs in the community not in an institutional setting. This is important since most institutions have formal standards that guide staff in client selection and service, which may eliminate some youth from participating. Third, the service provided by street workers is not initially requested by youth. The worker is required to "reach out" and take steps to alleviate any fear, suspicion or hostility that might exist. Finally, programs are heavily dependent on the relationship between youth and staff. This final characteristic also is endemic in the first three features and the comment of the RL in Exhibit 7-1 highlights the key role of their relationship.

Exhibit 7-1

A San Antonio Roving Leader's Philosophy

I'm interested in the whole kid, in helping him do better in life. Recreation is just the hook to get into a relationship with him. It's what I use to collar him. If I organize a basketball game, kids are there. You have to have some way to get them in. If I told them to meet me in church or school, I wouldn't get any of them, but ask them to play basketball and they will be there. However, slowly but surely, I can then get them into different community organizations as our relationship strengthens. Now, I work with some ministers, and on Sundays I go around and pick some of them up and get them involved in the community churches. At first, just once a month then more. Eventually their attitudes to church and school change. I've seen this happen with a bunch of kids. We won't change all of their lives, but at least those who need help now have someone they know and trust to get it from.

❖ ❖ ❖

RL programs currently exist in several cities in the United States and Canada. While each has a unique history, in all cases the principles and practices pioneered in the early outreach efforts prevail. Two of the largest contemporary programs are operated by PARDs in Austin and San Antonio, Texas.

In both cities, RLs target children ranging in age from ten to eighteen. Although they come from diverse backgrounds, the youth share many characteristics. Most are relatively poor. Many live in single-parent families headed by a mother or grandmother. In some cases, the father or mother is in jail, is dead, or has never been part of the household. Many are exposed to gangs, drugs and alcohol at home or in their neighborhoods and schools; have witnessed violence, in some cases against members of their own family; have behavior problems at school; and in some cases have been suspended. A few have been arrested for offenses such as shoplifting or selling drugs.

For the most part, youth with whom the RLs come into contact lack structure and consistency in their home lives. They have few or no positive role models, and in most cases have no one who pays personal attention to them or offers emotional support. They have had little or no opportunity to go outside their neighborhoods to see how other people live or to develop recreational, cultural and other interests. In some cases, heavy responsibilities have been placed upon them at an early age, such as taking care of younger siblings or doing a major portion of the housework.

The San Antonio Program

The RL program in San Antonio was launched in 1972 in response to the question "How can we reach youngsters who are hanging-out on street corners and not coming to our community centers?" The commitment to outreach emerged from managers in the San Antonio PARD who perceived it to be a rational strategy for addressing this question.

The original leaders were hired with federal CETA job training funds. When CETA funds were terminated in the early 1980s, many recreation positions in the city were lost. Preference was given to replacing staff in recreation centers who were no longer funded, so the RL program was eliminated. It was allowed to die because at the beginning of the 1980s recreation services for at-risk youth were not perceived to be critically important to the city.

By 1992, the public's and decision-makers' perceptions of the role of recreation services had changed. Juvenile crime had grown exponentially and there was a public outcry demanding that the city's leadership address the problem. Some major decision-makers in the city were personally impacted by this crime wave, which resulted in them being highly sensitized to it:

- A council member's son was an innocent bystander victim in a drive-by shooting.
- The city manager was robbed of his wallet in the driveway of his home by two youth.
- The Mayor resided in a district of the city in which violent crime was occuring.
- His successor had a son who was picked up by police on a playground for being out after curfew.

These personal experiences coincided with a shift in philosophy when a mayor was elected who was more proactive toward prevention. City Council members were under pressure to respond to the community's concerns and turned to the PARD for advice. The movement to restore the RL program was further accelerated because some individuals who had personally benefitted from involvement in the original RL program twenty years previously were now in influential positions on the City Council or on city staff.

This convergence of factors resulted in the RL program being resurrected in 1992. Initially, money came from a UPARR (Urban Parks and Recreation Recovery) grant and from the San Antonio Housing Authority, which had received federal grants for alleviating drug abuse. The city also included some general fund support. Over time this support has increased as the grant funds have declined.

The targeted geographic areas include public housing communities and areas of minority populations with relatively low incomes. These areas have some of the highest crime rates in the city, and the youth served are considered to be at-risk. Although service areas are identified, fixed boundary lines do not exist. The RLs can go where they feel they are needed, and are not confined to where the department thinks they should be or where they would like them to be. The program's goal is to take a preventive approach to crime and violence through providing recreation programs where traditional facility-based programs are not available. The specific objectives of the programs are to:

- reach out to at-risk youth who do not participate in, know about, or avail themselves of traditional recreational activities and other social services offered by the city;
- teach youth the importance of team play, not merely as a sports concept but as a way of life;
- develop youth's self-esteem and the importance of respect for themselves and others, regardless of neighborhood, skin color, or belonging to a particular group or organization; and
- provide, and make youth aware of the numerous services available to the youth and their families.

Austin Program

The RL program in Austin was created as part of the city's Social Fabric Initiative, which began in 1996 with the City Council's approval of funding to enhance youth programs and services. By electing a council committed to advocacy and funding for youth programs, Austin's citizens sent a message that youth services were a priority. The initiative provided funds for a variety of programs which formed a fabric, or net, designed to support youth who have fallen through cracks in other social structures. Two council members, both former PARD advisory board members, provided important leadership for the initiative.

Although regular programs had attracted considerable numbers of teens, many others had not been attracted into programs. As one RL observed:

> *The recreation centers don't have the resources to actually get out into the community as much as we are out there. It wasn't just like I said "okay, this program is happening Wednesday night at Zaragosa and go ahead and go." I have to tell kids three weeks in a row, and go talk to the parents... In some cases, parents are unwilling to let them go because they think there is nothing but kids hanging-out there, or maybe bad things are going on there, or they may have heard a couple of bad things. These kids and parents just don't take the time to find out what is going on at the recreation center.*

The RL program was thus created to provide outreach to youth not currently served by the Austin PARD. Described by the organizers as a "recreation center on wheels," RLs rove their communities, carrying equipment and supplies for impromptu games, crafts and athletic activities. The activities, however, serve primarily as a "hook" through which the leaders connect with youth. RLs spend their time at housing projects, apartment complexes, parking lots, street corners and sports centers seeking out youth in need of positive, fun ways to spend their time. The Director of the RL program in Austin described their role in Exhibit 7-2.

Exhibit 7-2

The Roving Leader's Mandate

"How many of us in our careers have said, 'Geez, if my hands were not tied, I could do this, this, and this with these kids?' This is what the Department empowers the RLs to do. There are legal parameters we have to abide with, but we say to them, "You go out into this particular area of town, seek out youngsters who are either doing nothing constructive or are engaged in anti-social activities. Work with them. Determine on the spot what needs to be done to move them in a positive direction—recreational activities, ping-pong games, basketball games, job referrals, taking them to a clinic, working with their families, or whatever.

"The RLs have a lot of flexibility—much more than our staff in recreation centers—and that is a key to their success. They are not social workers, but they know where those services are available. If a leader comes across an individual who has been kicked out of school, for example, then he knows all the school principals in the area, knows the kid's family, and can try to resolve the behavior that precipitated the suspension. That's what a RL does."

Five principles guide the work of the RLs. First, they seek to address issues in a holistic manner, which requires RL's to build relationships with youth and with their teachers, parents and other extended family members. Second, they have the flexibility to "roam," rather than being tied to a fixed site. This freedom allows them to deal with spontaneous situations and issues that arise with the youth they serve.

Third, to reach out and work in-depth with this group, an individualized approach is necessary. An RL and an assistant are assigned to an area of the community. Within this area, RLs are not tied to a particular site. In some cases, youth are referred to the program by teachers, juvenile justice officials, or other sources in the community. Initially at least, there was little expectation that the RLs would serve large numbers of youth, which meant they could invest effort in building in-depth relationships with youth and their families. While a goal of most traditional PARD programs is to serve high numbers of participants, Austin's RL program focuses on investing the threshold amount of effort on individual youth, that is needed to positively impact them.

Fourth, staff learn about, and work with, multiple social service agencies and their resources in order to better serve youth and stretch limited resources. Finally, the structure of the program means that there is less direct supervision than at site-based programs. This increased autonomy allows RLs to be more responsive to the changing needs and circumstances of the youth they serve.

The RLs in Austin began their efforts with door-to-door surveys in neighborhoods with profiles suggesting they were likely candidates for the program. Questions addressed the recreation resources that were being used, the number of minors in households, and problems parents and youth would like to see ameliorated.

Survey respondents expressed appreciation that they had been consulted and that their needs and opinions were valued. This was an encouraging indicator of community cooperation and support, which is a prerequisite for RLs to be able to integrate effectively in their assigned areas. Survey respondents commented especially on the lack of recreation centers or programs, high crime rates, and inconsistent trash pickup. The surveys increased awareness of the willingness of RLs to work with residents to solve community problems. RL's positive actions reinforce their standing in the community. For example, when an RL supplies a citizen with a contact number that results in improved trash pickup, it builds trust and respect which provides an opening for introducing families and their children to other services offered in the community.

In Austin, the RL program's objectives and the means identified for achieving those objectives are listed in Exhibit 7-3.

Exhibit 7-3

Roving Leader Program Objectives and Means for Achieving Objectives in Austin

Objective (as a result of participating in the program, participants will:)	Means for Achieving Objectives
increase their perceptions that they are involved in experiences that are meaningful (safe and secure activity environment).	a) provide settings (e.g., building, place to hang out, activity, group) where youth/teens can feel a sense of belonging b) encourage youth/teens to participate in organized or drop-in recreation activities at APARD recreation centers or other facilities c) provide opportunities to interact with other youth/teens in a positive manner d) provide mentoring support from caring and interested adults e) provide opportunities to take part in community service activities f) provide means for achieving a sense of belonging without having to join a gang or upon leaving a gang
increase their repertoire of free-time experiences and abilities (new experiences).	a) help remove barriers to youth/teens participating in activities in other neighborhoods, by providing opportunities for and transportation to participation in events outside the neighborhood or local community (e.g., field trips and special events) b) provide opportunities to participate in recreation activities in the community c) encourage youth/teens to participate in organized or drop-in recreation activities at APARD recreation centers or other facilities d) provide opportunities to increase activity skills

Exhibit 7-3 Continued

Objective (as a result of participating in the program, participants will:)	Means for Achieving Objectives
increase the resources that they feel they have to help deal with difficult personal and family issues (avoidance of risk behaviors).	a) provide adult mentors to talk with teens about difficult issues b) when issues are beyond staff capacity to provide guidance, provide referrals to appropriate organizations and agencies that can provide youth/teens with assistance
increase their motivation to be in or stay in school or alternative school settings, and achieve or maintain passing grades (school achievement).	a) show interest and discuss advantages of youth/teens staying in school b) create partnerships with schools in the community c) provide access to opportunities to gain tutoring assistance d) provide educational tours to community colleges, universities, local businesses
increase their ability to make positive choices about issues such as drug and alcohol usage, sex, and gang membership and activities (avoidance of risk behaviors).	a) create an atmosphere where youth/teens feel comfortable discussing issues with program staff b) utilize services of outside organizations (as feasible) to provide information about drug and alcohol abuse, and safe sex/ abstinence practices
increase their trust and respect for other youth/teens, adult mentors, and other authority figures (mentoring).	a) provide opportunities for youth/teens to interact with positive adult role models (e.g., Roving Leaders, center staff, and other community youth/teens leaders) b) provide opportunities for youth/teens to interact with other teens in an environment that encourages trust and respect c) provide an atmosphere where adults do what they say they are going to do and keep their promises
increase their citizenship, leadership and/or job skills (job and other skills).	a) provide workshops, training sessions, and guest lectures b) provide incentives for teens/youth to become involved in these activities c) provide opportunities to display leadership and/or good citizenship, or demonstrate work skills d) identify opportunities for youth/teens to make a difference; i.e., volunteer experiences e) build awareness of the value of having good leadership and job skills
increase their knowledge of persons from other backgrounds and neighborhoods (cultural awareness).	a) provide opportunities to interact with teens from other recreation centers and ethnic and cultural backgrounds

Program Design

The San Antonio program has five RLs who are funded from Community Development Block Grant allocations and one who is paid out of city general funds. The RLs work Monday, Wednesday, Thursday, and Friday from 3:00 p.m. to 9:00 p.m., and Tuesday and Saturday from 1:00 p.m. to 9:00 p.m. However, work hours are flexible to accommodate different events and needs. The geographical coverage of the program is synonymous with the service areas of existing community centers. Although the RLs have a base at these centers and may bring participants to them for activities, they primarily work in the surrounding neighborhoods. In three areas, the RL has an assistant. In the summer an additional three assistants are hired.

Although the primary target clientele is youth aged 6 to 19, there is special emphasis on youth who are younger than 16 because they often cannot get to recreation programs at the centers and because it is felt that younger age groups are more malleable so there is greater potential for positively impacting them.

The San Antonio RLs operate primarily out of the back of their vehicles. They supply their own automobiles, but the city reimburses them with a mileage allowance. The RLs seek out traditional youth hang-outs, especially in close proximity to the housing projects, such as parking lots, street corners and sports centers. They offer activities such as basketball, volleyball, softball, football, and quiet games. The RLs talk to them, counsel them, encourage them to stay in or return to school, gain their confidence, and help keep them involved in positive activities.

In Austin, RLs work in eight designated areas, some of which have recreation centers and some of which do not. In all areas, the RLs are supported by at least one assistant. Working hours vary depending on the day and planned activities. Roving leaders carry pagers and cell phones which youth use to contact them, sometimes late at night if they are having problems.

The array of programs Austin RLs offer is extensive and includes caving, camping, hiking, canoeing, mountain biking, fishing, tutoring, community/park clean-ups, freestyle break dancing, athletic activities, anger management classes, the Kids on Bikes Program, gardening, fine arts/music programs, graffiti wipe-outs, and visual art programs. Special events include the Ladies Night Out retreat, the Get Hopping Easter Egg Hunt, Water Day at Lake Long, and Super Saturdays, which are held once a month in conjunction with the Travis County Juvenile Department. On these days, RLs provide three hours of activities that highlight cooperation, communication, leadership, and trust building.

Many of these activities take participants out of their communities and put them in recreation situations with youth from other areas of the city. As they mix and get to know each other, superficial boundaries crumble. For example, Ladies Night Out brings about forty girls together from different parts of the city. According to one of the program leaders:

> *At first they didn't mingle too well but then they started talking and...they stayed up all night. At the end, the people that they didn't want any contact with, they started having contact with them. They kinda of became friends. We had guest speakers come in, and they motivated the girls to think about life and the tools they will need to be successful. There were friendships that developed, and we are going to do it again some time in August so these girls will have a chance to come back together again.*

Program Leadership

The key to the program's success is the staff. It is the leadership not the program content, that is important. RLs have to gain and retain the trust of youth, their parents, and the institutions which cooperate with them; they have to be able to organize and teach recreational activities; and to know the array of referral services that are available to support youth.

Whether it is camping, bowling, boating, or going to the rodeo, many RL participants experience some activities for the first time. Indeed, some of the activities are new to the RLs themselves, especially such high adventure pursuits as caving and hiking (specialists are brought along to teach these skills). One of the leaders noted that through the program, participants get to experience the positive things that go on outside their community "because nine times out of ten when they are involved in recreation at home, it is not a positive kind of recreation. The activities show them there is something else they can do, go out and have a good time, and not get into trouble."

These types of experiences create bonds between the RLs and the participants. While the activities attract teens to the program, it is the relationship youth establish with the leaders that makes them stay. Because of the individualized nature of the program, it was not anticipated that RLs would work with many youth. In a number of communities, however, leaders have been confronted with a large number of youth who want to be involved. Over time, a compromise has evolved. Leaders plan and operate programs serving larger numbers at specific community sites (e.g., parks, housing projects), but they also target selected individuals for more in-depth involvement. When targeted participants appear to be ready, RLs help them shift to recreation center-based programs.

Roving leaders are involved in much more than the provision of recreation experiences for the participants:

> *We are not just Roving Leaders going out there conducting activities. We are turning into surrogate parents. We are not only helping the parents, we are helping the brothers, the sisters, the aunts, the grandmothers; they all have problems and we get calls, we get pages. The job just entails so much more than dealing with a couple of kids, putting them in a recreation center.*

By getting out in the community, RLs see not only the youth, but all elements of their environment (home, school, neighborhood). This enables them to better tailor their relationships and services to the particular needs of each youth. RLs can provide structure, encouragement, and personal attention where these are lacking in children's lives, while also serving as positive role models.

RLs are dedicated, outgoing individuals who care about their jobs and the youth with whom they work. They must be able to communicate with youth on their level, without sounding preachy or talking down to them. The job requires that they understand principles of youth development. They must be willing to work long hours in the outdoors, operate out of their vehicles, knock on doors in rough neighborhoods, and work without the security of a fixed facility or a precise daily schedule. Above all, RLs must have patience and a strong desire to see youth succeed and have fun.

One of the RLs' greatest assets is that they do not pose a threat to youth with whom they interact. They are not there to inform on, or to arrest youth; they are there to say, "We're going mountain biking; if you think you can hang, let's go out and have some fun." Flexibility is also important. Leaders can respond to what participants need, when they need it. For example, if a teen has been suspended from school and his/her parents do not speak English, an RL can go with the teen to the school and help work out reinstatement. In Austin, for example, a parent who was frantic because her son had run away from home called a RL. Because of the trust and respect the leader had developed with the teens in his area, other youth informed him of the runaway's whereabouts. The RL convinced the teen to contact his mother and return home.

In San Antonio, all RLs were recruited from the neighborhoods in which they work. A local person was considered more likely to be successful than an individual from elsewhere within the department who has to get to know the "territory." Thus, the leaders were well-known and respected in the targeted neighborhoods before working in the RL program. They did not have to sell themselves to the community, since some familiarity and, hence, trust between them and the neighborhood parents and youth already existed.

In Austin, the opposite approach was taken. RLs were purposely assigned to areas in which they had not previously worked or lived. Supervisors felt that this would force RLs to more fully investigate problems and opportunities in their assigned areas, rather than assuming they understood the needs and resources of the community based on their past contacts and experiences.

Staff Attrition

Although Roving Leaders work long hours, the job can be very rewarding, as attested to by one Austin RL:

> *To me, I don't need the pat on the back or the newspapers....To me, it's just the kids that make it worthwhile. When they run up to me and say, 'oh, I missed you and I love you.' That's what this job is about. It's not the money, it's not the hours...it's just being there for them when they need you. On this job, you can't go on vacation, because kids don't know what vacation is. If they need you at 1:00 in the morning on a Sunday, they're going to call you. And it's their emergency. And it might be something real small. But it's important to them. And to me, that's why we're here.*

Clearly, the work of an RL is more than a profession, it is a *calling*. This work has to be done by inspired individuals. It is not enough to be well-trained in the recreation field.

Nevertheless, working with at-risk youth on a daily basis, and seeking to address their problems and positively impact their lives, is emotionally exhausting. As an Austin RL program supervisor pointed out:

It's hard to find staff who have a real love for recreation because that's what it is all about. And who don't mind that the hours are going to be crappy and that they are going to encounter a lot of emotional baggage, teen pregnancy, shootings and stabbings, some youth going hungry...that kinda stuff. That they could look beyond that and go, "I've gotta continually help this child, let me find the resources," shows they are really unselfish.

Even when quality staff are recruited who enjoy the job, retaining them for an extended period of time can be difficult. Burn-out by staff is frequent. Staff often work longer than an eight-hour day and are called to deal with difficult situations as they arise, irrespective of whether they are officially at work. The extended hours take time away from family and other responsibilities. Some RLs see themselves as being indispensable and have a hard time spending time away from the program when they are not officially on duty.

Unfortunately, this high level of dedication is not rewarded with a commensurate salary. While low pay is a reality for all youth development workers, it is particularly pernicious in this context given the stress and hours associated with the job. While both PARDs have attempted to raise salaries for the lead staff members in the program, salaries are still lower than other jobs the RLs could pursue. In addition, due to budget constraints a number of the RLs do not receive full benefits as part of their compensation package.

Together these factors result in a high rate of staff attrition which undermines the building of staff-participant relationships. In Austin, there were 21 RLs in September, 2000, comprising 8 full-time RL supervisors, 6 full-time assistant RLs and 7 part-time RL assistants. Six months later, 9 RLs had left the program (a supervisor, a full-time assistant and 7 part-time assistants) and only three of these positions were filled because of departmental budgets being frozen.

The high attrition makes it hard to maintain program momentum, continuity and quality. In addition the ongoing advertising, hiring, rehiring, recruiting and training processes are both expensive and time consuming. These ongoing processes make it hard to maintain program momentum, continuity and quality.

Training

Each month, the RLs in San Antonio come together for a special seminar geared to furthering their skills and exchanging ideas. They are also encouraged to participate in training programs offered by other city departments and non-profit social service organizations. The department has developed a manual which is used in the initial training for a new leader or assistant. This is supplemented by the new hire going into the field with an experienced leader for a few days.

In Austin, an orientation is conducted for new staff members, which includes information about department policies and procedures. Staff meetings and daily contacts enable RLs to exchange ideas, share referrals, and brainstorm solutions to issues that arise. Formal training is conducted by outside experts in areas such as behavior management, identifying drug problems, and responding to family problems.

Cooperation with Other Agencies

For many youth targeted by the RLs, there is a loss of confidence in, and/or a lack of understanding of, established institutional support systems. Thus, part of the mission of the RLs is to establish links between their clientele's needs and organizations that can help meet them.

This requires cooperation with an array of other agencies and organizations. For example, in San Antonio, "Operation Cool It," which included a curfew, was launched to help deal with gang violence issues in one part of the city. When the city initiated the curfew, the area's councilman was opposed to its implementation. He wanted alternatives of what else could be done with youngsters from 7:00 p.m. to 10:00 p.m. at night. In response, the city funded expanded hours of operation at recreation centers. The Council authorized the Health Department to go into recreation centers to undertake screenings and immunizations. RLs directed their clients to these services. The Police Department brought mobile jails and substations into the area. Social workers came in to walk the streets with RLs, and this combined effort cleared up many of the area's problems. The total initiative was coordinated by the neighborhood's RL.

In Austin, the program has benefited from a close association with the Austin Police and the Park Police. RLs have gone on "ride alongs" with police, who point out hot spots and share their knowledge of areas they patrol. The program has also gained the support of professionals associated with other community agencies. A social worker who worked with a non-profit agency, noted that "the program has provided another avenue for children to have a positive form of recreation and mentoring. Programs such as these are needed to help teach children a better direction in life. Consistent exposure to this program within the community will show residents another side of the City of Austin."

Program Costs

In San Antonio the annual budget for personnel, car allowance, equipment and supplies is approximately $200,000 and this amount has been consistent for a number of years. In Austin, the initial budget was approximately $500,000 and was increased over three years to almost $1 million. During the fourth year, however, budget cuts were proposed by the City Council reflecting the reduced revenue available to the Council because of a down-turn in the economy. Cuts led to staff reductions and the hiring of more part-time staff who would not receive full benefits. The cuts had a negative impact on the relationships established between program personnel and the youth they served. Many of the program's participants had significant instability in their lives, and loss of contact or diminished contact with the RLs served as another example of the "system" letting them down.

Program Impacts

In San Antonio, over 2,000 youth are registered annually in the program. No accurate records appear to exist to indicate the number of youth with whom the RLs have in-depth contact or the average length of contact the RLs have with participants. Over 850 youth are registered in Austin and it is estimated that they have in-depth contact with approximately 200.

Although the Austin program had strong support within the PARD and from some city council members, the program was still vulnerable to budget cuts because it was unable to demonstrate program impact relative to issues that were important to the city, i.e., juvenile crime reduction, improved school performance as measured by higher staandardized test scores, and youth staying in school and graduating. From the beginning of the Austin program, questions were raised by the city's budget staff as to whether the RL staff was working efficiently when each was involved with only 45-50 youth in a given year. The key element of the RL program is its commitment to working intensively with specific individuals, but there were no effectiveness measures demonstrating the success of the approach. The program relied on reporting the number of youth served and amounts of time RLs spent with youth as key outcome measures, but these output measures were not convincing to city officials that the program was having an impact.

If an RL worked with three individuals for five hours, this generates 15 contact hours. Contact hour numbers were not scrutinized until the department was targeted for budget cuts. The contact hour measure is a classic case of inappropriately using an efficiency measure to determine effectiveness, i.e. program outcomes. Contact hours are appropriate for determining the cost per hour of service, but they do not describe the program's impact.

Neighborhood residents are aware of the program's positive impact. If there were attempts to cut the program, the RLs were confident that parents, church leaders and business leaders in their neighborhoods would vigorously and vociferously make their opposition to cuts known to the council. In addition, council members are kept informed of how the programs work and the esteem with which the programs are held in the community. However, none of these factors enabled budget cuts for the program to be averted, mainly because the nebulous nature of the program outcome data.

Collecting school records and crime statistics has been a formidable task due to the difficulty of securing them from both the schools and the police. Consequently, a survey was devised by Texas A& M University to measure changes in youth behavior and attitudes as a result of their participating in the RL program. It was anticipated that the availability of this type of information would solidify the case for maintaining or increasing funding. The survey is shown in Exhibit 7-4.

Exhibit 7-4

Roving Leader Program Participant Evaluation Form

SCHOOL					
Grades (GPA/TAAS status)	Failing everything/ No effort (Below 50%) 0	Failing majority of subjects/ little effort (50-59%) 1	Just passing (60-69%) 2	Passing most subjects (70-89%) 3	Honor Roll Top 5% of class (90+%) 4
Attendance - tardies/absences	Dropout/Doesn't attend school 0	Excessive UA/ excessive tardies 1	Excessive tardies/ occasional UA 2	Occasional tardies/ Few EA 3	Good attendance/ No tardies or UA 4
Referrals for misbehavior	Expelled/ALC or DIL 0	Suspended or excessively referred 1	Occasional referrals/ISS 2	Occasional misbehavior not warranting formal referral 3	Good behavior 4
BEHAVIOR					
Involvement in high risk behaviors	Involved regularly with violence, drugs, gangs, alcohol, or sex 0	Involved with at least two or more high risk activities on a regular basis 1	Occasional involvement in high risk activities 2	Experimented, but little involvement with some high risk activities 3	No involvement with high risk activities 4
Ability to solve problems (Conflict resolution)	Unable to resolve conflicts without abusive and/or violent behavior 0	Sometimes able to resolve conflict appropriately 1	Occasional ability to resolve conflict appropriately 2	Usually able to resolve conflicts appropriately 3	Always able to resolve conflict appropriately 4
Interaction with people in a positive manner	Never interacts in a positive manner with people 0	Sometimes interacts in a positive manner with people 1	Occasionally interacts in a positive manner with people 2	Usually interacts in a positive manner with people 3	Always interacts in a positive manner with people 4
COME/COMMUNITY					
Quality of parental involvement in youth's life	Abusive homelife (physical/verbal). No positive parental involvement if any 0	Some involvement with parents but usually negative 1	Occasional positive parent involvement and interaction 2	Usually has positive parent involvement and interaction 3	Positive parent involvement in all aspects of child's life 4
Degree of connectedness to community resources	Not connected to any community resources 0	Connected to some resources but not on a regular basis 1	Connected to some resources on a weekly basis 2	Connected to some community resources on near daily basis 3	Connected to many community resources on near daily basis 4
Respect shown to parents at home	Always disrespectful to parents 0	Rarely shows respect for parents 1	Occasionally shows respect for parents 2	Usually shows respect for parents 3	Exemplary behavior toward parents 4

Lessons Learned

Before initiating an outreach effort, it is important for city officials to ensure that the program is sustainable over the long-term. Directing money into short-term programs that cannot be sustained is likely to be counterproductive. Those advocating improved approaches to youth development programs consistently emphasize that short-term, one-shot programs exacerbate the distrust of institutions prevalent among these youth by creating expectations and a level of service and then failing to sustain it for the long-term.

Too often youth services are conceived as a short-term band-aid solution, which means the long-term nature of the issues is only temporarily addressed. The consequences of lack of funding and program continuity for outreach efforts, whose *raison d'etre* is to establish trust and relationships with youth in the community, are that youth often feel less hopeful and empowered than before the program was launched. The problem is thus exacerbated, not ameliorated. Unfortunately, however, many of the funding decisions are made by elected government officials who have short-term, and personally self-sustaining, political agendas to fulfill.

Another factor contributing to the lack of commitment to sustained funding is that outreach programs are by definition not facility-based. There is a tendency for cities to give priority in times of budget shortages to operating programs emanating from physical facilities. There is a sunk capital cost which the residents have invested in facilities and their return on this very visible investment is not forthcoming if funds for operating them are not made available. In contrast, there are no tangible facility assets which are not being used if the RL programs are cut. Hence, from a political perspective, this is frequently viewed as a more palatable and expedient solution to budget cuts than reducing staff levels at facilities.

It is also more challenging for an agency to demonstrate *accountability* for the effectiveness of RL programs than for regular facility-based programs. A corollary is that elected officials have more difficulty collecting political kudos for supporting resources for such a program since results cannot easily be quantified. Without being able to show that the program has been effective, it is difficult for an agency to convince elected officials that it is using its limited resources responsibly. Again, this contributes to the vulnerability of outreach programs being cut in times of economic downturns. Ironically, it is during these times when the need for them is greatest!

RL programs challenge the conformist idea of serving as many youth as possible by focusing on one-on-one time with individuals. They target the most difficult to reach youth who are not connected to resources in their community and who are most adversely affected by external life issues. Unfortunately, as the pressure to justify programs grows, supervisors feel the need to show statistics pertaining to the number of children served rather than focusing on the smaller number of youth for whom the service was originally intended. Further, the consequences of pressure for accountability in terms of reporting contact hours leads to emphasizing serving more youth with site-based activities designed for those who are less disadvantaged and who are easier to serve.

Finding ways to avoid *staff burnout* is critical to program success. Outreach programs hire highly dedicated individuals who are willing to put in long hours meeting client needs. Unfortunately, the job can be all consuming, leaving little time for recovery, personal time and family or other obligations. While the RLs may not perceive the long hours to be detrimental immediately, in the long-term there is a high probability of staff burn-out. Supervisors need to be careful not to set performance expectations that make workers feel they must devote all of their life to their work responsibilities. Holding sessions on self-care and providing "permission" for workers to turn off their beepers is imperative.

Staff training is critical. To be on the streets dealing with community, youth and family issues requires skill in areas such as human relationships and child psychology. In addition, workers need to be skilled in forming community partnerships and working with individuals from diverse backgrounds. While many agencies conduct pre-service training, the need for ongoing in-service efforts is critical.

Sources

1. New York Times (1949). *Worker assigned to the streets.* April 24, p.61.
2. Trolander, J.A. (1987). *Professionalism and social change.* New York: Columbia University Press.
3. Bannon, J. J. (1972). The Roving Leader: A new look.. *Parks and Recreation*, 7(2), 22-24.
4. Thompson, J. K. (1999). *Caring on the streets: A study of detached youth workers.* Binghampton, NY: The Haworth Press.
5. Bernstein, S. (1964). *Youth on the streets: Work with alienated youth groups.* New York: Association Press.
6. Austin, D. M. (1957). Goals for the gang worker. *Social Work*, 2(4), 43-50.

Some of the material for this case study came from the following publications:

Baker, J. E., & Witt, P. A. (2000) Backstreet beacons: Austin's Roving Leaders. *Journal of Park and Recreation Administration*, 18(1), 87-105.

Bocarro, J. N. & Witt, P.A. (2002, in press). Reaching out/reaching in: the long term challenges and issues of outreach programs. *Journal of Park and Recreation Administration.*

Bocarro, J.N. (2001) *Mobile beacons: Roving leaders and the communities they serve.* Unpublished doctoral dissertation, Texas A&M University, College Station.

Crompton, J. L. & Witt, P. A. (1997). The roving leader program in San Antonio. *Journal of Park and Recreation Administration, 15(2)*, 84-92.

Witt, P. A., & Baker, J. E. (1999, March). Make a R.E.A.L. difference. *Parks and Recreation*, 70-80.

Witt, P. A., Crompton, J. L. & Baker, J. E. (1999). Taking it to the streets. *Trends*, 35(4), 41-45.

Section 3

Comprehensive Programs

CHAPTER 8

A MATURE YOUTH SERVICES PROGRAMS:

PHOENIX PARKS AND RECREATION DEPARTMENT

Background

Phoenix's population grew from 789,704 in 1980 to 1,321,045 in 2000. In the 1990s it was second in total population growth among the country's large cities, behind only New York City. This rapid growth and the city's changing demographics presented special challenges to all government and non-profit service providers. According to the 2000 census, whites constituted 71% of the city's population, Hispanics, who may be of any race, made up 34% of the population. 29% of households had children under 18. People of mixed heritage or not reporting ethnicity comprised 20%.

In 1980, Phoenix Parks and Recreation Department (PARD) opened the South Phoenix Youth Center next to one of the city's inner-city high schools. The center was built in response to requests from teenagers who said they needed a safe place to hang-out. This center offered a "one-stop-shop" for youth recreational and social services needs. The center undertook a three-pronged approach to services: recreation, employment services and prevention services. The opening of the center initiated a journey that has led the PARD to being one of the most highly regarded providers of youth services in the country. The philosophy and structure of Phoenix services in general, and youth services in particular, have been cited as national models that other cities seek to emulate. This case study provides a synopsis of that journey and the PARD's accomplishments in serving youth, with emphasis on the most recent years.

Prior to 1985, youth services were offered at various facilities but the services were rather fragmented and many times the focus was on populations other than adolescents. In 1985, the department expanded its youth service efforts by developing a mobile recreation outreach service in response to concerns expressed by West Phoenix residents. Parents were concerned at the lack of structured activities for teens given the emergence of increased juvenile delinquency activity. With the support of a local council member, the community secured general purpose funding to provide the City Streets Program which offered mobile recreational, educational, social, and cultural activities to teens. Outreach sites included malls, schools, park sites and local youth gathering places.

In creating the City Streets program, the PARD drew upon the philosophy, approaches and programs that had been developed at the South Phoenix Youth Center. These included mens/womens support groups, pre-employment preparation and recreational special events (e.g. car, talent and modeling shows).

By 1990, the City Streets concept had been extended to all areas of the city, and in 1991 the PARD further emphasized its commitment to youth by identifying youth-at-risk as a priority for the next decade. This commitment was reinforced through a 1993 *Summit on Youth - Youth Empowerment in Action (Y.E.A.)* sponsored by the Mayor's Office. Approximately 100 youth and 100 adults participated in the summit, which was sponsored by a major utility company. The invited adults included youth-serving agency representatives, school district superintendents, and business leaders. Teens included high school leaders, department program participants, and youth "alleged" to be involved in gangs. Through workshops participated in by both youth and adults, the summit addressed seven program areas:

- interagency cooperation, communication, coordination and collaboration;
- youth employment;
- curfew ordinance;
- gun ordinance and gang violence;
- youth offender community service;
- youth preparatory skills; and
- at-risk youth prevention and intervention services.

Each workshop was led by a professional moderator. The discussion began by providing participants with a general background of the issues. Youth and adult participants then held separate discussions to clarify issues and identify possible solutions from their respective perspectives. The two groups then rejoined to develop a list of recommendations which were presented to all summit participants at the closing session. The format provided equal opportunity for youth and adults to formulate recommendations.

The summit enhanced awareness of the need for comprehensive youth programming and services, and it provided momentum for further action. Several city staff committees were formed to discuss services for youth that would address the summit's recommendation, and the PARD convened an internal Youth-At-Risk Task Force comprised of 29 department staff members to develop program priorities and issues. To accomplish its work, the PARD task force was divided into six subcommittees:

- program inventory/overlap analysis;
- marketing-promotion;
- youth serving agency network model;
- unmet programs, needs, and deficiencies;
- school recreation analysis; and
- alternate funding sources.

After reviewing reports from the subcommittees, the task force recommended that youth services be increased throughout Phoenix with a special programming emphasis on at-risk youth. Specific recommendations included:

- creating a computerized inventory of youth programs offered in the community;
- seeking funding sources for after-school and summer programs;

- placing more emphasis on life skills;
- brokering services with other agencies to expand program offerings;
- developing a staff training program for all part-time and full-time staff who work with youth;
- increasing expertise in grant writing; and
- expanding late-night program offerings.

In response to the city's youth at-risk task force report, in 1993 the City Council made revisions to its comprehensive city youth policy. The policy reaffirmed the city's commitment to maintain and improve the quality of life for all youth. The foreword to the document stated:

> *Youth are our community's most precious and treasured resources and represent tomorrow's work force and community leaders. When we value our youth, they grow up to value themselves and to enrich our community. When we meet the physical and emotional needs of our youth, they grow up healthy in body and mind, able to help others. When we give our youth the necessary resources, including our time and energy, they grow up empowered to make significant contributions to our community. Our hope is that this policy will be the basis for a strengthened and renewed commitment by our community to our youth.*

The youth policy outlined five primary goals:

- To gain a better understanding of issues affecting youth and their families in Phoenix and current efforts to address their needs.
- To promote community agreement on goals and priorities.
- To establish a clearer understanding and consensus on the roles to be played by various jurisdictions and organizations in the service system.
- To guide the city in making decisions and developing its role in serving youth and their families.
- To identify funding and non-financial strategies for the city's involvement in youth services.
- To ensure youth participation in city government.

The policy recognized the following principles:

- The city is not alone in its concern for children and youth.
- A window of opportunity is available to make necessary and basic changes.
- Prevention and early intervention are critical components for successful program models.
- Need identification and service options are critical areas of concern.
- Service prioritization is key to meeting the basic needs of youth.
- Regional cooperation is a viable solution to problem identification and program resolution.
- Programs will be evaluated and funded based upon identified needs.
- An efficient delivery system will meet future challenges.

In addition, based on recommendations made by the citywide and PARD task forces, the Department recommended, and City Council approved, the creation of the At -Risk Youth Division in the PARD. The charge of the division was to centralize department youth programs and special services for at-risk youth. The division was asked to provide administrative and programming support to the city's four geographic-based park districts; to help access grant funding; and to build community partnerships. To form the division without additional cost, it was recommended that:

- staffing be reallocated from existing positions;
- grant funds be pursued to expand the program;
- existing youth facilities be coordinated by the new division; and
- program evaluation surveys be developed by local universities.

It was envisioned that the division would administer outreach youth programs, clarify accountability, and prepare staff with the necessary skills to provide youth related services.

The creation of the division was not without controversy within the department. Some staff felt that the department had moved too far from the traditional role of PARDs. One staff member even left the department because she felt that dealing with drugs, sex and domestic abuse was not part of the parks and recreation mandate, believing that they better belonged in the social services department. However, most staff embraced the idea believing that the recreation agency was too focused on "games and sports," rather than on dealing with community issues and problems.

The PARD director at that time responded to those concerns by stating:

> *My staff say we are becoming counselors and social workers. That's fine, I believe we should be. My philosophy is that if a young man comes in on drugs or a young woman comes in who is pregnant, we have to help. Young ladies come to my female staff and say "I'm pregnant, will you come home with me and help me talk to my mom." They are scared, so of course we help. We often adopt these kids. We respond as best we can to whatever they need. I would not have a problem with my Department being called a Department of Community Services.*
>
> *Our job is to make young people whole in any way we can, and offering wholesome recreation activities is only one aspect of that. It's a way of reaching them. It gives us an opportunity to help them straighten out other parts of their lives that are not good. You have to do this work one case at a time. If you talk about doing it by the masses or in general terms, it will fail. Follow-through is critical and that is our limiting factor. We don't have the manpower or money to follow through at the level we should.*

In a 1993 planning document, the department listed a working definition of youth at-risk to guide program development design:

> Those teens, regardless of ethnic background and socioeconomic status, whose lives are affected by such factors as abuse, neglect, lack of educational opportunities, lack of positive leisure activities, poor peer relationships, behavior and discipline problems, low self-esteem, lack of positive role models, dysfunctional home environment, and other factors that impact normal growth and development.

To ensure that youth interests were well represented in program planning, the department created teen councils throughout the city comprised of youth who attend particular recreation centers. These councils meet twice a month to plan recreational, social and community service projects. Each council provides a member who attends the monthly citywide Teen Parks and Recreation Board meeting. This board self-appoints a Chair, Vice Chair, Secretary and Treasurer. In addition, a representative of this board sits as a youth advisor on the PARD Advisory Board.

At all levels, teens advise staff on programs and topics of mutual interest. The boards help set youth programming policies and procedures. The Teen Parks and Recreation Board is responsible for development, funding, and implementation of the annual teen conference, which is attended by over 300 youths. Additionally the Board is responsible for special events, youth logo, youth slogan, and recommendations to PARD staff on future youth programs and facilities.

PARD's program philosophy and offerings have evolved to the point where it is now the most comprehensive youth services program among large American cities. The nation's sixth largest city has refined the role of recreation departments in serving youth by introducing such programs as: (a) providing diversion and community service programs for adjudicated youth; (b) providing job training and drug counseling programs; (c) finding shelter for homeless or abused kids, and (d) being the first department in the nation to set up a procedure for tattoo removal. The PARD's vision is far reaching in its intent and focus. The central philosophy guiding the At-Risk Youth Division is that "prevention is the building block; youth are our greatest resource." The division tries to go beyond serving youth who "enter through the front door" of facilities and programs, by identifying and serving youth who are not connected to regular services and facilities.

The division's current priorities are:

- Maintaining and fostering relationships with a variety of private, quasi-public and governmental agencies, educational institutions, professional staff and volunteers to ensure the service delivery network meets the needs of youth and reflects the objectives and intent of the Mayor and City Council.
- Ongoing training of staff related to youth development and professional development.
- Serving as a monitor and research body to identify trends and issues relevant to the youth population.
- Serving as an advocate for youth.

- Developing and institutionalizing programs and services that benefit youth.
- Applying for and administering funds through contracted service providers, monitoring contract compliance and service delivery.
- Becoming a central coordination body for the Phoenix Activity City after-school program.

Since 1993 the division has had two different heads, both of whom had their roots in the field of social work. Their backgrounds have been appropriate given the focus of services, and the desire to get beyond being perceived as solely a "fun and games" entity. The current division head worked previously for the County juvenile justice division and has strong ties to other youth agencies in the community.

The major responsibility for dealing with youth issues remains with staff members working at the various recreation centers. To supplement their efforts and develop citywide programs, the At-Risk Youth Division has grown from 11 (in 1993) to 52 FTEs. This includes 27 full-time, 10 grant funded positions and approximately 70 part-time staff.

The budget grew from around $400,000 in general-purpose funds and over $230,000 in grants in 1993, to over $2,000,000 in general purpose funds and $700,000 in grants in 2000. A surcharge of 25 cents imposed on each round of golf played at city golf courses goes into a city fund (approximately $150,000 per year), and helps to support a youth recreation internship program that provides jobs for youth at the recreation centers, youth golf clinics and staff training.

To supplement the city's resources, the division secures federal, state, and private foundation grants. To facilitate the grant writing process, a full-time grant researcher and coordinator were hired soon after the division was formed. In its first full year, the division submitted 25 applications for funds, of which 15 were successful, yielding almost $1 million in additional resources.

To support this grant application work, a resource library of data reports, and statistical findings related to youth has been developed. Programs funded by outside sources request applicants to demonstrate identifiable causes, existence of need, and/or current trends relating to the proposal issue. Community assessments and community readiness plans are also collected. This library ensures data are readily available for inclusion in grant proposals.

The unit has received strong support and citywide acclaim for providing central coordination of quality youth programs. This support is illustrated by the reassignment of programs to the division, e.g., Parental Responsibility, PAL (Police Athletic League), Accept the Challenge, New Turf and Rites of Passage. These programs were formerly in other city units such as Equal Opportunity, Human Services, the City Manager's Office, Youth and Education Office and Police. Several departments contract with the At-Risk Youth Division to provide prevention and intervention services that they are not equipped to provide. (Exhibit 8-1 describes some of the programs offered by the division).

Exhibit 8-1

Overview of Selected Programs

- **Project BRAVE.** Using a three-year Local Law Enforcement Block Grant ($126,000 per year), Project BRAVE facilitates domestic violence prevention workshops for youth aged 6 to 19 years (approximately 4,000 per year) who might be subject to abuse in their homes. The program was created at the request of the police to assist in building a prevention arm to counteract the cycle of family violence. The division collaborates with a number of other departmental and community organizations in presenting this program.
- **Project SCRUB** (Stop Crime Remove Urban Blight) is a collaboration between the At-Risk Youth Division, Maricopa County Juvenile Court (MCJCC), and the Human Services Department. The program is responsible for providing diversion to two-thirds of all Phoenix youth involved in status offenses for the first time. It provides constructive supervised community service for court ordered youth offenders with 16 to 400 hours to complete. Community service hours are undertaken through organizations such as: Neighborhood Services, Real Estate, Human Services Departments, Neighborhood Block Watch, Fight Back Associations, and various Community Resource Officers, which are all involved in restoring distressed neighborhoods. The program is funded through general-purpose funds ($146,000 per year).
- **First Offender Program.** The At-Risk Youth Division partnered with Maricopa County Juvenile Court to create the First Offender Program. Youth who commit certain status or misdemeanor offenses, including shoplifting, criminal damage, trespassing, theft, and disorderly conduct, are referred to the program by the court. The program is offered in-lieu of being assigned to a county probation officer. It requires that juvenile offenders and their parents attend a three-hour workshop called "Power of Choice". Youth are required also to complete eight hours of community service.
- **Young First Offender Program.** After tracking the background of participants in the First Offender Program, it was noted that a disproportionate number of youth offenders were under 13 years of age. This resulted in the Young First Offender program created in collaboration with the Maricopa County Juvenile Court (MCJCC), and the City's Human Services Department. Like the program for older youth, this offering is designed for children who commit a first misdemeanor offense. It is an alternative to them becoming involved with juvenile court, and eliminates monthly probation services fees charged to the youths' families if they are placed on traditional probation. Its objective is to deter delinquent behavior before it progresses to more serious offenses and subsequent incarceration. Children do three hours of supervised community work and three hours of supervised recreation which exposes them to positive recreational activities. This program is funded through $80,000 in general-purpose funds.
- **Curfew Diversion Program.** The At-Risk Youth Division implemented a Curfew Diversion Program in collaboration with Maricopa County Juvenile Court, Phoenix Police and New Choices of America. This program eliminates the need for police to detain youth at a local police precinct. Instead of taking youth to a local precinct, police take them directly to the nearest community center involved in the program. Police aides then process the paper work while recreation staff provide supervision and recreational activities until parents pick up the detainee. It was reported that the program resulted in a 50% reduction in curfew violations.

Exhibit 8-1 Continued

- **Operation AIM**. Operation Attendance is Mandatory (AIM) is a collaboration between the City's Youth and Education Office, the Human Services Department, the City Auditor and Prosecutor's Office, Phoenix Police, the At-Risk Youth Division and the Maricopa County Juvenile Court. The collaboration involves four School districts, and 107 schools within the City of Phoenix. The objective is to reduce truancy which impacts overall juvenile crime in communities. The program is funded through a $125,000 Local Law Enforcement Block Grant.
- **PAL**. Historically, the Police department implemented its Police Activities League program. In the mid-1990s the city reassigned administration of the program to the At-Risk Youth Division. The program seeks to build relationships between youth and the Police, and provides recreational, educational and social programs for 10 to 18 year old youth at six youth centers staffed with Recreation Coordinators.
- **Employment and Training.** The City Council approved an increase of 25 cents per round of golf played at the City's five courses to assist in developing additional programs for at-risk youth. This yields approximately $150,000 per year that is used to provide youth with job training. The Recreation Internship Program is a result of that fund. It has placed former interns into part-time positions throughout the department. The interns participate in a 12-week work experience and are required to complete 30 hours of education related workshops and 90 hours of field experience. Approximately 45 interns are employed at facilities throughout the city each fall and spring semester.
- **Plan-It League**. The At-Risk Youth Division collaborates with Phoenix Mercury/ Phoenix Suns staff members who provide young women with positive role models to facilitate development of basketball skills and provide overall career awareness. The program has two components: the PLAN-IT Internship Program for high school young women and the PLAN-IT League, a youth basketball league for girls aged 9 to 14. The interns meet with personnel from the professional Suns and Mercury basketball organizations on a weekly basis.
- **X-TATTOO Program**. The At-Risk Youth Division together with the River of Dreams, a non-profit organization, members of the Arizona Society of Plastic and Re-constructive Surgeons, Valley Vocational Services, and youth serving agencies provide laser removal of visible gang tattoos for at-risk youth and adults within Maricopa County. X-TATTOO seeks to provide participants access to productive and non-violent futures by removing tattooed gang insignia. Almost 350 individuals have had tattoos removed.
- **Phoenix Activity City (PAC)** is an after-school program that currently services over 100 schools, with plans to extend to 180 schools. The program curriculum consists of nine elements, and aids in providing specialized prevention services to the sites. The elements are: life skills, educational support, social/peer interaction, physical activity, cultural awareness, fine arts, crime reduction and fun. The program's annual budget is $4 million dollars.

❖ ❖ ❖

The division commissioned several evaluation studies from faculty at Arizona State University. Additionally, the diversion program has developed a statistical database to track juvenile crime trends. These statistics are evaluated on a monthly basis. Major programs that have undergone comprehensive evaluation include: The Thunderbirds Teen Center, the South Phoenix Youth Center, the Young First Offender Program, the Recreation Internship Program, and X-Tattoo.

The division is responsible for administering over 20 youth programs and services citywide, which include recreation, employment and training, diversion, prevention services and cultural arts. Additionally, it has become the central clearinghouse for responding to grant funding submissions. Over the last four years, the division has become the coordinating body for a large portion of Maricopa County's diversion services, which includes five diversion programs with partnerships with other city departments and the county.

The division continues to operate two comprehensive youth and teen centers. Many times, these centers serve as the "safety net" in the community to reach youth after school and on weekends when traditional social service agencies and schools are closed. Both centers play a central role in the advocacy and engagement of youth in local school and community systems.

The South Phoenix Youth Center serves youth aged 13 to 21. The mission of the center is to "provide positive alternatives and promote positive self-development of youth by any means necessary." The mission is met by providing a variety of programs and special events, school activities, and information and referral services. In addition, the center offers community linkages with other government and social service agencies, educational institutions, and businesses.

The Thunderbirds Teen Center opened more recently with a vision of providing a wide variety of innovative, affordable, non-traditional recreation programs to neighborhood youth 13 to 19 years of age. Its primary goal is to equip youth with an inventory of skills and positive experiences that will help promote positive self-development while decreasing juvenile delinquency and high school drop out rates. The center is unique in Phoenix in that it features a fully integrated computer music studio, which incorporates many facets of computer technology such as a 24-track recording studio, computer sports leagues, tutorial services and software. Collaborative efforts with North Canyon High School led to over 15 joint projects including Grad Night, intramurals, drama, spring fling, the City Streets support group, guidance counseling and job training. These collaborations were pivotal in reaching Limited English Proficient Students in the surrounding area.

What's Next?

In the future, the division hopes to be a catalyst for adding youth centers in underserved areas of the city and reassessing and expanding the definition of "youth" so it extends up to 23 year olds. This is consistent with the division's focus on offering a variety of services that support the transition of youth to adulthood and meets the need for training and education among the "Baby Bust" generation.

The present division head has big aspirations:

I would like this division to be recognized as one of the most successful leadership and cultural diversity programs for youth in America. I would like to create an extraordinary experience for youth. This experience would arm youth with the skills and motivation to create positive change in their community. Our hope is to create a place that listens to youths' fears, frustrations and aspirations; a place where they can know themselves and their peers better, to discover their personal values, and learn the skills to act on their beliefs; and finally, a place that enables youth to develop respect for racial and cultural differences through education for leadership, human relations and citizenship.

Consideration has been given to changing the division's name to Youth Development. While the at-risk youth label helps focus political attention on the division's ability to decrease risk-behaviors, the division is so well accepted within the community and city government that the change would probably have little negative political impact. If the division had tried to make this change in the early 1990s, it would not have been able to capitalize on community concerns about youth risk behaviors and the willingness of government to put resources toward reducing anti-social behavior.

In summing up the division's success, its head says: "We are at the table, not fighting or begging to be part of the action. We are thought of as part of the team of professionals trying to deal with youth issues in the community." Indeed, at budget time a number of other city departments seek to align with the PARD and the division in order to garner money and support for their services.

Lessons Learned

- A central feature of the Phoenix approach has been the integration of young people's ideas into service delivery. Department staff believe that youth input ensures services and vision are appropriate and attainable. Trying to create a responsive service system is impossible if youth are not given a voice in program and facility development.
- While the separation of services for at-risk youth into an independent division was timely and necessary, there is a danger in separating too far from the day-to-day activities of the rest of the department's youth services. Significant cross-fertilization and cultivating of the division's mission with that of the rest of the department is essential to success. What was initially perceived as an "administrative only" role for the unit evolved into substantial involvement in programming.
- A diversified staff (race, gender, age and education) is essential for programmatic success. An ethnically diverse staff, that includes individuals from a number of different service backgrounds (recreation, arts, education, social work, justice studies, psychology), produces a more comprehensive and responsive approach for dealing with the needs of at-risk youth.
- Grant administration is time-consuming and staff intensive. Its merits must be weighed against accomplishing other division priorities. If grants are to be sought, an administrative support system needs to be in place to support grant writing and administration.
- Developing close partnerships with the Juvenile Courts and the Police Department are keys to success for this type of programming. The "buy-in" of law enforcement and the courts, substantially expands the potential range of youth at-risk services that can be offered.

- Research and evaluation tools must be implemented in order to discern program effectiveness and promote continuous improvement. Like many other departments, the PARD did this by linking with a major university.
- Systems need to be set up to capture program data needed to meet the requirements of city government and external funders.

Sources

Manny Tarango, At-Risk Youth Division Head, Phoenix Parks, Recreation and Library Department

CHAPTER 9

P.L.A.Y. TEAM PROGRAMS

The city of Virginia Beach has a population of 440,000. Data from the city's public schools show a significant change in the ethnic composition of students from 1991 to 2000. In 1991, 74% were Caucasian and 19% African American, but by 2000 these ratios had changed to 64% and 27% respectively. The crime rate for juveniles in Virginia Beach is the lowest in the region.

Nevertheless, when the city undertook a survey of its residents as part of its ongoing strategic planning process to find out what they perceived to be priority issues the city should be addressing, one of the five priority areas identified was at-risk youth. To respond to this identified need, a Strengthening Families task force was convened to encourage a collaborative approach among youth-serving agencies in creating increased opportunities for school-age children beyond current instructional hours. This task force recommended establishing a Youth Opportunities Office to coordinate efforts, believing it would ensure optimal use of shrinking resources and promote collaboration among all agencies providing services to youth in Virginia Beach.

The Virginia Beach Park and Recreation Department (PARD) is one of the multiple agencies constituting the Youth Opportunities Team. Other agencies involved include: City Public Schools, Community Services Board, Juvenile Court Services, Public Health, the Youth Opportunities Office, the Volunteer Council, and the Virginia Beach Departments of Agriculture, Housing and Neighborhood Preservation, Police, Public Libraries, and Social Services.

The overall vision for youth created by the Youth Opportunities Team is All Our Children Are Well. This African phrase was adopted from the Masai tribe, who greet each other by asking, "And how are the children?" The response is, "All the children are well," which shows the emphasis the Masai place on youth in their community. The Virginia Beach vision is that their community will make the same level of commitment to youth.

The PARD's contributions to this vision focused on the creation of its P.L.A.Y. (Promoting Leisure Activities for Youth) unit. The unit's goal was to provide prevention programming. Its mission statement specifies five objectives:

- To provide a safe and structured environment in which to grow and learn;
- To act as responsible and caring adult mentors;
- To provide opportunities to develop marketable skills and increase life skills, thus providing a healthy start for a healthy future;
- To provide the opportunity for achievement, recognition, a sense of belonging, goal setting, a sense of purpose and self-esteem building;

- To increase the resiliency of youth by exposing them to positive behaviors in an environment that decreases their exposure and/or involvement in risk-taking behavior; and
- To create opportunities for youth to give back through community service.

Identifying Target Areas

The first task was to identify target areas in Virginia Beach that had the greatest need for prevention programs and a lack of existing recreational opportunities. The PLAY Team used existing data to select four areas for more detailed assessment. The data used for this purpose were:

- The geographic location of youth under age 25 who had committed a crime.
- Substandard housing and percentage of persons under the poverty level in each planning area.
- Age profiles of each planning area.
- Number and type of dwelling units in each planning area.
- The geographic location of citizens receiving food stamps.
- PARD's fee waiver data.
- Number of children attending school in each planning area.
- Number of children enrolled in PARD's Before and After-School Programs.
- Number of youth memberships sold at each PARD center.
- Number of youth memberships sold at the Hilltop, Indian River, and Mount Trashmore Y.M.C.A. centers.
- Recreation opportunities in each planning area.
- Youth pregnancy data.
- Number of youth in each planning area participating in city-wide athletic leagues.
- Subsidized housing in each planning area.
- Title 1 schools in each area.

Analyses of these data suggested that the greatest need for prevention programs was in four planning areas: Aragona/Pembrook, Bayside, Holland, and Oceanfront. Within these four planning areas, there are a total of 20 neighborhoods. The existing recreation opportunities in each of these areas were deemed to be limited. They are shown in Exhibit 9-1.

Exhibit 9-1

Potential Recreation Opportunities in the Four Selected Planning Areas

	Bayside Borough	Oceanfront/Cooke	Holland	Aragona
Neighborhoods	Campus East Lake Edward Pembroke Meadows Wesleyan Forest Haygood Weblin Place	Atlantis/Seabridge Square Piper's Landing Trailer City 15th and 16th Streets Friendship Village West Oceana Gardens	Chimney Hill Pecan Gardens Scarborough Square	Aragona Village Pembroke Manor Pembroke Lakes Pocahontas Village County View
Number of Youth	6108	2528	5419	1151
Civic Leagues	8	8	3	4
Sibsidized Housing	1	5	1	1
Recreational Opportunities				
Recreation Centers	1	1	1	0
Parks	5	3	5	8
Private Recreation	0	0	0	0
Schools	6	3	6	2
Churches	6	11	3	2
Open Spaces	0	2	0	0
Swimming Pools (Public)	2	1	1	0
Golf Courses	0	2	1	0
Tennis Courts	0	2	0	4
City Sport Leagues	2	2	2	3
Private Sport Associations	1	1	2	1

The program was piloted in two neighborhoods, and over a multi-year period has been incrementally extended to all 20 neighborhoods in the target area. In each neighborhood a needs assessment is conducted. Typically, this involves the PLAY team hosting a block party with free food, games and music, at which attendees complete need assessment forms. The information is used to guide development of future programs and services.

Community outreach is a vital part of the PLAY Team's mission. Each member of the team is assigned a geographic area of the city. They are the liaison for community recreation centers, the schools in the area, and the neighborhoods within that community. The PLAY Team staff visit schools during the students' lunch periods twice a month to maintain a connection with the youth and promote PLAY Team programs and services. They collaborate with the schools in various ways, such as being on the PTA Board, assisting with organizing school social events such as dances, and serving on a variety of school committees.

Programs

The needs assessments reflecting different neighborhood interests have resulted in a wide range of program ideas emerging. A brief description of several of them is given below.

W.A.V.E. (Working All Virginia's Environments) is a year-round program for ages 12-17. The primary objective is to provide youth with recreation, education, and conservation hands-on experiences in a safe and social setting. Participants work in outdoor activities with a variety of organizations and affiliations throughout the Commonwealth of Virginia including Virginia State Parks, National Wildlife Refuges and others who share an interest in Virginia's environment. Activity options include: hiking trips; learning how to map wildlife from the Department of Game and Inland fisheries; working on the West Neck Creek Development Project; archeology; arts & crafts; back-country maintenance; geology; historic clothing and furnishings; and historic preservation.

Rites of Passage provides female participants between the ages of 13 and 17 the opportunity to explore different cultures. It is an eight week unit that offers both education and recreation components. Participants learn the importance of recognizing their role in life, positive decision making, and healthy relationships. There is a graduation ceremony for those who successfully complete the program

Survivor Beach Style is a collaborative effort between the PLAY Team and the site coordinator of the Virginia Beach Public School's Ropes and Initiatives Course. The purpose is to provide opportunities for participants to develop personal confidence and a positive self-concept while encouraging the development of problem solving and communication skills. The Survivor program consists of team building activities, trust activities, and cooperative games, as well as high and low activities on the Ropes and Initiatives Course. Between 10 and 12 participants are chosen by the guidance staff and the In-School Suspension Coordinator at area schools based on the following criteria: poor attitude in school, inappropriate social behavior, and/or academic failure.

The Mobile Activity Center is a recreation center which tours the City of Virginia Beach and provides those in the targeted areas programs and services they might not be able to access because of their lack of transportation. The unit is parked in apartment village play areas, cul-de-sacs, neighborhood parks, or on grassy parts of townhome complexes. It is designed to increase motor and social skills, awareness of community resources, awareness of family violence solutions, and safety awareness. Staff encourage success in school by assisting with homework and recognizing youth's achievements. Activities offered include arts and crafts, sports, and special events.

Playing Smart was made possible through a grant from Virginia Partners in Prevention. It focuses on education, leisure activities, and healthy relationships. The goal is to increase participants' self-esteem and empower them through knowledge to make informed choices regarding sexual activity. The target population is 10 and 11 year old males and females. Students are selected from area schools based on the following criteria: family history of teen pregnancy, family management problems/conflict, poor school attitude, and/or inappropriate social behavior. Biweekly sessions held for four weeks include one hour of education and an hour of recreation. A graduation ceremony is held at the end of the program, and each participant receives a free membership card to Virginia Beach PARD's Recreation Centers.

A component of the program is experience with the "Baby, Think It Over" simulated care doll. The doll is used as a parenting simulation. It cries at random intervals and requires round-the-clock care on the part of its "parent." This simulation is a challenge to the young adult. It teaches him or her more about the responsibilities of parenthood than any amount of lecturing could. Many students who use the doll say afterward that it motivated them to wait to have children.

The simulation is demanding. It requires the child to be "on call" by his or her "baby" 24 hours a day from Friday evening until the following Monday evening. He or she must drop what they are doing, with no warning, whenever the "baby" needs attention. The device used for caring for the doll is strapped to the youth's wrist with a tamper-proof bracelet. The doll cries frequently (but briefly, if its "parent" is attentive). It wakes the youth at night, and possibly other family members. If extra equipment has been provided, the youth must take it along wherever he or she goes (equipment may include a diaper bag, car seat, and clothing).

Energy 2 Burn was designed by the American Council on Exercise (ACE) in cooperation with the National Fitness Leaders Association to introduce physical activity into the lives of youth once a week for 5 weeks. One PLAY Team member is ACE Certified and meets with the fourth grade population. The first 10 - 15 minutes involve educational sessions on health related topics, and the remaining class time is filled with exercise activities. Each child keeps a log book of his/her physical activity and completes written assignments. At the conclusion of the program each child receives a certificate of completion.

Safety Camp is a week long program designed to educate third grade students on safe living. Volunteers from both city agencies and private businesses present interactive, hands-on classes to educate these students on potentially hazardous situations and how to react to them. Safety Camp is held during the Public Schools' Spring Break. Students are bussed from six different recreation centers to make the program accessible to all who are interested. The target population for Safety camp is those students who are "at risk." Lunch and snacks are provided daily by the Virginia Beach Public School's Food Services. Safety presentations include: kitchen safety, bus safety, sports safety, fire safety, gun safety, and traffic safety. The police make a special helicopter landing during the week to demonstrate rescue response. In all, youth attend over 20 different safety presentations during the week, which are interspersed with multiple opportunities to "just have fun." At the conclusion of the week, children compete in the Safety Olympics before being rewarded with a free bicycle helmet and other gifts at the closing ceremony.

The Questing for Success Camp was created to offer at-risk middle school youth an opportunity to participate in an educational recreation camp during the week of Spring Break at minimal cost to the parents. The goal of the camp is to teach alternate approaches to resolving issues that regularly confront middle school youth. The 40 youth participants are identified through referrals made by school guidance counselors.

Educational sessions address such topics as handgun violence, healthy relationships, HIV/STD's, nutrition and hygiene, first impressions/interview skills, conflict resolution, self esteem, money management, stress management, and first aid. Recreational activities focus on team building, communication skills, and cooperation. The camp is open to fifty middle school aged youth based on the following criteria: economic status, behavioral history, family status, and/or criminal records.

The R.E.A.L. (Responsible, Educated and Learning) Youth program is designed to heighten self-awareness, enhance self-esteem, develop leadership skills, identify personal strengths, and challenge youth to achieve self-fulfillment. Youth learn the importance of higher education and giving back to the community. Over 30 youth are served in this program and the targeted population is at-risk youth between the ages of 11 and 17. They come together to coordinate and implement monthly meetings, hold fund-raisers to help raise money for trips, and listen to guest speakers who discuss different topics related to HIV, Cultural Diversity, Education, etc. Activities include participating in Clean The Bay Day, adopting a Nursing Home, coordinating and implementing activities at the Children's Hospital, and restoring a neighborhood park.

Beach Girls' Cheerleading is intended to provide female adolescents aged 11-17 with cheerleading activities. The year-round team of 20-35 members participates in fund-raising and community service projects, city-wide special events, team trips and monthly life skills educational sessions, i.e., Hygiene, Etiquette. Individuals are targeted who have a desire to learn about the sport of cheerleading, but lack the opportunity or ability to join other teams; such as their school or cheer organization which require tryouts.

The Regional Girls Basketball League's goal is to heighten self-awareness, enhance self-esteem, and challenge at-risk girls to achieve self-fulfillment through the medium of athletics. The objective is to reach girls who have not had the opportunity to participate in programs such as this; to educate and encourage wholesome competition by utilizing leisure time wisely in an effort to enhance emotional, educational, and cultural values; and to promote sportsmanship and character building.

Fighting Invisible Tigers is a stress management course targeted at teens aged 12-16 who are having trouble dealing with frustration, anxiety, and anger. The 10 week program is an introductory level course on dealing with stress. After completing the sessions, members of the group should:

- Know the difference between a state of stress and its effects on health and well being.
- Be able to evaluate current stressors, stress levels, and methods of coping.
- Experience the benefits of a range of life skills: physical activity, relaxation, assertiveness, supportive relationships, life planning, and positive "self-talk".
- Feel empowered to care for themselves and seek help and support when needed.

Evaluation

Evaluations of all the programs are comprehensive. Typically they comprise three separate elements: evaluations solicited from parents; students' assessments of the quality of the programs; and pre and post tests measuring students' knowledge or attitude before and after the program. Illustrations of these evaluation instruments using the Questing for Success Camp program as the example are given in Exhibits 9-2, 9-3, and 9-4.

Exhibit 9-2

Parent Evaluation

1. Has your youth shared any positive feedback with you concerning the 2001 Questing Camp? If so, what was the nature of his/her feedback?

2. Has your youth shared any negative feedback with you concerning the 2001 Questing Camp? If so, what was the nature of his/her feedback?

3. Do you feel that the 2001 Questing Camp provided your youth with a meaningful experience? If so, how?

4. Please share your comments concerning the fee for the program?

5. Please share any additional comments which you feel will serve to benefit next year's program.

Name (optional) ______________________________

Exhibit 9-3

Participant Evaluation

Please rate the following information sessions using the scale below.

	5 Excellent	4 Good	3 Average	2 Not very good	1 Poor
Domestic Dating Violence	5	4	3	2	1
School Violence	5	4	3	2	1
Stress Management	5	4	3	2	1
Street Violence	5	4	3	2	1
Positive and Negative Influences of Media	5	4	3	2	1
Nutrition & Fitness	5	4	3	2	1
Responsible Thinking (Part 1)	5	4	3	2	1
Responsible Thinking Activity	5	4	3	2	1
Options, Choices & Consequences	5	4	3	2	1
Responsible Thinking (Part 2)	5	4	3	2	1
Responsible Thinking Activity	5	4	3	2	1
Peer Pressure (Part 1)	5	4	3	2	1
Peer Pressure (Part 2)	5	4	3	2	1
Body Language	5	4	3	2	1
Diversity	5	4	3	2	1
Alcohol Awareness	5	4	3	2	1

Please rate the following activities using the scale below.

	5 Excellent	4 Good	3 Average	2 Not very good	1 Poor
Rec Ctr Swim/Bowling	5	4	3	2	1
Jail Tour	5	4	3	2	1
Ropes Course (First Trip)	5	4	3	2	1
Hiking Trip	5	4	3	2	1
Golf Trip	5	4	3	2	1
Ropes Course (Second Trip)	5	4	3	2	1
Recreation Day Red Wing Park	5	4	3	2	1
Group Games and Activities	5	4	3	2	1

What was your least favorite session and why? ______________________________

What was your most favorite session and why? ______________________________

What was your least favorite thing about camp? ______________________________

What was your most favorite thing about camp? ______________________________

Would you recommend this camp to any of your friends? ______________________________

Would you attend a camp like this again? ______________________________

NAME (optional) ______________________________

Exhibit 9-4

The Questing for Success Camp Pre/Post Test

For each statement below, please indicate how much you disagree or agree with each. There are no right or wrong answers. Please circle only one response for each statement.

	Pre Test Results				
	Strongly Disagree SD	Disagree D	Neutral N	Agree A	Strongly Agree SA
1) I know a lot of safe places to hang out.	SD	D	N	A	SA
2) There are a lot of adults who are interested in me.	SD	D	N	A	SA
3) I am able to get along with friends.	SD	D	N	A	SA
4) I must stay out of trouble.	SD	D	N	A	SA
5) I respect authority figures.	SD	D	N	A	SA
6) I am creative.	SD	D	N	A	SA
7) I can succeed in life.	SD	D	N	A	SA
8) I try to treat others with respect.	SD	D	N	A	SA
9) I try to solve problems in a positive manner.	SD	D	N	A	SA
10) I have a desire to keep trying when challenged.	SD	D	N	A	SA
11) I know about a lot of activities in my community.	SD	D	N	A	SA
12) I can turn to adults for help.	SD	D	N	A	SA
13) There are other people my age who like me.	SD	D	N	A	SA
14) I must obey the rules.	SD	D	N	A	SA
15) I respect adults.	SD	D	N	A	SA
16) I can set goals.	SD	D	N	A	SA
17) It is important to me to always do my best.	SD	D	N	A	SA
18) Teamwork is important.	SD	D	N	A	SA
19) I try to control my anger.	SD	D	N	A	SA
20) I want to improve my people skills.	SD	D	N	A	SA
21) I am interested in participating in programs in my community.	SD	D	N	A	SA
22) There are adults who will look out for me.	SD	D	N	A	SA
23) I am an O.K. person.	SD	D	N	A	SA
24) I should be punished if I break rules.	SD	D	N	A	SA
25) I respect people in charge.	SD	D	N	A	SA
26) I can deal with problems that might come up in the future.	SD	D	N	A	SA
27) It is important for me to do well in school.	SD	D	N	A	SA
28) Cooperation is important.	SD	D	N	A	SA
29) I try to listen to the opinions of others.	SD	D	N	A	SA
30) I am interested in sports.	SD	D	N	A	SA
31) I am interested in programs that take place after school.	SD	D	N	A	SA
32) Adults are willing to help me with my problems.	SD	D	N	A	SA
33) I am wanted by the people around me.	SD	D	N	A	SA
34) I must follow rules if I want to participate.	SD	D	N	A	SA
35) I respect those who stay out of trouble.	SD	D	N	A	SA
36) I like to try new things.	SD	D	N	A	SA
37) It is important for me to stay in school.	SD	D	N	A	SA
38) All players need a chance to play.	SD	D	N	A	SA
39) I can settle arguments without fighting.	SD	D	N	A	SA
40) I like the arts.	SD	D	N	A	SA

Questing Camp Pre/Post Test Results

Summary Report
Summer 2001

Score Categories	Analyzed Observation	Percentage of Total
Near the same score = NS	8 of 40	20%
Exactly the same scores = ES	1 of 40	2.5%
Slight positive change = SPC	9 of 40	22.5%
Positive change = PC	12 of 40	30%
Slight negative change = SNC	4 of 40	10%
Negative change = NC	6 of 40	15%

- 52.5% increase in observed positive responses from Pre to Post Test
- 25% increase in observed negative responses from Pre to Post Test

The questions in Exhibit 9-2 are spaced down a sheet so there is more room for parents to write responses after each question than is shown in the figure. The participants' rating scales are shown in Exhibit 9-3. On the actual instrument, two lines are made available under each item on which participants are encouraged to elaborate and explain their reason for their rating of that item. The attitude/knowledge test shown on Exhibit 9-4 is adapted from the Protective Factors Scale (see Chapter 5) and is taken at the beginning of the program and again at its completion, so the program's impact can be evaluated. Thus for example, the annual summary of these comparisons shown was able to report a 52.5% increase in positive responses from the pre to the post test.

In addition to the P.L.A.Y. Team's evaluation increases, the Youth Opportunities Team, which is the consortium of all the Virginia Beach agencies involved with youth, has its own "Indicators of Success." Their list of indicators is more generic, offering a macro perspective rather than the micro perspective of individual programs which is the P.L.A.Y. Team's focus. Their Indicators of Success list is shown in Exhibit 9-5.

Exhibit 9-5

Indicators of Success

Youth report meaningful involvement in the community
Youth report positive experiences with adult mentors
Youth report feeling safe in their families, schools, and community
Youth Opportunities Office is adequately staffed to address actions outlined in Plan
Number of developmentally-appropriate programs and services available for ages 0-6
Number of children ages 0-6 enrolled in programs and services
Outcomes for children, ages 0-6 and their families, enrolled in programs and services
Number of grants which target areas prioritized in Youth Plan
Dollar amount of grants received for youth initiatives
Number of agencies represented in the Youth Provider Network
Number of new/enhanced collaborative efforts
Outcomes of new/enhanced collaborative efforts
Increase in number of youth and families participating in programs and services

Exhibit 9-5 Continued

Number of youth employed
Number of youth volunteers
Number of youth volunteer hours
Number of youth programs incorporating protective factors/building developmental assets
Number of youth opportunities associations
Number of new/enhanced neighborhood-based youth opportunities
Number of businesses implementing family-friendly practices
Number of people served by a community school
Number of services available at a community school
Reduction in the number of youth involved in risky behavior
Increases in the number of youth who are members of councils, committees and boards
Youth feel their opinions are taken seriously
Increase in the number and diversification of members on the Youth Opportunities Team
Number of city departments and community agencies that submit Youth Action Plans
Number of new and/or enhanced partnerships with businesses and agencies
Number of staff, parents, businesses and communities trained in Youth Development approaches
Number of adults trained to partner with youth
Number of how-to-guides distributed
Number of active members on the City-Wide Parent Involvement Advisory Group
Diversification of members on the City-Wide Parent Involvement Advisory Group
Number, location and utilization rate of computers set-up for public use
Number of visits to Youth Connections website
Number of visits to the Youth Opportunities website
Results of database survey
Number of media spots portraying positive images of youth
Number of forums for community input
Number of youth involved in the evaluation process
Decrease in risk factors perceived by youth
Increase in protective factors perceived by youth

❖ ❖ ❖

Source

Jeff L. Bass, Department of Parks and Recreation, Virginia Beach

Section 4

Specific Programs

CHAPTER 10

TEENS IN ACTION

In the past 20 years, few cities in the United States have changed as dramatically as North Miami. In 1980, the population of North Miami was 40,000, of whom 92% were White. By 2000, the ethnic composition of the city changed significantly and the population increased to 60,000. Exhibit 10-1 shows that North Miami is now a culturally diverse inner-city community, in which household incomes are predominantly in the low to moderate range. Over the past ten years, the average age of the city has declined as older residents have died or moved elsewhere. Expanding populations of African American and Caribbean Blacks, and of Cuban, Central and South American Hispanics have moved into the city. They reside predominantly in low-cost single-family or multi-family homes. The relatively low per capita income reflects that many are employed in relatively low-paid service or laborer jobs, and that there are a relatively large number of people per household.

Exhibit 10-1

PROFILE OF RESIDENTS OF THE CITY OF NORTH MIAMI IN 2000

Race/Ethnicity	
Non-Hispanic White	20.9%
Haitian	20.5%
African-American and other Black	25.5%
Hispanic	25.6%
Language Most Often Spoken at Home	
English	61.4%
Spanish	16.4%
Creole	14.4%
Household Income	
Under $20,000	29.3%
$20,000-$50,000	32.8%
Over $50,000	14.9%
Refused to Answer	23.0%
Own/Rent	
Own	56.5%
Rent	43.1%

Evolution of Teens in Action

The old North Miami police station was renovated into a small 12,000 sq. ft. community center. This was the first "new" programming space made available to the Parks and Recreation Department (PARD) in three decades. Because of the proximity of the community center to the North Miami Senior and Junior high schools, and the large number of students flowing into the downtown area after school, a programming priority was to move students off the streets by involving them in recreation programs after school. Accordingly, the PARD staff created an after-school drop-in teen club. The initial goals were to provide a safe place where:

(1) teens were in a positive and supportive environment;

(2) cultural diversity was respected and encouraged;

(3) teens were able to talk to staff about personal, school and family problems;

(4) personal growth was encouraged.

A month before the center opened, PARD staff discussed the possibility of forming a teen volunteer group to help with programs and special events. Shortly thereafter a North Miami high school student arrived at the center seeking volunteer hours to meet requirements for the countywide Silver Knight's Award (a prestigious community award). This student was instrumental in recruiting a few more teen volunteers to assist at the July Grand Opening of the new community center. PARD staff observed that the eight volunteers who had assisted at the "new" community center's grand opening evolved into a social group as a result of the bonding that occurred through their volunteer involvement.

Staff recognized that other high school students were looking for opportunities to satisfy their community service mandate which must be fulfilled as part of the requirements for high school graduation in Florida. Thus, staff were able to recruit 120 teens to volunteer in organizing the city's annual Thanksgiving Parade. A meeting of the volunteers for this event was held early in the school year and it was used also to solidify them into a teen club that was eventually named Teens in Action (TIA). After two months, membership expanded to 40 teens. PARD staff consciously strived to create a positive, supportive club environment and to informally mentor the TIA members. In a few short months, what had begun as a small group of high school students seeking volunteer hours had metamorphosed beyond a volunteer organization into a social group whose goals reflected those listed above in the first paragraph of this section.

Staff encouraged interactions among teens from different ethnic and cultural backgrounds, and created opportunities for them to work together, while making the meetings both fun and a learning experience. Popular themed special events like Caribbean Food Festival Day, a Sadie Hawkins type dance, Valentine's Day Dating game, and A Blast From the Past (a 50's dress up day) were planned and implemented by TIA students. Quickly the group grew to over 100 students.

Exhibit 10-2 lists the themes used to recruit youth to TIA. The community center is within walking distance of both the North Miami Senior High and Middle Schools, which reduces the need for arranging transportation to the site and facilitates teen involvement. An array of TIA opportunities has evolved including:

- Special events for TIA volunteers such as Caribbean Jam dance, potluck dinner, and the Blast From the Past Fashion Show.
- Assisting in city events such as the Winter Carnival, National Thanksgiving Day Parade, and Halloween; working children's holiday parties throughout the year; and creating activities for these parties (storytelling, dance contests, etc.).
- Computer lab attendants at three centers throughout the year, including the Senior Adult Center.
- Conducting a free tutoring program at the community center throughout the year, with particular emphasis on computing.
- Assisting in city recreation programs such as athletics and gymnastics (set-up and breakdown of equipment, working with children, etc.).
- Organizing community holiday food and toy drives and fund-raisers (e.g., bake sales).
- Attending regular TIA meetings held bi-weekly.

Exhibit 10-2

WHY VOLUNTEER?

1. To meet your community service requirement.
2. To facilitate exchange of knowledge between yourself and the community.
3. To build self-esteem.
4. To have an impact.
5. To help others.
6. To gain a perspective on life.
7. To gain leadership skills.
8. To build your resume.
9. To test yourself.
10. For fun!

There are different levels of commitment and involvement among the TIAs. A core of approximately 50 students are involved regularly, while the remainder participate periodically when they are available. Flexibility in accommodating the volunteer commitment and club activities into the teens' schedules is a key consideration when planning the program.

The TIA Computing Program

TIA's computer tutoring and lab attendant services is the "flagship" program for which it has received widespread kudos. A survey undertaken for the city of North Miami identified community needs. The highest-ranking request from residents was for computer classes. Since 95% of the 7,000 students enrolled in North Miami elementary schools qualify for free lunch and breakfast programs, PARD staff recognized that few residents could afford a computer even though there was widespread recognition that computer training was a key skill for obtaining a good job.

The PARD lacked resources to respond to this need. However, the early success of TIA caused staff to seek more complex volunteer assignments to challenge them. It was thought that instructing TIAs to teach job-related computing skills to seniors, peers and children would enhance their level of personal satisfaction and growth. The best way to learn anything is to teach it. Hence, it was anticipated that TIAs would enhance their own computing abilities as well as develop communication, organization, and social skills and a sense of responsibility. Thus, the PARD contracted with North Miami Senior High School, and with Metro-Dade County Public School Board to be a "Dade Partner" site. This agreement channeled more students into the TIA program.

The PARD did not have any computers. However, seven were acquired when they were phased-out of City Hall and another eight were donated by the Dade County Inner City Games agency. Software was purchased for $2000. Two computers were assigned to the Griffing Senior Center, five to the renovated police station, and eight to Sunkist Grove Community Center. At each center, space was adapted for the computer labs.

TIAs were recruited for the tutoring program. They underwent extensive screening by a part-time coordinator (who was a MIS student at a local university) to ensure they were qualified to tutor in specific subjects. Some became qualified as math/science tutors, others in English/reading, and a few in all subject areas. Other TIAs were trained as computer lab technicians. A grant of $500 was secured from a local hospital to pay for training workshops. As the TIAs received more specialized training, they designed and created their own website at www.tiaallstars.cbj.net so they were able to communicate with each other through this site. The TIAs included representatives from a variety of cultural and ethnic groups, and when they were assigned to the three free computer labs they enhanced residents' awareness of the positive contributions young people from all the city's ethnic groups could make to others.

Benefits and Evaluation

The major contribution of TIA was the benefits its members accrued from participation in it, but a corollary of their involvement was that they provided hundreds of hours of free labor to the PARD. Given that increases in the PARD's budget in the previous five years were barely adequate to keep abreast of inflation and provided no resources for new services, this volunteer labor was significant.

Students selected by PARD staff for the TIA program benefited materially by receiving credit for their community service. Staff could only manage a fixed number of student TIAs so participation is selective. Hence, TIAs enjoy some prestige and the recognition of being leaders among their peers. They are required to meet given standards of behavior and academic performance to remain in the TIA program.

The PARD staff prepared a TIA Manual which provides details of the expectations PARD has of TIAs and details of the programs in which they can become involved. The basic rules are listed in Exhibit 10-3.

Exhibit 10-3

TEENS IN ACTION RESPONSIBILITIES

1. ATTENDANCE
   - It is mandatory that you come to work on time.
   - You must contact the TIA coordinator via e-mail or call at least 48 hours in advance to notify a change in your schedule unless there is an unexpected emergency.
   - It is your responsibility to sign in and out, and complete the TIA Sign In Sheets properly and thoroughly.
2. SCHEDULES
   - It is your responsibility to keep track of and follow your work schedule.
   - It is your responsibility to obtain updated or revised schedules for each month.
   - It is your responsibility to complete volunteer timesheets on a weekly basis.
3. DRESS CODE
   - You must have proper ID. This includes a school picture ID, a North Miami Public Library card, and teen membership card.
   - You must wear your volunteer shirt to work.
   - No short shorts, sandals, sunglasses, hat or caps allowed.
   - Please come to work in a professional and presentable manner.
4. ETIQUETTE
   - Respect each other and your superiors at all times.
   - Be polite, courteous, and patient.
   - Conduct yourself in a professional manner at all times.
5. BEHAVIORAL SKILLS
   - No excessive socialization.
   - No horseplay.
   - No sleeping.
   - No walkmans or CD players.

As a volunteer, you are considered an employee of the City of North Miami. Although this is an unpaid position, you are receiving community service hours to compensate for your volunteer time. As a City employee, we ask that you conduct yourself in a professional manner at all times during your tenure with us.

Volunteers are responsible for completing timesheets on a monthly basis. Credit will not be given for hours worked without submitting a timesheet. Timesheets are due no later than Saturday each week.

All forms (applications, waivers, etc.) must be completed and notarized prior to the volunteer's service commencing.

On-going feedback is provided by staff to the TIAs. Examples of feedback recognizing both positive and negative behavior are shown in Exhibit 10-4.

The staff receive feedback from both TIAs and their parents by requiring them to fill out simple surveys. The TIA's survey has four questions:

- What did you like least about the recent event?
- What did you like most about the recent event?
- If you were the coordinator of this event, what would you have done to make it more interesting?
- Other comments.

Exhibit 10-4

Sample Feedback on Positive and Negative Behavior

Positive Feedback to TIA's

I would like to thank each of you for the excellent job you did during the Gymnastics and Dance Exhibition held on Friday. You exhibited maturity as a Teens In Action Volunteer and represented the group as a whole wonderfully. During the Gymnastics and Dance Exhibition you were all able to adapt and take on new responsibilities to help staff members properly execute the production.

Again, thank you for all of your work and continue to do well!

Negative Feedback to a TIA

Dear John Smith:

Your behavior and attitude at the North Miami Community Center today was completely unacceptable. You were rude and disrespectful. At your age, you should be aware that you are expected to carry yourself in a professional, mature, and respectful manner. You have failed to pick up your completed volunteer hours form at the time I advised you to do so and as a result, the form is no longer up to date and is considered invalid. I have completed another volunteer hours form and you may pick it up two weeks from today, Wednesday, at the North Miami Community Center at 3:30 p.m. with an apology.

If you have any further questions, you may contact me at (305) 892-3020 or via e-mail.

TIA Cordinator

Negative Feedback to the School

During TIA meetings, Rita Jones behaves inappropriately. She is constantly talking, and does not pay attention. She is rude and disrespectful. After a mandatory conference with Rita it has become obvious that her attitude and behavior will not improve. We have mentioned to her about making effort to improve her behavior and she has not done so. Based on four previous incidences and our mandatory conference regarding her behavior, we have come to the conclusion that Rita Jones will be terminated from the Teens In Action program as of today. She will receive hours that she earned excluding the four incidences in which she misbehaved.

Similarly, the parents' feedback questionnaire consists of five questions measured on a 5 point scale from Strongly Agree (5) to Strongly Disagree (1):

- Do you feel the Teens In Action program has benefitted your son or daughter?
- Have your child's grades improved in school as a result of the program?
- Has your child's behavior changed positively?
- Has your child's behavior changed negatively?
- Has your child become more conscious of his/her responsibilities at home?
- Other Comments (an open-ended section).

Lessons Learned

Traditionally PARDs have viewed volunteers as an external resource that enables them to extend, supplement, and enhance their range of services. This role of the TIAs was recognized and periodically was tangibly rewarded when the Miami Heat and Florida Marlins professional franchises provided them with transportation, free tickets and refreshments for some of their games. However, this external resource role was a corollary and not the central goal of the program.

The central goals articulated in the second paragraph of this case related to benefits accruing to the TIA members in the form of encouraging tolerance of cultural diversity; facilitating social interaction; and enhancing status in the community, personal growth, and self-image. These benefits are identical to those which many youth seek from participating in traditional park and recreation programs. Thus, PARDs should view the creation of meaningful opportunities for volunteering as a recreational program they offer. That is, volunteering is a legitimate end program in itself, not merely a means for developing additional programs.

TIA demonstrates how programs can effectively be initiated in multi-racial, low-income communities even when minimal resources are available. The success of the program was validated by the Metro-Dade County Public School Board when it recognized the city of North Miami PARD as "Dade Partner of the Year" for the TIA program. The program showcases positive actions by teens which provides some partial counter-balance to the "bad press" about teens which predominates in many communities.

Source

Jim Stamborski, Recreation Superintendent, City of North Miami.

CHAPTER 11

TOTALLY COOL, TOTALLY ART:
NRPA'S FIRST NATIONALLY BRANDED PROGRAM

The prevailing model among PARDs is to develop and initiate new programs at the local level. The challenges of communicating among agencies make it difficult for PARDs to be aware of, and to implement, best program practices from other communities. Thus, PARDs invest considerable time and energy in developing quality programs when similar programs have been implemented successfully elsewhere by other PARDs. If they were familiar with these previous efforts, much of the developmental costs and inevitable mistakes that accompany new initiatives could be avoided.

Other youth serving organizations, such as the Boys & Girls Club, YMCAs, YWCAs, Girls Inc., and 4-H have developed and tested high quality programs at a few locations and then disseminated them to all of their program sites across the country. This "branding" approach to program development enhances the programmatic expertise available to their local staff; reduces both the time and monetary resources needed to initiate a new program; and ameliorates many of the frustrations that inevitably occur when new programs are launched. Branded programs offer substantial gains in both efficiency and effectiveness to local communities in developing high quality programs for youth. A similar approach is needed in the parks and recreation field.

In response to this need, the National Recreation and Park Association (NRPA) is planning to distribute several standardized branded program models to local PARDs. Each of the programs will be replicable and designed to support developmental assets in one or more of the following areas: education and culture; physical and mental health; and workforce development and career opportunities. Each branded program will be successfully piloted, implemented and evaluated by one or more PARDs and will be adaptable to the needs and resources of other PARDs.

The First NRPA Nationally Branded Program: Totally Cool, Totally Art

Austin PARD's Totally Cool, Totally Art (TCTA) program was selected as NRPA's first nationally branded youth program, because of its consistent record of excellence; the portability of the program concept and design to both small and large communities; and the existence of evaluation data demonstrating the program's successful outcomes. TCTA was created by staff at Austin PARD's Dougherty Arts Center. During each program year, visual arts classes are offered to teens (mainly 13-16 year olds), twice a week (Monday/Wednesday or Tuesday/Thursday) at PARD recreation centers. Six separate four-week sessions are delivered at each of the fourteen participating centers.

TCTA is not a traditional arts and crafts program. The classes are conducted by artists who have a passion for the art medium they teach. TCTA's philosophy is "process-oriented" emphasizing the process of art making, instead of the actual product. Through the creative process, each participant has opportunities to enhance creativity, promote self-esteem, and foster respect for others. The adolescent comes to understand that there are no right or wrong answers, only the individual's point of view. Goals of the TCTA program are:

- to develop teens' sense of belonging, and teens' feeling that they have safe, positive, and creative environments in which to participate during available free time (Safe Places and Sense of Belonging);
- to provide opportunities for new experiences which will increase participants' knowledge, skills and possible interest in art as a career field (New Experiences);
- to increase teens' trust and respect for other teens, adult mentors, artists, and other authority figures (Respect and Trust);
- to increase teens' ability to work cooperatively with other teens and communicate effectively in a group (Team Work and Communication); and
- to enhance teens' ability to make creative and positive choices through self-expression (Art Education).

Exhibit 11-1 shows how these goals are operationalized and the indicators used to evaluate the extent to which the goals are achieved.

Exhibit 11-1

Totally Cool, Totally Art Goals Matrix

Goals	How to achieve this goal:	Indicators that TCTA is meeting the goal
Safe Places, Sense of Belonging: To increase teens' sense of belonging, and teens' feeling that they have safe, positive, and creative environments in which to participate during available free time	• Create a positive, supportive art class and mentoring environment • Provide an environment that respects the ability and and creativity of each participant • Provide opportunities for teens to be responsible and make positive choices through their participation in art activities	• Teens bring their friends to share their experiences • Teens demonstrate consistent high attendance rates • Teens provide valid explanations for their absences • Teens work with each other to achieve goals • Teens show pride in their recreation centers
New Experiences: To provide opportunities for new experiences in order to increase participants' knowledge, skills, and possible interest in art as a career field	• Provide opportunities for youth to be exposed to and participate in a variety of art media • Provide professional artists and quality arts supplies and equipment for teens to enable them to gain an appreciation for and skills in the visual arts • Provide opportunities for teens to expand their imagination, creativity, and self-confidence through their involvement in art activities • Provide teens with information about other community arts opportunities and possible career choices for people who are interested in the arts through resource lists, field trips, guest speakers, and other activities	• Teens ask questions and develop new communication skills • Teens show enthusiasm for new media • Teens apply new skills outside of TCTA time and pursue further education in the arts

Exhibit 11-1 Continued

Goals	How to achieve this goal:	Indicators that TCTA is meeting the goal
Respect and Trust: To increase teens' trust and respect for other teens, adult mentors, artists, and other authority figures	• Provide opportunities for youth to interact with adult role models (center staff, artists, and other adults) who keep their word and create a supportive learning atmosphere • Utilize both recreation center teen leaders and artists as collaborative program leaders so teens can benefit both from contact with different artists while maintaining consistent contact over time with center teen leaders • Provide opportunities for youth to interact with other teens in an environment that encourages respect and trust • Provide opportunities for teens to create and strengthen friendships with other teens • Provide opportunities for teens to learn responsible behavior through care and use of art supplies and equipment and through following curriculum directions and rules • Provide opportunities for teens to act responsibly in the storage and protection of their own and others' art work	• Teens communicate more openly with adults • Teens are respectful of their surroundings and recreation center rules • Teens are willing to ask questions and to ask for help • Teens introduce friends and families to mentors and artists • Teens show ability to work out conflicts with others
Teamwork and Communication To increase teens' ability to work cooperatively with other teens and increase teens' ability to communicate effectively in a group	• Structure opportunities for teens to share ideas, supplies, and other resources and to resolve problems and conflicts through collaborative efforts • Provide opportunities for teens to improve their ability to communicate and gain feedback about their ideas, thoughts, emotions, and experiences through their art work • Provide opportunities for teens to learn about the activities and involvements of other program participants through program newsletters • Provide opportunities to gain knowledge about and better understand cultural diversity through discussion of art from various cultures and historical periods in TCTA	• Teens are supportive of other teens • Teens participate in constructive problem-solving • Teens mentor other younger teens • Teens welcome new participants to the program
Art Education: To increase teens' ability to make creative and positive choices through self-expression	• Provide opportunities for teens to learn new or strengthen existing visual arts education concepts and skills • Provide opportunities for teens to make creative choices about the content and product of their own artistic endeavors • Provide opportunities to discuss and analyze the criteria and decision making processes used to select art work for exhibition at the open house • Provide opportunities for teens to gain recognition and increase their pride in their accomplishments through exhibiting selective art work at the culminating open house event • Provide experiences through the arts that relate math, history, language, etc., and thereby increase interest in school	• Teens use self-expression in their artworks • Teens communicate new ideas to their mentors and peers • Teens develop a new vocabulary • Teens express interest in and commitment to finishing art projects • Teens seek other opportunities in art outside TCTA

Program Structure

The TCTA program begins at approximately 5:00 p.m. with a one hour activity organized by the Teen Coordinator from the host center. This activity may include preparing a meal, eating and socializing, and / or completing homework. From 6:00-8:00 p.m. a class in a particular art medium is offered by one or more practicing artists who are assisted by the Teen Coordinator. Group size at each site is limited to 20 teens, so there is a 20 to 2 ratio (Teen Coordinator and artist). The Teen Coordinator manages the program at the site while the artist teaches the class.

Exhibit 11-2

Kelly's TCTA Experience

Kelly is a 14-year-old who spends two evenings a week at the Community Recreation Center in Austin, Texas. Kelly arrives at 5:00 p.m. with her friends and sits down for a slice of pizza and time to focus on homework. Kelly's teen leader helps with homework and checks on the progress of Kelly's grandmother, who was just released from the hospital. About 6:00, Kelly puts away the school books and runs outside to greet the two arriving artists, who will teach a printmaking class this evening as part of the Totally Cool, Totally Art (TCTA) program. Kelly is excited about the art project, a 12" woodcut print that will be a gift for Kelly's grandmother. Kelly can't wait to begin, but sits quietly as the artists/instructors explain the evening's activities: how to safely use the Japanese woodcarving tools, which formal art elements work well in this medium, and how to begin.

Before TCTA, Kelly did not come to the recreation center regularly. She would occasionally stop by and sign up for an activity, but would not show up. Instead, Kelly would most often hang out at the park with her friends. Now, thanks to TCTA, Kelly is totally engaged, totally involved, and totally motivated.

Community recreation centers throughout Austin host the program for two nights a week at each center. The centers offer six four-week sessions. TCTA's artists teach at two different centers each week, and every four weeks they rotate to two new centers. For instance during session one, Installation Art is featured at one center on Mondays and Wednesdays and at another on Tuesdays and Thursdays.

Art media differ each year. Computer and claymation, monumental sculpture, storytelling, photography, blacksmithing, computer animation, film-making, printmaking, installation, conceptual art, portraiture, painting, and drumming are some of the activities that have been included. Exhibit 11-3 provides a more comprehensive list of activities that may be incorporated. Which media are offered depends on local teens' interests and the art resources available in the community.

Newsletter: The TCTA coordinators create one newsletter during each four-week session, and distribute it to participants and staff at each recreation center. This helps provide continuity for the overall program by including information about staff, dates for future sessions, brief reports about programs at particular sites, and publicity about arts events throughout the city.

Young Artists' Exhibitions: An important component of TCTA is the opportunity for participants to have their work publicly displayed and recognized. Program staff arrange for participants' art work to be displayed at local malls and other public venues. In addition, the program sponsors two exhibitions each year to showcase the artwork and enable the teens' parents, friends, and the general public to view it. One exhibition is held after the third set of four-week classes, and the other is held after the sixth session. City leaders, and other dignitaries attend the exhibitions which give them a better understanding of how the funds they budget for the program are being used.

Exhibit 11-3

Possible Activities to include in the Program

- *Music*
  Choral
  Classical
  Jazz
  Solo, Recital
  World
  Drumming
  Experimental

- *Design Arts*
  Graphics
  Layout
  Prototypes
  Logos
  Packaging
  Advertisement
  Fashion

- *Theatre/Performing Arts*
  Mime
  Playwright
  Puppets
  Storytelling
  Technicians/Designers
  Costumes and Sets
  Plays, Musicals

- *Dance*
  Ballet
  Folk/traditional
  Jazz
  Modern/Contemporary
  Tap
  Creative Movement

- *Visual Arts*
  Clay
  Fiber/Textiles
  Glass
  Metals/Jewelry
  Paper
  Wood
  Drawing
  Painting
  Photography
  Printmaking
  Public Art/Installation Art
  Sculpture
  Found Objects
  Mosaic

- *Media Arts*
  Animation
  Audio Arts
  Computer Arts
  Documentary
  Video/Film
  Radio
  Television

- *Folk Arts/Crafts*

- *Literature*
  Poetry
  Zines
  Short Stories
  Chap Books
  Book Making

Several awards are given at each exhibition. Two awards are presented to the students who best exemplify the spirit of TCTA (i.e., commitment, interest, creativity and ability to work with others). Awards are also given for each medium to students who have shown the highest level of dedication to that medium. The awards ceremony gives public recognition to teens' accomplishments and supplies them with tangible reinforcement of their aptitude in the form of medals and plaques. The intent is to reinforce teens' sense of pride in their involvement and accomplishments.

Advanced Referrals: TCTA artists identify students who are ready for more advanced art classes. The staff places students in existing advanced art classes or creates classes to accommodate them at the Dougherty Arts Center or elsewhere if existing opportunities are unavailable. Partnerships with local art schools, museums, and arts and cultural organizations testify to the success of the advanced referral component of the program. Staff encourage students to complete scholarship applications from local art institutions. Participants are responsible for completing the forms and returning them to the Teen Coordinators. Referrals are based on artistic merit, dedication to a particular medium, attendance, enthusiasm, project completion, and desire to follow-through on opportunities.

Staffing

Artists encourage teens to learn new, or strengthen existing, visual arts skills through studio instruction. They teach all areas of the art-making process, from conception and creation to completion and presentation. Artists help in exhibiting the artwork at the Young Artists' Exhibitions and provide advice on its proper storage and care.

The artists prepare a lesson plan for each session. This encourages them to consider the significance of the material being presented, how it links to the goals of TCTA, time constraints, and to identify any special arrangements that may be required. Lesson plans serve as a means of communication between the artists, TCTA Program Coordinators, and Teen Coordinators. In developing lesson plans, artists determine how they will use the activities to enhance productivity, creativity, problem-solving, higher level thinking skills, including abstract thinking, the capacity to learn in other content areas (such as reading or math), and meta cognition (i.e., the process of analyzing one's own thinking and learning processes).

Teen Coordinators are employed at each center to facilitate teen programs, including TCTA. Their TCTA responsibilities include recruiting participants, securing an appropriate space for the classes, taking attendance, completing program paperwork, and disciplining students. Coordinators guide and supervise each teen participant along with the artists. Their task is to facilitate a friendly working partnership among students, staff and artists.

Program Coordinators provide overall management of the TCTA program. They are responsible for supervisory and administrative duties, which include hiring and supervising the artists and promoting the program in the community. Coordinators schedule and facilitate citywide meetings among artists and staff, establish budgets for art supplies and special events, and monitor all expenditures. They distribute, collect and review artists' lesson plans, supply request forms, and prepare program forms. They also collect evaluation survey data from program participants and compile an attendance database based on information supplied by the Teen Coordinators at each site.

Staff training is an important part of the program. Joint training sessions for both artists and Teen Coordinators are held at the beginning of each program year. At these sessions, program goals, policies, and procedures are explained. In addition, Teen Coordinators meet the artists, and learn about and experience some of the art activities planned for that year. Topics for training include program objectives, staff responsibilities, purpose and management of exhibitions and special events, paperwork, policies and procedures, curriculum development, and program evaluation.

Site Considerations

Accessibility and space are key considerations when selecting TCTA sites. Getting students to sites is challenging because many participants do not have easy access to transportation. However, operating the program at multiple sites means that participants are likely to find a program within walking or biking distance. In some cases, van transportation has been arranged to deliver participants to the sites.

The amenities needed at the sites where TCTA is conducted are another important consideration. The Recreation Centers need to have running water, electricity, chairs and tables, a work space that can get messy, cleaning supplies, adequate storage space for artwork and supplies, and places to display finished artwork.

Program Evaluation

Evaluation has been an important part of the TCTA program from its inception. Reports have been used to sustain city council support for the program, and data have been used by staff to fine-tune the program efforts from year to year.

The evaluation process has included collecting and analyzing data in the following areas:

- *Workload*: Number of participants served, total hours of participation, etc.
- *Program Costs:* Cost per unit of service.
- *Program Quality and Satisfaction*: Participant ratings of the quality of selected site and leader characteristics, along with ratings of the overall value of the program.
- *Program* Outcomes.

Each of the evaluation measures is described in the following paragraphs.

Workload Statistics. Registration and daily attendance data are collected and maintained in a master database. This enables program organizers to access information on registration demographics (age, birthday, ethnicity, gender, parent contact phone numbers) and attendance per site across the entire program. These data collection efforts were initiated during the first year of the program, so benchmarks are in place against which subsequent trends and improvements can be monitored. The database makes it easy to generate program statistics after each session. The following are examples of some of the statistics generated across the first five years of the program's operation.

- Over the first five years of the program, 1,387 different teens participated in at least one program session. Of these, 31% participated in only one session, 55% in two to six sessions, 14% in seven to twelve sessions, and

2% in 13 or more sessions. In the fifth year teens registered for an average of 2.8 sessions and averaged 13.2 days of participation.

- Over the first five years of the program, 74% of the teens attended during only one year, while 19% attended for two of the years, and 8% of the teens attended from three to five years. Participants averaged 3.6 sessions over the five years.
- The number of participants increased from 287 the first year to 468 in the fifth year. Part of the increase was attributable to adding more sites, but some was also due to the program's greater visibility, better recruiting, and word-of-mouth endorsements from current participants.
- The program organizers sought to fill each program session to its capacity. There are two ways to report program capacity: the first method is based on enrollment numbers, while the second refers to how many days teens actually participated in the program. The program was designed to handle 20 teens per session per site. The program increased from 65% of enrollment capacity to 73% over the five year period. Based on percent of possible participant days, the program operated at between 44% and 57% of capacity in each of the five years.
- Approximately equal numbers of males and females were attracted to the program each year.
- The program was designed to focus on 13-16 year olds. However, some centers included 11 and 12 year olds who showed the maturity to participate. During the fifth year, 29% of the children were 12 or younger, while 71% were 13 years or older.
- Participation by race remained consistent across the years. During the fifth year, the distribution was 42% Hispanic, 39% African-American, 19% White, and 2% Other (mainly Asian). The percentages approximate the profiles of the communities the program serves.

Program Costs. The program has tracked expenditures to facilitate comparisons from year to year. Using both cost and participation data, cost per hour of service was calculated. Over the first five years, the cost per participant hour has decreased from $11.64 to $9.38. As program capacity increased, the cost per hour of service declined. Given the high quality of the program and demonstrated positive impact on participants, stakeholders in Austin felt that the program was cost effective.

Program Quality and Satisfaction. Surveys have been developed to assess both program quality and participants' satisfaction. These are usually administered during the last program session of the year. This procedure misses teens who have participated in earlier sessions, but does provide a snapshot of teens' program perceptions without over-taxing participants and staff. Ideally, surveys should be filled out after every session. However, this means that teens participating in multiple sessions would have to fill out the instrument on multiple occasions which would over-tax both participants and staff.

Participants have consistently reported that their overall experience in the program is positive; that they would recommend the program to others; and that they would sign up again for the program. They also give high marks to the quality of the program staff, and the caliber of supplies and materials used in TCTA.

Program Outcomes. Again, surveys are administered to all teens participating in the sixth session. The survey questions are designed to determine if participants have improved their attitudes, knowledge or behavior as outlined in the program goals. The survey data indicated that participants showed increases in several areas as a result of participating in the program. In general participants increased their ability to get along in a group; their knowledge of community resources to use during free time; and their understanding that there were adults who cared about them. Teens also indicated that they increased their interest in art and would do more art in the future as a result of participating in the program.

The surveys showed that many teens encountered difficult situations in their lives which negatively impacted their self-esteem; their desire to remain in school and their perception that they will accomplish meaningful things in the future. The program was important to these teens not only for the opportunity to be involved in art activities, but also because it facilitated access to adult mentors who could help them deal with some of the negative issues with which they are confronted outside the program. In addition, the results indicated that teens increased their ability to do art and share ideas with other teens and use their imagination.

Interviews conducted with those attending TCTA indicated that many would be sitting at home or watching television if they were not participating in the program. The teens reported that the program provided an antidote to hanging out on the street or engaging in unstructured activities. They saw the program as an antidote to boredom and reported that it acted as an incentive to attend school, since this was a prerequisite for participating. Some teens saw TCTA as a vehicle for pursuing an existing or potential interest in art.

Lessons Learned

TCTA is a prototype program that demonstrates the feasibility of developing nationally branded youth programs based on outstanding offerings currently delivered by park and recreation agencies. Branded programing is a mechanism for disseminating best practices. A key to success is identifying programs that have a strong track record of performance and a format that is adaptable to communities of varying populations and local conditions. Evaluation evidence demonstrating or confirming a program's quality and impact will help the diffusion process, since this provides evidence to other agencies of the viability of the programs. Evaluation data also can be useful in convincing local funders that the program is worth their investing in it.

Exhibit 11-4

Contents of TCTA National Program Materials

Model Program Manual
- Overview
- Mission and Philosophy
- Goals Program Design
- Rules and Guidelines
- Art Curriculum and Media
- Newsletter, Exhibitions, and Special Events
- Program Evaluation
- Recruitment and Retention Strategies
- Advanced Programs
- Staffing Overview
  - Artists/Instructors
  - Administrators
  - Youth Leaders
  - Publicity Coordinator
- Training/Staff Development
- Resources
- Budget

Staff Manual
- Job Duties and Responsibilities
- Forms and Reports
- Policies and Procedures
- Leadership Resources

Publicity Examples
- Newsletter
- Recruiting Poster
- Press Releases
- Exhibition Invitations

Virtual Studio (Pictures of various art media)

Model Powerpoint Presentation
(Boiler plate for making presentations to potential funders)

Evaluation Materials
- Procedures
- Forms
- Example Report

The dissemination of branded programs can only occur if there is a willingness among program developers in local PARDs to share their experiences, and help develop the materials necessary to franchise the program. In the case described here, Austin PARD, supported by NRPA and National Recreation Foundation funding, developed descriptive materials showing not only how the program was designed and evaluated in Austin, but also how it might be adapted for use in other communities. Austin PARD created a program video, a picture gallery for some of the art media that they have used, and examples of advertising materials, newsletters and press releases that have been generated by the program. They were also willing to share their program manual, evaluation procedures, instruments, and reports. The program is disseminated on a CD and its Table of Contents is shown in Exhibit 11-4.

Sources

Maria Cicciarelli and Carlos Pineda, Dougherty Arts Center, Austin Parks and Recreation Department.

National Recreation and Park Association (2002). Totally Cool, Totally Art National Program Manual and related materials.

Witt, P.A. (2000, March). It's Totally Cool, Totally Art. *Park and Recreation*, 35(3): 64-75.

CHAPTER 12

INVOLVING YOUTH IN DESIGNING SERVICES:

THE KETTERING S.T.A.N.D.

PARDs in a number of communities have developed effective mechanisms for ensuring that youth have a voice in identifying issues and in service delivery processes. In Kettering, Ohio, the Recreation, Parks and Cultural Arts Department (RPCAD) has played a major role in coordinating planning and service delivery. The formation of a youth council, Kettering S.T.A.N.D. (Students Taking a New Direction) was a central feature of this process.

Sometimes more insights can be gained from reporting the early stages of launching an initiative, than from describing mature established programs where staff may have forgotten details of the early challenges they had to surmount. Hence, this case traces the formative years in the evolution of Kettering STAND and compares it with a more mature youth development program in a community in Illinois that KSTAND aspires to emulate over time.

Youth Summits

Kettering has a population of 57,502. Youth 19 years and under constitute 22.5% of the population. Minorities make up 4.8% of the population, and 9.5% of the households are headed by females.

The Kettering City Council and Kettering School Board held a joint strategic planning meeting to identify priority areas of community concern. The need for an annual youth summit emerged as one of the top three priorities, with the other two being more use of Kettering schools and other facilities as "service delivery centers" for Kettering neighborhoods, and developing an awareness campaign specifically designed to promote all the benefits of living in Kettering.

In response to the first priority, the Healthy Youth Task Force was formed. Initially, it was comprised of school and government officials, and a few community members who expressed an interest in getting involved. The Director of Kettering RPCAD chaired the committee. The initial project undertaken by the Task Force was to sponsor a youth summit. Over 300 Call-to-Action invitations were sent to businesses, civic and church organizations. Two hundred and fifty people, mainly adults with a few youth representatives, attended this summit. Participants were from government agencies, non-profits, and schools, and their charge was to identify youth issues and resultant program delivery strategies for Kettering. The purposes of the summit were to:

- further understanding of the issues that were facing youth;
- share experiences and available opportunities for serving youth;
- raise the community's awareness of youth needs; and
- develop a community-wide task force charged with formulating an action plan for growing healthy youth.

In his opening remarks to the summit, the RPCAD Director quoted from a study completed by the National Commission on the Role of the School and the Community in Improving Adolescent Health that reported:

> *For the first time in the history of this country, young people are less healthy and less prepared to take their places in society than were their parents. And this is happening at a time when our society is more complex, more challenging, and more competitive than ever before.*

The Director also noted that Kettering, like many suburban communities, was changing. There were more single-parent families and two-parent families with both parents working over 40 hours per week, thus decreasing parental supervision during after-school hours. In addition, more families were moving in and out of the community during the school year, which decreased the stability of school attendance. These, and other circumstances provided challenges to enabling youth to grow up as productive citizens.

In additional remarks at the opening session, the wife of the Governor of Ohio reminded the audience of Abraham Lincoln's observation that the future of this nation rests with how well it treat its children:

> *A child is a person who is going to carry on what you have started, sit where you are sitting, and when you are gone, attend to those things that you think are important. The child will assume control of your cities and towns and states and move in and take over your churches, your schools and your businesses. The fate of humanity is in the hands of children.*

She noted that community coalitions and partnerships have been recognized as key to effective youth development efforts. This reflects a change in strategic approach from focusing mainly on the person, to a more ecological approach where attention is paid not only to individuals, but also to the milieu in which they live, and the community and governmental organizations that provide services for them. She listed four features that were characteristic of successful partnerships:

(i) *Enable a strong core of partners* who come together and work closely during the early stages of the coalition.

(ii) *Create a comprehensive and widely shared vision* that permits every individual in the community to feel part of the coalition's mission.

(iii) *Form small area units* to promote broad-based memberships and thus engage many volunteers in the efforts. As Margaret Mead observed: "Never doubt that a small group of thoughtful, committed people can change the world. In fact it's the only thing that has."

(iv) Develop a *diverse range of prevention activities.*

As a result of the Youth Summit, the following priorities were identified:

- reduce the risk of children being abused and neglected;
- provide additional family and youth counseling services;
- reduce the dropout rate in Kettering schools;
- reduce incidents of youth violence and high-risk behaviors;
- shut down "prime time for juvenile crime;"
- provide after-school and summer jobs programs;
- expand parks, recreation, physical fitness and arts programs; and
- increase joint use of public facilities for before and after-school programs.

After the summit, the Healthy Youth Task Force formed two sub-committees (Youth in Action and Prevention Services) to deal with the identified issues. Both of these task forces used the Search Institute's 40 Developmental Assets model as the basis for their work (Exhibit 3-1). Through the Youth in Action subcommittee, a few interested youth were recruited to help organize a second youth summit the following year. The profile of attendees at this summit was approximately 50% youth and 50% adults. At the conclusion of this second summit, a group of students formed a youth council and named themselves Kettering S.T.A.N.D. (Students Taking A New Direction). At the time of writing this case, KSTAND had been in existence for 18 months.

Creating a Voice for Youth

The official mission of KSTAND is to create a supportive atmosphere where students can identify their needs, and address those needs by providing service to the community and social opportunities that are both positive and rewarding. KSTAND strives to be youth driven. The group hopes to make a difference in the lives of peers by providing opportunities for youth to come together in a welcoming constructive environment.

A core group of 25-30 youth meet regularly to identify priorities and create an agenda for future action. To become a member, students must complete a "Pledge to Help" form. Eligible students must be in grades 6-12 and either reside in Kettering or go to a public or private school in Kettering. KSTAND participants are fairly diverse, representing most segments of the youth community. Both middle and high school students participate, although there are many more middle school participants. Organizers hope that as middle school students move on to high school they will stay involved, thus increasing the involvement of high school students over time. Most of the initial members are still active. However, due to other activities, e.g., sports, band, entering high school, or a heavy academic load, some are not as involved as they were at the beginning.

Meetings of KSTAND are held at the Kettering Recreation Complex at 7:00 p.m. on the first Monday and third Thursday of each month. Generally the meetings last one hour. The executive board meets at 6:00 p.m. before each regularly scheduled meeting. The executive board is comprised of three chairpersons and seven sub-committee chairpersons elected by KSTAND members. A sample of the responsibilities of a co-chair is listed in Exhibit 12-1.

Exhibit 12-1

Kettering STAND Co-Chair Responsibilities

1. Co-Chair #1 Responsibilities
   - Develops agenda
   - Co-leads group assembly and executive board meetings.
   - Representative for Healthy Youth Task Force Meeting; meets quarterly at the Government Center at 1:00 p.m.
   - Checks Kettering KSTAND's voice mail regularly and returns messages; updates voice mail message regularly.
   - Responsible for leading games and activities at the start of the meeting.
   - Monitors Social sub-committee chair
   - Monitors Publicity and Marketing sub-committee chair
2. Co-Chair #2 Responsibilities
   - Develops agenda and co-leads meeting
   - Representative to Volunteer Advisory Council Meeting
   - Monitors Fund-raising sub-committees
   - Monitors Annual Community Service sub-committees
3. Co-Chair #3 and Secretary Responsibilities
   - Takes and distributes minutes
   - Co-leads meetings and develops agenda.
   - Representative for Parks, Recreation and Cultural Arts Advisory Board Meeting
   - Coordinates phone tree
   - Monitors Youth Summit sub-committees
   - Monitors Teen Lounge sub-committee

Among the reasons teens get involved with KSTAND are for opportunities to give back to the community, and contribute to improving the quality of life for youth in the community. Members benefit in many ways from their participation. A 17-year-old female indicates that she

> *"joined KSTAND as a favor to a friend. Now almost two years have passed and I have stayed with the group because of the ambition the kids have in everything we do. We work as a team and have built friendships and trust."*

Other participants cite the opportunity to give back to the community and being involved in the decision making process as central benefits of their involvement.

KSTAND participates in approximately one community service project a month. The nature of their participation ranges from setting up and cleaning up at community events, to organizing children's games and obtaining sponsors for the youth summit. Service projects have included volunteering at such events as Cabin Fever Reliever; the Annual Youth Summit; Safe On Saturday; Kids Fest; and the Mayor's Annual Tree-Lighting. KSTAND was recognized at a Kettering City Council Meeting and was presented with the Mayor's Award for Youth Volunteer Service for "outKSTANDing" volunteer contributions to the community, and for donating their time and talent to provide needed services that enrich the quality of life for all.

KSTAND also participates in the annual Holiday-at-Home parade. A subcommittee decides on the float design. All members are encouraged to participate in the parade and construction of the float. They also received the Princess Award for the best small float in a recent parade. KSTAND members worked diligently each evening for a month to build the float.

KSTAND seeks to offer healthy social alternatives for youth. Movie night is held quarterly, featuring videos, basketball and pizza. Members participate in a day-long Student Leadership Training program, which incorporates team building and leadership exercises based on interactive games, a high ropes course and low ropes training. The training program is an excellent opportunity for members to get better acquainted with one another and develop and enhance their leadership skills.

Funding to support youth initiatives has been obtained from a variety of sources including: Ohio Department of Alcohol and Drug Addiction Services, Department of Human Services, City of Kettering, local business sponsors for individual events, and funds raised through efforts of the youth themselves.

The Third Youth Summit

The third youth summit was held a year after KSTAND was launched and was totally organized by its members. Thus, over the first three years of the summit, the profile of attendees shifted from 90% adult, 10% youth; to 75% youth, 25% adult. Almost 75% of costs for the third summit were met by in-kind contributions from local businesses and monetary donations from local organizations. Purposes of the third summit included educating youth about community issues; giving youth a forum to speak on issues; and recruiting more members to join KSTAND.

Over 140 youth from five Kettering area schools and approximately 40 adults attended the Summit. After hearing from a keynote motivational speaker, teens were divided into five breakout groups, each of which discussed a particular topic and made action recommendations. The five groups were called: Kettering PD Blue; Stop in the Name of Peace; KSTAND for the Future; So Called Media; and Kickin' it in K-Town. Emerging from the group discussions were recommendations that KSTAND organize a battle of the bands and advocate for a skate park and teen center. The teen center would have a dance room, arcade, basketball court, exercise room, snack area and meeting room for KSTAND. Teenagers wanted a place to call their own. The physical space of the teen center would create a "headquarters" for teenagers, while the symbolism of the center would reaffirm to teens that they are valued by the Kettering community. KSTAND is currently investigating locations for a teen center. When development of the center begins, KSTAND will be involved in its planning from choosing the name to providing input on the design and how it should be furnished.

A skate park feasibility and planning committee has now been formed with a KSTAND member as chair. The committee is investigating site locations, funding sources and designs, and holding public hearings to solicit input. Youth desire a place to skate without being harassed, threatened with arrest for trespassing on property, or issued a fine or citation. A skate park is considered by teens a higher priority than a teen center given that there are other facilities they could use to hang-out. Business owners were tired of skateboarders whom they perceived as adversely affecting their businesses so they supported the park. A youth committee was formed to guide development of a skate park

Other new teen facilities that were suggested included building a roller hockey rink, sports fields and a pool/billiards room. Summit attendees felt there should be more activities for students, like a gymnastics team and a swimming pool. Some attendees wanted more shops for teens in Kettering, and perhaps even a whole new mall. There was some feeling that there should be more opportunities for teens to have access to media, like having a teen radio station or TV programs. Other suggestions included using a room in one of the city buildings for dances, a climbing wall, basketball, craft classes and an after-school computer lab.

It was proposed that KSTAND could have more impact in schools by disseminating information to students through assemblies, announcements and talking to other students. Suggestions for improving the format of meetings were also made such as starting out with a fun activity, before moving to discussions of forthcoming events and organizing particular KSTAND activities. Holding KSTAND meetings at restaurants or at a school was another suggestion. KSTAND hoped to improve relationships with police officers and considered a sporting event with the Kettering Police Department as a vehicle for doing this. At present youth do not see police as being empathetic to youth and view them negatively as authority figures. Some teens believed that just as they may have misconceptions about law enforcement officials, many law enforcement officials might have misconceptions about teenagers.

C.R.O.Y.A. (Committee Representing Our Young Adults)

To learn from the experiences of others, similar youth action committees were identified in other communities. One of the oldest and most successful appeared to be CROYA. in Lake Forest, Illinois. The term "young adults" was chosen to dignify and signify the future role of youth in the community. CROYA is dedicated to young adults which means meeting needs perceived by young adults. Representatives from CROYA attended the second Kettering Youth Summit and provided insights from their experiences.

CROYA's mission statement is:

> *Lake Forest and Lake Bluff strive to provide a high quality of life for their young adults in an environment that promotes their growth and development. The cities charge CROYA with the task of helping the young adults identify and meet their own needs.*

CROYA has had a successful youth group and center for over 20 years. Five full-time staff members are hired jointly by the young adults and an adult board. Programs are designed to build confidence and self-esteem, develop leadership skills, and act as a referral to resources for peers whose needs cannot be met by CROYA. CROYA has its own facility adjoining the Lake Forest Recreation Center, consisting of a family room, full kitchen, an area containing a variety of information resources about teen issues, and staff offices.

CROYA has a board, comprised of representatives from the City of Lake Forest, the Village of Lake Bluff, and the local schools, as well as the student chairperson of CROYA's senior high youth committee. The board reviews CROYA's programs, oversees the budget and serves in a support capacity to the director and staff.

The "CROYA Process," which has been developed over the organization's 20 years of existence, is used as a basis for all program origination, planning, implementation and evaluation (see Exhibit 12-2).

Besides social events, programs offered through CROYA include:

- *High School Peer Training.* Through this program students develop listening and communication skills (approximately 120 high school students participate each year). Students gain confidence in their own abilities and become aware of the needs of peers. Once students finish the training, they provide service to the community (e.g., homeless shelter) and are involved in leading student retreats.
- *Junior High Peer Training.* This is a 12-week peer leadership program, which students must complete in order to be invited to participate in a conflict resolution program.
- *Retreats.* These events offer environments in which feelings are examined about self and others. Two are held each year in the fall and spring. The fall retreat focuses on developing basic communication and listening skills, while in the spring the focus is on current youth issues and is designed by peer leaders.
- *TAPS: Teenage Placement Service.* This is an information service for teens seeking employment. Employers and residents list jobs that teens can then apply to undertake. The program is a matching, not a screening service.
- *Community Service Programs.* CROYA members volunteer their time to help community organizations with projects.
- *Fund-raising.* These efforts help students appreciate and respect what they have by enabling them to invest personal effort in raising the funds needed for maintaining their programs and facility.

KSTAND organizers aspire to develop their group to the level of maturity that CROYA has achieved in its 20 years of existence. However, they recognize that the process will be incremental and that it took CROYA a long period of time to develop their underlying processes, facilities and programs.

Hiring a Youth Development Coordinator

The Kettering program evolved to the point where it needed to hire a full-time Youth Coordinator. An extensive interview process, which included KSTAND representatives, was used. The new coordinator reported that the teen interviews were the toughest part of the process. While Kettering administrators focused on questions that measured skills, judgment and experience, the youth focused on favorite movies, music and food. The goal of both groups was to determine whether or not the candidate was a good fit for the position. Administrators wanted

Exhibit 12-2

The CROYA Process

1) Youth suggest an idea for a program or event, or the community approaches CROYA to request help with a service project.
2) Staff listen and facilitate a larger forum of youth (e.g., weekly youth meeting or special meeting) in which to further discuss the "idea." The purpose is to ascertain whether enough young people are interested and if the proposal is viable.
3) The youth committee votes to proceed or reject the "idea."
4) If the vote is affirmative, a sub-committee is formed of youth volunteers. Chairs and co-chairs of the committee are selected out of a hat from those who have expressed interest. This gives all youth across all grades the opportunity to lead something, and avoids leadership becoming a popularity contest or becoming senior reliant.
5) The subcommittee lists everything that the program or event entails (location, permits or permissions, refreshments, guest speakers, logistics, security, chaperone needs, overhead costs, what to charge, pre-sales and promotion, transportation, schedule, materials, obstacles, etc.). Youth and staff break things down into doable parts.
6) The program is further broken down into tasks. Individuals take responsibility for various "doable parts" (refreshments, tickets and sales, promotion, set-up, contacting pertinent people or agencies, etc.).
7) Staff members are present at all meetings, facilitating the process, playing devil's advocate, and sustaining the momentum.
8) Future meeting dates and an overall timetable are set. Some meetings are during or after school, while others are later in the evening (also known as dinner meetings). Youth are assigned deliverables for each meeting, later coming together to report on progress, discuss obstacles, ask for help, etc.
9) As the program's launch time approaches, staff work closely with committee chairs to ensure youth are on schedule. In addition to meetings, frequent phone calls between staff and young people and among youth are necessary to check on progress and attend to last-minute details. A pre-event meeting takes place close to the appointed date.
10) On the day of the program or event, committee youth arrive early for setup and stay late for clean up. The youth run the program or event, with help from staff.
11) In the week(s) following an event (especially a new one), youth "process" the outcome at weekly youth meetings and sometimes via written evaluation forms. What worked and what could be improved upon are documented for the next time. Since many events are annual, CROYA youth and staff strive to learn from each event, so improvements can be made each year.

❖ ❖ ❖

to know if the candidate could do the job, while youth wanted to know if the candidate would be a good friend. The coordinator is responsible not only for ongoing and new KSTAND initiatives, but also for developing an internship program, coordinating the community's after-school program, and providing meaningful community service projects for the Satellite Juvenile Court to assign to offenders.

After-School Enrichment Program

Youth feedback at the summits and KSTAND advocacy resulted in creation of an after-school enrichment program. (This was actually proposed by the adults on the sub-committee, Youth In Action, as an initiative of the second Youth Summit.). The new Youth Coordinator is responsible for coordinating this effort. The program operates at nine elementary and two middle schools. An effort is being made to target sixth graders who, typically, are involved less with extra curricular activities.

The mission of the after-school program is to provide enrichment, as opposed to day-care. For each eight-week period, four programs are offered at each site. Clubs meet once per week for one hour. For example, a Martial Arts club, using instructors from a local martial arts studio, is held once a week at nine schools. The Cardinal Club, a fourth grade proficiency tutoring club with a parent serving as advisor, is offered at one of the elementary schools. Art Clubs, led by full-time art teachers, are held at several schools. At one elementary school, a former student and a current college student teach Theater Club.

Approximately 600 students participate in the after-school enrichment program. At each school, students register for clubs according to their interests. For some activities, there is a waiting list because of high demand. Expansion of the program can only occur if additional funding is available.

Satellite Juvenile Court

The Youth Coordinator coordinates the Satellite Juvenile Court, through which juvenile court offenders are assigned community service hours. KSTAND works directly with the Court to provide meaningful work and life skills training for juvenile offenders. Plans to expand the current program include, surveying offenders to identify their interests and experience before assigning them to a task. Jobs are designed to be productive, learning experiences.

Challenges for KSTAND

Teens and program supervisors identified the following five challenges facing the program:

(1) *Low high school membership.* More middle than high school students participate in KSTAND. Two factors are believed to account for this. First, many high school students are busier with school related and other outside activities. Second, many high school students do not wish to be part of a group that mixes with middle school students. To rectify this imbalance, efforts are being made to retain middle school students through their high school years, and to develop separate middle and high school branches. Middle school students appear to be more interested than high schoolers in social and volunteer activities. A key to building involvement may be to further develop these opportunities and focus on organizational and planning skills. As the group becomes

more established and its purpose and opportunities better understood, individuals who are attracted to the program will come with more focus and comprehension of its potential.

(2) *Lack of follow-through on projects and inconsistent leadership.* Sometimes participants agree to undertake specific responsibilities, e.g., develop a brochure or contact other organizations about co-sponsoring an event, but do not follow through on their commitments. This directly relates to part of the rationale for initiating a teen program, (i.e., to help teens realize they can have a strong voice in what happens to them), but a corollary of that voice is a responsibility to show leadership, take initiative and follow through on commitments. The program advisors make suggestions and offer advice, but try to avoid taking over the group or nagging at members. Teens tend to be overly optimistic about what they can accomplish, and consequently often underestimate the magnitude of the tasks to which they commit.

(3) *Limited diversity of group membership.* While Kettering is mainly a white, middle class community, KSTAND members and advisors want the group to incorporate diversity in terms of race, sexual orientation, and gender. To accomplish this, targeted recruitment efforts will have to be undertaken and efforts made to ensure that the group's participants welcome economic, sexual orientation and racial diversity.

(4) *Acquiring 501 (c)(iii) status.* Fund-raising is an ongoing issue. Achieving *501 (c)(iii) status* will make it easier to solicit foundation grants and other sources of private funds.

(5) *Creating a place of their own.* Teens desire to create a place of their own. This need was consistently raised at each of the first three youth summits. Ultimately, their expectation is that a teen center will be created, but in the interim, a priority task is to find space for a teen lounge, a place to hold meetings, and storage space to lock up supplies and equipment. Teens value spaces which are exclusive for their use, and in which they do not impede the activity of others, such as younger children and older adults.

Concluding Thoughts

The desire to emulate what CROYA has accomplished is strong, but KSTAND organizers are aware that it took many years to develop a teen center and put in place the facilitation process that CROYA uses so effectively. Despite multiple challenges in launching KSTAND over a two-year period, stakeholders in the community believe the program is progressing quite well. With the hiring of a youth development coordinator, the program is likely to receive added impetus and it is anticipated this will raise it to a higher level. Organizers offered the following advice to others who are interested in developing similar programs:

- Start small, only set goals that can reasonably be accomplished by a start-up program.
- Do not become discouraged if things do not proceed exactly as you had planned in the first couple of years.
- Obtain information about what similar programs elsewhere are doing and solicit advice based on their experiences
- Start with those activities that are of most interest to youth, e.g., social and volunteer activities, before taking on other activities.
- Limit how much control adults exert over the program. The process used by CROYA enables adult leaders to balance the positive and detrimental impacts of participants learning from their mistakes. Debriefing about things that went right and those that could have been improved after an activity is key to an effective learning experience.

Sources

Sheila Russell, Program Supervisor, Kettering Recreation, Parks and Cultural Arts Department. E-mail: Sheila.Russell@ketteringoh.org

http://www.ci.kettering.oh.us/recreation/KSTAND.htm

http://www.croya.com

Slayton, E.D. (2000). *Empowering teens: A guide to developing a community based youth organization.* Lake Forest, IL: CROYA Press.

The National Commission on the Role of the School and the Community in Improving Adolescent Health. (1990) *CODE BLUE: Uniting for Healthier Youth.* http://www.nasbe.org/healthyschools/codeblue.mgi

CHAPTER 13

PROJECT CHOICES

A few years ago, two teens approached the City Council about establishing a youth council to serve as an advisory group to the city on youth issues. This resulted in the formation of the Chattanooga/Hamilton County Youth Council (CHYC). The council's 44 representatives are recommended by principals and guidance counselors from each of the county's public, private, and parochial high schools, and there are also two home-school representatives. If teens demonstrate commitment to, and involvement in, CHYC activities, they can be nominated to serve for multiple years. The city designated Chattanooga Parks, Recreation, Arts and Culture Department (PRACD) as the coordinating department for CHYC activities.

The CHYC offers area students an official forum to air their concerns and to participate in the give-and-take of public discussion. The mission of CHYC is "to provide opportunities for youth to develop mature citizenship, leadership, a sense of personal achievement, and an understanding of government." The CHYC's programs focus on four areas: (i) providing leadership education and development; (ii) providing practical local government knowledge and experience; (iii) increasing communication between youth and adults; and (iv) providing service opportunities for young people to contribute to and benefit from their communities.

Challenges at Hamilton Place Mall

Chattanooga's Hamilton Place is the largest mall in Tennessee and it was "the" place for teens to see and be seen by their peers. Consequently, large numbers of unsupervised teens congregated at the mall, especially on Friday and Saturday evenings. Some negative incidents occurred, and feedback from shoppers, merchants and civic leaders indicated that the unsupervised teens were creating an uncomfortable atmosphere. It seemed likely that CHYC could have a role in ameliorating this situation.

Mall officials researched what other malls around the United States were doing to resolve this teen problem. They found, for example, Mall of the Americas in Minneapolis hired on a part-time basis, 15-20 parents of youth who hung-out in the mall. They were paid $18/hour to walk the mall on Friday and Saturday nights. Mall officials believed that hiring parents was effective because they already had a relationship with the teenagers, who usually followed their instructions without objection. Security personnel were called if parents felt they could not handle a particular situation. During the year before Mall of the Americas implemented its policy, the police department received more than 300 calls relating to youth problems at the mall. However, there was only one call in the year after the policy was implemented and the police calls have been at the single digit level each year since. Other malls, for example Asheville Mall in North Carolina, address their problem by contributing funds towards developing alternate youth activities in the community.

Based on their research and discussions with youth and city officials, Hamilton Place instituted a policy that allowed teens to be at the mall after 6:00 p.m. on Friday and Saturday nights only if they were with a parent or guardian. The policy is described in Exhibit 13-1. The Mall also indicated a willingness to fund activity alternatives for teens.

Exhibit 13-1

Hamilton Place Youth/Guardian Policy

On Fridays and Saturdays 6:00 PM till close:

1. Hamilton Place visitors under 18 are required to be accompanied by a parent or legal guardian 18 years or older on Friday and Saturday evenings after 6 PM.
2. Security will begin monitoring those entering the center at 6 PM.
3. Unescorted youth shopping prior to 6 PM on Friday and Saturday evenings must leave the mall by 6 PM or be joined by a parent or legal guardian.
4. Unescorted youth will be asked to leave the center after 6 PM on Fridays and Saturdays.
5. Individuals utilizing public or other forms of transportation must schedule their departure time to ensure compliance with the 6 PM Youth/Guardian policy.
6. Individuals in violation of the Hamilton Place Youth/Guardian policy or in violation of any posted mall rules who refuse to leave the mall when requested to do so by mall security officers may be prosecuted for trespassing.
7. Proof of age will be required if the age of the youth and/or parent or legal guardian is not easily determined. Those whose age cannot be determined and who lack identification will as asked to leave the property.
8. Acceptable identification is a photo ID from a state agency, school or employer.
9. Youth under 18 working in the mall will be allowed access without a parent or legal guardian. Proof of work status will be required and they must go directly to the place of employment, and must leave the mall at the conclusion of their work shift if after 6 PM on Friday and/or Saturday evenings.
10. One parent, over 18 years of age, may escort all of his/her children. Additionally, one parent or legal guardian, over 18 years of age may escort up to 3 youths, at least one of the youths must be the child of the parent or guardian.
11. Unescorted theater patrons under the age of 18 may only enter through the Food Court entrance.
12. Parents or legal guardians are responsible for the actions for the escorted youth.
13. Any person, violating the posted rules of behavior will be asked to leave Hamilton Place.
14. If an escorted youth is banned from the center, the adult escort will also be banned for the same period of time as the youth.
15. Security personnel are responsible for enforcing this policy and the procedures.

The Hamilton Place Youth/Guardian Policy is posted at all mall entrances.

Some teens reacted negatively to the policy. One teen said:

I don't like that teenagers can't go to Hamilton Place now without an adult. I'm 15, and I don't always want my parents to be taggin' along. There are a lot of responsible teens out there that don't require constant supervision.

However, some agreed with the need to control teen behavior at the mall, having seen, first hand the problems there:

I see Hamilton Place doing it as a means of protection instead of punishment. It's sad that everyone has to suffer because of the acts of a few, but it's good that Chattanooga now sees that teenagers need a safe place to go. Right now there is nothing else to do except walk around the mall.

The need to provide things to do was echoed by a CHYC member:

They need to build us a place and put together activities for us to do on weekends. Most of the places open to teenagers during weekend nights cost a lot of money. That's why we go to the mall.

Hamilton Place Mall officials, representatives from the CHYC, the Mayor's office, and the NAACP held several meetings to see what actions might be taken to alleviate this potentially dangerous situation. They realized that teens needed alternatives to hanging out at the mall during the evenings, on weekends and during the summers. Of these time periods, there seemed to be a particular need to expand summer weekend programming options. Both the PARCD and CHYC recognized that teens had considerable unsupervised and discretionary time, and that inadequate recreation opportunities too often led to anti-social and illegal activities. Thus, they involved teens from the CHYC as part of the planning process. It was recognized that venues should be established where teens could engage in in positive activities and hang-out with their peers in a safe, supervised environment.

Momentum from a Youth Summit

Coincident with the emerging challenges at Hamilton Place Mall, a youth summit was being planned and its outcomes directly related to the problems at the mall. A group from the Chattanooga Leadership (CL) program decided to sponsor the youth summit as their class project. CL is an educational forum created for adults to learn more about city departments, community organizations and the ways that they can become more actively involved in the community. PRACD staff pointed out to the CL organizers that youth needed to be integrated into organizing the summit; thus, the CHYC became centrally involved in planning the event. Their involvement of youth was perceived to be critical since similar efforts to address youth issues had failed in the past because youth were not centrally involved in the planning. The summit and its follow-up activities were perceived to be vehicles through which youth and adults could forge agreements and become agents of change. Out of the summit emerged a number of youth concerns and recommendations about ways to address them, and a Charter of Teen Principles (Exhibit 13-2).

Exhibit 13-2

Charter of Teen Principles

- Teens are best motivated by situations which are supportive, non-threatening and which offer variety.
- Teens are constantly testing values in their search for identity.
- Teenagers receive the greatest amount of enjoyment from two areas: relationships and music.
- Wherever they (teens) are at any given time, teens consider it their space.
- Self expression and respect are very important.
- Teens today can be likened to the teen culture that emerged in the 1960's that protested war, racism, and other negatives in society.
- Teens like to see and be seen.
- Major influences on teens are; peers, music, TV, family, and school.

While the CL members initially saw the need to improve primary and secondary education as the key issues, through discussions at the summit they came to appreciate the wider array of concerns that impacted the lives of young people in their community. A survey of 1500 area youth conducted in preparation for the summit identified five major issues that concerned teens: (a) places to go with friends; (b) education; (c) dating relationships; (d) personal health and well-being, and (e) future career opportunities (Exhibit 13-3).

Approximately 100 teens selected by principals and counselors from local public, private and home-schools participated in the summit. They interacted in small groups, identified sub-issues in each of these five topic areas, and generated strategies for their amelioration.

A recurring theme of summit attendees was the limited places for teens to socialize with friends. Clearly, that was the root of the problem at Hamilton Place Mall. The attendees recommended that more clubs or places that are teen-friendly; more opportunities for teens from different racial and social backgrounds to intermingle; and more things to do in the community (Exhibit 13-3). The summit resulted in the PRACD having an enhanced understanding of teens' perceptions of themselves.

The recommendations emerging from the teen summit challenged the community to address teen issues. To maintain the momentum created by the summit, CL sponsored meetings with student delegates and teen-serving organizations to identify immediately "doable projects."

Exhibit 13-3

Results from First Teen Summit

Places to go with friends*

More Clubs that are Teen-Friendly
Have "teen nights" at existing adult night clubs.
Do a "Battle of the Bands" event which local high school groups can plan.
Open teen clubs at Christian facilities.
Obtain parent involvement in development and acceptance of the club.
Have teen events in "neutral" sites like Coolidge Park.

Racial and Social Diversity
Develop sister school programs to promote interaction among schools.
Have diverse music at teen clubs.
Create after-game "5th Quarter" parties in a neutral place.
Acquire teacher and school support of diversity initiatives.
Create more neutral places like Coolidge Park.

Variety of Places to Go and Things To Do
Need more teen voices at political meetings/local decision-making.
More neighborhood parks.
Increase opportunities for outside activities.
Improve availability of information about things to do.
Be sure there are places that offer extended evening hours.

Education
College preparation
Hands-on education
Cultural diversity

Personal health and well-being
Personal self-image/self-esteem
Exercise and eating right
Teenage depression

Future career opportunities (what is needed to stay here and work)
Renovation of downtown
More things to do
Career information

*More details are given in this topic area since it most closely relates to the development of Project Choices, which is the central topic of this case study.

Material not included in text.

In its early stages, Youth Council delegates were involved in a number of community service activities. They also researched and presented to City Council the need for a teen center and what elements it should contain. Discussions about creating a teen center are still in progress. Finally, teens may be more successful soliciting community assistance and discounts for certain projects.

Developing the Response to the Youth Summit and the Challenges at Hamilton Place Mall

Meetings were scheduled between PRACD staff; the recreation committee of CHYC; and the Teen Alliance, which was a network of non-profit and governmental youth program service providers in the community, that included organizations such as YMCA, Boys & Girls Clubs, Girls, Inc., and Family and Children's services. After several meetings, program ideas and recommendations emerged which were the basis for an eight-week summer program called "Project Choices" (PC).

PC's goals were to provide positive alternatives that promoted positive self-development of youth. Its specific objectives were to:

- Create safe places where teens could hang-out with their peers, participate in positive activities, and meet new people.
- Increase the range and number of new experiences available to teens.
- Empower teens by fully involving them in program planning and implementation.
- Increase teens' sense of belonging through creating opportunities for them to feel they have worth.
- Increase employment opportunities for teens
- Improve relationships between teens and authority figures.

PC complemented PRACD's existing successful summer late-night hoops program and its Sunday afternoon concert series called Hang Time. The gyms were packed for late-night hoops games and the concerts typically attracted between 3,000 and 5,000 teens. However, PRACD staff had decided to phase out the Hang Time program because the large number of teens attending the events created concerns about security. The late-night hoops program was perceived to be a critical element in the overall PC programming effort, and three other major programs were added: Jammin' Jyms, Real Tight Saturday Night, and City of Hope. During the first summer over 4,000 teens participated in at least one of these PC activities.

Jammin' Jyms was scheduled at three recreation centers on Friday and Saturday nights from 7:00 to 11:00 p.m. The programs at each site varied depending on available facilities and program interest. Among the programs offered were free style art classes, drawing and painting, hip hop dance, song writing, photography, exploring the elements of urban art, music & song writing, modern jazz, art with a message/stained glass projects, creative designs/media sculpture and collage, and basic modern and jazz dance. Approximately 250 teens participated in one or more of the programs scheduled at the three program sites, and many of them were regular attendees.

Real Tight Saturday Night programs and events were scheduled on Saturday and Sunday nights between the hours of 8:00 p.m. and midnight, with times being dependent on the particular event that was being offered. Programs scheduled were ice skating, reggae concerts, car shows, battle of the garage bands, "70's" parties, "pooling around," hip hop concerts, and step competitions. Bowling was scheduled every Sunday night for teens and their families at a local bowling center. All events were offered at little or no cost to participants and their families. Concerts attracted up to 500 teens, while typical attendance at dances was approximately 150. Attendance at other events ranged from 50 to 100 participants.

The City of Hope Theater Production was designed to showcase the theater, dance, music, writing, and art talents of teens who participated in the PC programs. The theme of moving from despair to hope, reflected the sentiment of moving from frustration with the implementation of the Hamilton Place teen policy to the potential of PC. According to a PRACD staff member:

> *There was a lot of despair among young people who thought they had nowhere to go. When the youth came up with the ideas for Project Choices and the public and private sectors organized to assist in the development of weekend programs, youth began to see their community as a "City of Hope."*

The play was written by teens and it was based on their feelings about living where streets are unsafe and where "Trouble" (a character in the play) is always around. Through their interactions with "Hope Keeper," the teens believe again in their power to change the world by learning that "we have the power to change our surroundings. Hope means believing even when it seems impossible." Over 230 teens participated in the production.

Over 300 teens participated on one of 24 teams in *Late-Night Hoops,* while 1,300 spectators were in attendance for each of the eight weeks of the program. Centers also offered 3 on 3 basketball leagues, talent shows and other recreation activities and sports competitions.

Organization and Staffing

All of the programs were organized, planned, and implemented by teens. PRACD staff and CHYC members met five times before the program started and once a week during the eight weeks in which the program was offered.

In addition to using department personnel, 23 jobs were created for teens as support staff or instructors. Teens comprised 60% of paid employees for the overall program. They were hired as program and facility monitors, logistics coordinators, scorekeepers, and art and dance instructors. In a few cases, teens who were perceived to be leaders in their communities (even if in a gang) were hired. These individuals were proud of their involvement in the program, liked wearing a staff tee shirt, and in some cases became involved in other PRACD programs (e.g., volunteers in the summer day camp program). Since their leadership was respected by other teens, their involvement helped increase teen participation in the program.

The Chattanooga Police Department, PRACD and teen and adult volunteers provided security at the larger events. Police were located around the Late-Night Hoops program site, with emphasis being given to parking lots and facility perimeters. Recreation staff assisted the police by patrolling entrances and exits, the sites themselves, and by helping with the parking lots. The main responsibilities of the volunteer security monitors were to observe the crowd and notify the police or recreation staff of any potential conflicts or disturbances. They also assisted recreation staff at other event sites where the police were in charge of traffic control, while recreation staff assisted by setting up barricades and fencing where needed.

At major venues, everyone was subjected to a "pat-down" body search by recreation staff and volunteers before entering a program site. Performers also were screened. In some cases, local celebrities participated in event screening to ease any tension or discomfort with the process. During concerts, if performers used any type of gang signs, inappropriate language or dancing, performances were stopped immediately. Teens and their parents felt that the imposition of the security procedures created a safe environment for participation.

The cost of "Project Choices" was $72,385 during its first year of operation. Of this amount Hamilton Place provided $10,000, and promised an additional $15,000 for the second year of the program. The city provided $54,000. A key to keeping the costs low was the willingness of partners to cooperate with the PRACD. For example, the Urban Art Institute at no cost, served as the site for several of the Real Tight Saturday Night events and some of the art classes; the bowling center gave teens a 50% discount; a local ice rink provided a 50% rental discount; and the Chattanooga Police Department provided security for events at no cost to the program.

To reach more teens, a new site at a downtown church was added to the program in the second year since it is close to where a large group of teens reside. Plans are also underway to start a TV show featuring events and programs in which teens will participate during the summer months. The show will be aired on Friday or Saturday nights. Movies in the parks on alternate Saturday nights are another proposed new feature of PC.

Program Evaluation

The following evaluation approaches were used:

- *Attendance* was tracked. At the bigger events, site coordinators issued wristbands to program attendees, and the number of wristbands given out each night was recorded. Hand-held counters were used at other events to record attendance. At some of the recreation center-based activities, teens signed a log sheet when they entered the building.
- The *number of teens volunteering* at events was tracked to determine the degree of teen involvement in the program.
- *Surveys* were distributed to participants to ascertain perceptions of program quality and satisfaction. Participants gave high ratings to the quality of the events, with a large majority indicating that they would come again and recommend the programs to others. The mayor and city council were pleased with the overall acceptance and quality of the events.
- *Program staff and volunteers observed teen-adult interactions.* There appeared to be increases in positive interactions between teens, staff and the police, and police reported that teens were engaging in fewer negative behaviors. The police donated their time to security, since they saw the events as positive alternatives to teens hanging-out on the streets. The police reported that problematic incidents in the community seemed to decrease. The police intend to more accurately track these outcomes in future years. Disciplinary

problems at events appeared to decline, while teens who were either paid as staff or used as volunteers appeared to benefit from the responsibility and recognition they received.

- Program staff felt that teens had benefited in other ways from their participation in the program, including:
  a) Decision-making skills – Young adults learned ethical decision-making and problem solving through leadership development, career exploration activities, hands-on experiences, service to others and positive social interaction.
  b) Community Service – Teens increased their understanding of the rewards to be obtained from giving back to their neighborhoods and communities. Life Skills – Teens established positive and rewarding relationships with their peers, adults, and authority figures. Opportunities were available for teens to engage in positive activities that enhanced their skills, social development and tolerance, and acceptance of diversity.

The city is committed to continuing the program maintaining its level of investment in it, even though the overall PRACD budget has been reduced in response to downturns in the economy.

Lessons Learned

An early response to an issue can stop problems from escalating. Waiting for a serious negative incident to occur before responding to teen issues shows a lack of responsive leadership. Undertaking thorough community assessments to identify problems and then proactively working with all stakeholders facilitates the avoidance of problems. This also helps to develop the broad constituency needed to stimulate political action and funding.

Teen involvement is essential. The PRACD saw its role as enabling teens to be involved in all aspects of program planning and evaluation. This improved relationships between teens and professionals, enhanced teens' sense of self-worth, and helped teens develop job related skills. The leadership of CHYC attracted other teens to events since they felt a sense of ownership in them.

Teen Council membership should be monitored. Appointments to a teen council should be monitored. In some cases youth are selected who enjoy the status of being appointed but who fail to invest effort in the work of the council. Some youth may be too shy or feel intimidated by more articulate members and this may restrain them from being fully contributing members of the council.

Hiring youth to work in the program. Hiring youth as program staff may encourage them to pursue a park and recreation career. It encourages them to model appropriate behaviors for their peers and enables adults to see teens performing in a positive manner.

Creating good relationships with the police is critical. In the current case, police donated their security services because they believed the preventive role of PC resulted in a net gain in the use of their resources. Police involvement with teens fostered improved relationships and made it easier for them to deal with problematic situations that may arise elsewhere in the community.

Start small and increase offerings over time. In this case, staff reported that they offered too many activities, and spread themselves over too many events. Teens also felt that overlapping activities were available at the same time. In future years, the number of activities offered at the same time will be reduced.

Providing transportation is key for younger teens. Transportation is required to enable younger teens and those without cars to attend events. Efforts are being made by PRACD to persuade the local transportation authority to operate buses late enough in the evening to enable teens to return home from events.

Source

Janice Miller and Barbara Readnower, Chattanooga Parks, Recreaion and Cultrual Arts Department.

Section 5

After-School and Summer Programs

CHAPTER 14

THE TIME FOR KIDS INITIATIVE IN PORTLAND, OREGON:

CHALLENGES OF EFFECTIVE MULTI-PARTNERING

Like many other states, communities in Oregon are experiencing a shortage of funds for public education. Measure 5, the state's tax limitation legislation, was passed by referendum in 1990, and its effect was to substantially limit options for expanding educational funding. Portland is the state's largest urban area and during the 1990s large numbers of ethnic migrant families settled in the city, especially Russians and Eastern Europeans, and Latinos. The language and cultural challenges of responding to the needs of these new children meant that the difficulties confronting Portland schools were accentuated.

The guiding vision of the Portland Parks and Recreation's (PP&R) Recreation Division is "We create recreation opportunities that can change people's lives and bring the community together." The Division believed that creating after-school programs targeted at the educationally disadvantaged was consistent with operationalizing this vision. Thus, it proposed and developed the Time for Kids Initiative (TFKI) which was a three year pilot program designed to enhance academic achievement and thus contribute to alleviating the perceived educational crisis in Portland.

The vision for the TFKI pilot program flowed from the Division's overall vision statement: "To create recreation and education opportunities that can change people's lives, bring the community together and increase the personal assets of Portland's youth." The program was intended to provide high quality, after-school programming which offered more depth and structure than traditional drop-in programs. Its focus was on youth development, rather than the more traditional goal of skill development. PP&R positioned itself to align with a central problem in the community and sought to demonstrate that it could contribute to alleviating that problem.

PP&R viewed this pilot program as an opportunity to serve as a broker of services rather than as a direct service provider. The intent was to partner with other organizations to shape a common mission which would best leverage the limited available resources. PP&R visualized an approach where partners representing a range of agencies and organizations would have equal status at the table in the planning, implementation and evaluation of programs, while PP&R's role would be to facilitate and coordinate the overall service delivery. PP&R staff recognized that this approach would be challenging. The recreation manager observed, "When everyone has resources, it's relatively easy for partners to cooperate. However, in situations like this where there is an acute shortage of resources, partners are tempted to revise their perspective and view prospective collaborators as competitors for the same resources, rather than partners."

Program Context

The pilot program was undertaken in two of the city's underserved areas: North Portland and Outer Southeast Portland. These two areas had a high proportion of low income residents and relatively little service infrastructure to serve them. These two areas received most of the ethnic migrant families who moved into Portland in the 1990s. North Portland received most of the Latino population- - which traditionally was not a major ethnic group in the city- -while Outer Southeast received most of the city's influx of 60,000 Russians and East Europeans.

The guidelines given to PP&R for administering the TFKI by the city council were:

- Ensure that TFKI is collaborative. This meant involving and utilizing the expertise of a wide range of non-profit community-based organizations, and recognizing them as equal partners in vision, funding and program evaluation. The emphasis on collaboration was intended to minimize gaps in program planning available to the targeted youth. PP&R's mandate was to serve as a service broker to facilitate on-site service delivery.
- Develop a comprehensive out-of-school hours program focused on two middle schools (6th-8th grades), one in each targeted area, since this was the age range in which the council perceived the juvenile delinquency problem to be most acute. PP&R had a full-time community recreation staff member resident at both of these schools, so some essential existing infrastructure was already in place. (Since much of Portland's indoor recreation program is dependent on the use of school facilities, PP&R has full-time staff based at 13 Portland schools. Before recent budget cuts, PP&R had part-time staff in an additional 30 schools. They were there for most of the school day and are responsible for organizing after-school programs).
- Ensure the Initiative is well evaluated. The rationale for a pilot program is to test whether desired outcomes are achieved. If they are attained, then the implication is that consideration should be given to expanding the TFKI beyond the initial targeted neighborhoods.
- Programs should be accessible (geographically, financially and culturally) to unserved or underserved youth.
- A broad array of programs/activities should be offered to meet a wide range of youth interests, with particular emphasis on programs designed to promote academic achievement and personal enrichment of youth.

The city council allocated $200,000 per year from the general fund to finance the program for three years. Although the council could only commit to one year's funding at a time, there was a clear understanding and recognition at the outset that if the pilot program was to provide meaningful evaluation data, it would have to be funded for the full three year period.

Program Development

A broad invitation to participate in the TFKI was sent to all non-profit community organizations which it was believed might have an interest. They were requested to extend the invitation to any other organizations that were not on PP&R's list which they thought may have something to offer. Approximately 50 potentially interested partners attended the first meeting. The group met every two weeks for three months discussing and defining the scope, depth and content of the TFKI program. By the end of this period the group had self-selected itself to approximately half its original size, as some of the initial organizations realized they did not have the capacity needed to participate.

The Search Institute had recently completed a study with the Multnomah County Commission on Children and Families (Portland is in Multnomah County). Over 10,000 youth in sixth, eight and tenth grades were surveyed using the Search Institute's model of 40 assets to identify what was missing in their lives. The study concluded that youth in Multnomah County had an average of only 19 of the 40 assets identified as essential for youth to grow up healthy, caring and competent. The TFKI collaboration group used the study results as a basis for selecting the 10 assets they deemed to be most important to Portland's youth, and mandated that any TFKI funded program should be designed to contribute to one or more of them. However, when the program proposals were received, they all focused on just three of these assets:

- Academic achievement;
- Developing work and/or life skills; and
- Community involvement/community service.

This suggested that these are the three assets which PP&R and its partners were best equipped to develop.

The collaboration group also extended the original mandate from the city council to focus the programs exclusively on the middle schools. The group recognized that inadequate academic performance and delinquent behavior at the middle schools had been nurtured through earlier experiences at the elementary schools. Thus, to positively impact 6th through 8th grade youth, efforts had to be made to address these issues at an earlier age. As a result, programming was extended to include outreach programs to 3rd through 5th graders at some elementary schools in the targeted areas.

Each of the collaborative partners interested in participating in the TFKI was required to write a proposal to PP&R requesting part of the $200,000 budget. An example of a completed proposal is shown in Figure 14-1. There were two types of partners: (i) those who offered year-long programs which were often school-based or school-linked and, (ii) those whose contribution consisted of offering programs that often covered a single topic, subject or activity.

Exhibit 14-1

A Completed Proposal Form

1. **Organization**

   Oregon Council for Hispanic Advancement (OCHA)

2. **Program Description**

   The goal of the OCHA/Time for Kids after-school enrichment program is to ensure the educational success of Latino students by implementing an after-school program that offers academic support and recreational activities. Twenty Latino 3rd, 4th, and 5th grade children from James John Elementary will participate in this program. The academic component will focus on strengthening students' math and literacy skills. To meet the diverse academic needs of participants, one-on-one tutoring and small group learning will be utilized extensively. For example, the class will be divided into teams composed of 4 to 6 students with comparable skills in a particular content area such as math or reading. This structure allows staff to personalize instruction and provide intensive tutoring.

   The children's classroom teachers will be consulted on a regular basis to ensure that academic activities are adequately addressing the individual needs of students and helping them meet, exceed, or improve toward their grade level benchmark. Program staff will also use culturally-based curricula published by the National Council of La Raza (NCLR), the nation's largest Latino advocacy organization.

   In addition, the program will integrate academics with a spectrum of recreational and community service activities. These will balance academic instruction with fun activities that teach participants teamwork, increase cultural awareness, and develop neighborhood pride and involvement (see list of partners in #4).

3. **Program duration**

   The program will run for the entire school year, beginning September 8 through June 23; classes will be held Monday-Thursday from 2:00 p.m. - 6:00 p.m. Fridays will be dedicated for planning meetings with teachers or parents as well as OCHA staff meetings. Staff will be contracted from August 30 to June 23 and located on-site from 12:00 p.m. to 6:00 p.m.

4. **Partners**

   OCHA has established strong partnerships with several agencies during the past summer and this school year. We expect to continue this collaborative effort in order to provide participants with diverse, high-quality educational and recreational activities. The following is a list of confirmed program partners and their roles.

   - *Multlomah County Library*–students will visit the St. Johns branch on a weekly basis to learn how to effectively utilize the library's resources, obtain library cards, learn about the Internet, and cultivate good reading habits. In addition, culturally-based storytime will be provided by the Library Outreach in Spanish (LIBROS) program.
   - *Campfire*–Americorp volunteers will teach children the importance of community involvement and help them plan a service program that positively impacts their neighborhood.
   - *Saturday Academy*–Saturday Academy staff will make 8 visits to teach youth math concepts using creative, hands-on activities.
   - *St. Johns Community Center*–children will have access to a variety of recreational opportunities ranging from organized sports to arts and crafts activities.

Exhibit 14-1 Continued

- *Police Activities League (PAL)*–students will have access to recreational opportunities at PAL's Youth Center and participate in their Spring Break activities.
- *James John School*–participants will have access to computers and educational software that help them build their academic and technology skills.

5. **Time for Kids primary objective**

Participants are meeting, exceeding or showing improvement toward their grade level benchmark.

6. **Marketing and recruitment**

Children participating in OCHA's summer enrichment program at James John Elementary will be given priority to transition into the after-school program. In the event that all positions are not filled, students will be recruited through a teacher nomination process. Every 2nd, 3rd, and 4th grade teacher will receive a description of the summer program as well as a nomination form. Students will be chosen based on two main criteria: (1) student demonstrates a need for additional academic assistance, and (2) teacher is willing to participate in preparing the student's academic plan and/or provide educational materials for the student to use after school. Following the nomination process, the family will be contacted to obtain parent/guardian consent. It is anticipated that approximately 15 students will transition from the summer program to the after-school program.

7. **Transportation**

Transportation will not be provided to participants in the OCHA after-school program. Parents will be asked to take responsibility for the daily pick-up of their children. Because of the proximity to recreational sites such as St. John's Community Center, additional transportation will only be necessary for daylong field trips. During such excursions, OCHA will utilize its agency van and rent additional vehicles as needed.

8. **Family/youth involvement in program planning**

Latino children and families were actively involved in the planning phase of the proposed program. Students currently participating in OCHA's after-school enrichment program were asked to write what they would like to do next year. Given that many students will transition from the summer into the after-school program, every effort was made to incorporate participants' ideas into the program design. During a recent parent meeting, parents also provided concrete suggestions regarding program goals, activities, and design.

9. **Family/youth input in ongoing project design**

OCHA's after-school program will commence with an orientation for children and family members to describe the program, reiterate the goals set for the school year, and recruit parents as classroom volunteers. Two additional parent potlucks will be held during the school year as a way to bolster family involvement and obtain feedback regarding project design, implementation, and evaluation. Students' input will also be obtained during recreational event planning.

10. **Enrollment fee**

The program is *free* of charge.

11. **Project location**

The after-school program will be implemented at James John Elementary located in North Portland.

Exhibit 14-1 Continued

12. Number of youth served.

Twenty Latino children will participate.

13. Registration process

Registration materials will be sent home with children two weeks prior to the end of the school year. Parents will also be contacted by phone to give them a description of the summer program, answer any questions they might have, and encourage them to complete and return registration materials promptly. In addition, families that have difficulties filling out forms will be given the option of attending a registration meeting at the school in order to receive individual help during this program.

14. Attendance

Attendance will be taken daily and parents will be contacted regularly to encourage student and family program participation.

15. Project evaluation

OCHA will evaluate the after-school program as follows:

1) Grades–students' academic records will be monitored to gauge their progress toward their grade level benchmark.
2) Student survey–pre- and post-tests will assess children's attitudes toward Latino culture, family, community, and school.
3) Parent survey–questions will gather descriptive statistics regarding parent educational attainment, language spoken at home, educational expectations, homework assistance, and parental school involvement.
4) Student attendance–every child will achieve at least a 90% attendance rate.
5) Family involvement–number of family volunteers and parents participating in at least one event.

16. Program staff

All program staff are bilingual/bicultural and have experience working with youth in educational and recreational settings. Individuals will also have a demonstrated ability to administer evaluation tools, an interest in working with Latino youth and families, and enthusiasm for the program.

The whole committee of prospective collaborative partners met to rank the proposals. This process was a complete failure because people were unable to focus on what was best for the overall program and instead insisted on defending and advocating their own proposals. Given this experience, the larger group unanimously agreed to PP&R's suggestion that a small group working with PP&R should rank the proposals. The Funding Committee was comprised of representatives from a community based organization, school principals from the two middle schools, an organization serving ethnic populations, and a PP&R staff person. The ranking of proposals by this committee was accepted by the larger group. The challenge was to select programs that offered different kinds of programs and sought different outcomes: "We didn't want to fund only art programs or only those that sought academic achievement as their outcome." During the three years of the pilot program, 17 partners, representing 32 programs, serving 21 sites were funded. A list of partners, showing the program they offered and its location is provided in Exhibit 14-2.

Exhibit 14-2

List of Partners in the TFKI

Sponsoring Partner	Program	Location
North Portland		
AKA Science	Hands in Science	James John
Boys and Girls Club	Bilingual Science and Technology Project	St. John's Community Center
Campfire	Youth Volunteer Corp	James John Ockley Green George
James John Elementary	Project Safe Summer Academic Enrichment Recreation	James John
Headwaters to Ocean	H_2O	James John Ockley
Multlomah County Library	Wired Words Science Odyssey	Columbia Villa James John
Northwest Passage	Instrumental Music	James John Columbia Villa Beach
OCHA	Latino Summer After-School Project for Latino Youth	James John James John
Oregon Building Congress (OBC)	Introduction to Construction	Tubman
Police Athletic League	Violence Free Spring Break	PAL Center
Portsmouth Trinity Lutheran Church	Portsmouth Community Garden	James John Ockley Green
RACC	Videography Project	Ockley Green
Tears of Joy	Drama Club	Ockley Green
Outer Southeast		
Asian Family Center	Asian Leadership Club	Floyd Light Alice Ott
AKA Science	Hands on Science	Gilbert Heights
Brentwood Darlington	After School Enrichment Project	Lane Middle
Headwaters to Ocean - H_2O	H_2O	Alice Ott, Woodmere, PAL, Boys/Girls Club, Kelly
Lents Boys and Girls Club	Summer Sports Camp	Gilbert Heights
Marshall Caring Community	Summer Peace Camp	Mt. Scott
Northwest Passage	Instrumental Music	Lane, Woodmere, Binnsmead
OCHA	Latino Summer Program Latino After-School Program	Gilbert Heights Gilbert Heights
Oregon Building Congress (OBC)	Introduction to Construction	Lane, Binnsmead, Floyd Light, Alice Ott
Portland Impact	Extended Day Project	Woodmere
Police Athletic League	PAL and Parks for Kids	Harold Oliver & PAL Center
Tears of Joy	Latino Youth Theater Masks and Murals	Alice Ott Alice Ott
Mult. County Library	Library Club	Woodmere

The primary goal of the TFKI was to improve academic performance. Hence, the central element in the program was 30-40 minutes of homework tutoring immediately after school. Tutors were students supervised by adults, and recruited from high schools. An effort was made to match the TFKI students with tutors from the high school which the students would attend when they left middle school. In Oregon, starting with the 4th grade, all students are required to do a specified number of hours of community service. This is usually part of their health education requirement and they receive credit for it. Thus, the TFKI staff from PP&R recruited tutors by connecting with the school counselors responsible for the community service component of the curriculum. In addition to the academic credit they received, the tutors were able to report their experience on college application forms and this likely enhanced their chances of being accepted at their college of choice.

In this way, TFKI became one of the smorgasbord of activities the high school offered their students to meet this requirement. Students who were interested were required to interview with the PP&R staff supervisor. Tutors were required to commit for one full semester. The interview was used to reinforce the extent of their commitment (e.g. every Monday, Wednesday and Friday, or whatever); clearly articulate their role and PP&R's expectations; and to identify the academic areas in which they were most qualified to tutor. Special efforts were made to recruit students who were both bilingual and bicultural.

Typically, tutoring was held in the school cafeteria. The TFKI students were there after school; picked up their snack; then went to the tutoring table which corresponded to their homework assignments. One or two tables were assigned for each subject area with one or two tutors at each, and each table could accommodate up to 10 students. Thus, each evening as many as 12 tutors were needed, which meant that approximately 20 had to be recruited each semester. In addition to the tutors, PP&R hired an adult at each site for ten hours a week to oversee and supervise the program for a couple of hours each evening. Grades were assigned to the tutors by the school counselors, but PP&R staff were required to complete evaluation forms on each tutor's performance. The forms were provided by the counselors and they addressed attendance, quality of work, and commitment. The tutoring component of the TFKI was not intended to be part of a mentoring effort. Mentoring was seen as a one-on-one year long commitment that went beyond providing assistance with academic studies.

Only after the homework tutorial time had been completed were the youth allowed to participate in the array of TFKI leisure class activities. It was their "admission ticket" into the classes. Students did not receive homework tutoring unless they had been in school that day. Before this rule was instituted, some youth skipped school, but were so eager to participate in the art, dance team, music, hoops program or whatever, they showed up for the tutorial session. This was also a mechanism for increasing school attendance, which itself is likely to be a contributor to improved academic performance.

Some of the youth in the TFKI were referred by teachers who saw they were having difficulty with their school work. In the first week or so, such students often tended to be resentful that they had been referred to the program since it was a public manifestation of their deficiencies. The types of unorthodox challenges facing some of these children are unimaginable to most people. An example is given in Exhibit 14-3. However, in most cases, they quickly came to enjoy the leisure activities, and were also motivated by improvements which occurred in their academic grades.

Exhibit 14-3

The Need for a Light Bulb!

A child in one of the schools was doing badly on homework assignments. He was obviously bright and intelligent but did consistently bad homework assignments- -sometimes not handing in anything. When a counselor questioned the boy in-depth seeking an explanation for his poor work, it emerged there were no working light bulbs in the boy's home! It goes dark at 4:30 p.m. in Portland in the winter. Thus, by the time he got home from school, there was no light available so he could not do his homework. After coming to the after-school program, everything changed. The PP&R supervisor commented, "We simply cannot understand the range of problems that some people have in their lives."

Staff Training

Staff training was limited because very little funding was available to support it. PP&R did have the report and results of the Search Institute's asset study to use as an initial introductory training tool. In addition, before the program was launched, one full-day retreat was held for all PP&R staff involved in TFKI. This did not extend to the tutors. Experts were brought in to advise and guide them. A key resource for PP&R was the Oregon Mentoring Institute (OMI). Their staff provided the training at one of these day retreats and made available at no cost to the PP&R an extraordinarily comprehensive set of materials, training programs, and manuals which substantially accelerated the PP&R staff's learning curve, and which the PP&R used extensively in subsequent additional internal training sessions. Two other valuable sources of assistance with staff training were the Northwest Regional Education Laboratory and The Mentoring Partnership. Over time, key lead staff were identified as mentors for their peers, so they could pass along the experience and expertise which they had acquired.

The results of the training and the experience gained by staff through involvement with the TFKI were mixed. Some were excited by the program, reveled in the opportunity to engage in asset based youth development, and were effective. However others, in the words of the recreation manager, "Just didn't get it." They remained in the traditional recreation mode of "recreation for the sake of recreation and diversion" with which they felt comfortable, and made no effort to redirect the thrust towards asset building.

Outcomes

One of the innovative features of the TFKI was its strong commitment to evaluation. The evaluation was designed to be two tiered, consisting of partners designing an evaluation of their individual projects and independent evaluators assessing the TFKI as a whole. Evaluation of the individual projects was based on a list of objectives developed by the partners in the early stages of the collaboration. At that time, each approved project was required to identify a primary objective which would form the basis of their individual project's evaluation. A comprehensive evaluation of the TFKI program also was commissioned from an external firm of consultants. The consultants' overall evaluation was drawn from data developed by PP&R, and the individual evaluations of each program which the partners were required to undertake under the terms of their funding agreement with the PP&R. The consultants' evaluation was comprised of four main elements:

- Attendance and Registration Analysis
- Student Attitude Survey
- Family Assessments
- Partner Assessments

Evaluators noted that "all of the data over the period of the initiative, creates a picture of a program that has struggled with challenges, but has accomplished some important outcomes for kids."

Registration and enrollment data and attendance records were collected by the partners. Partners forecasted a minimum and maximum number of participants when they signed agreements with the PP&R. This was used as the "expected performance" measure in the evaluation. A majority of programs met or exceeded minimum enrollment goals, and half of the programs met or exceeded their maximum expectation.

The Student Attitude Survey was a self-esteem inventory consisting of a 10 question instrument for use with elementary school children, and a 22 question survey which was completed by middle schoolers. A pretest was administered in the first or second class session, and a post-test in the last class. In over half of the partner programs statistically significant positive increases occurred.

Family Assessments to evaluate level of family support were undertaken in interviews with a sample of parents/guardians identified from the registration lists. A standard questionnaire was developed to guide the interview and ensure it covered key areas which included:

- Satisfaction with the child's experience in the TFKI.
- Confidence in program and staff.
- Importance of program goals to parents/guardians.
- Barriers to program participation.
- Level of parent/family member participation in programs.
- Strengths and weaknesses of programs.
- Suggestions for program improvements.

Interviews were conducted by phone, and in the language identified as the primary language of the household whenever possible. The International Refugee Center of Oregon provided interviewers who were able to communicate with Russian and Spanish speaking families. The Asian Family Center provided interviewers for contacts with families that they served.

Partner Assessments were undertaken by interviewing key people representing each of the collaborating partners. A set of 14 questions was developed to guide the interviews.

Analysis of the data generated from these four sources led to the following overall conclusions and recommendations:

- The TFKI had the support of participating families, school personnel and community-based organizations because it supported family aspirations for children's success, an education agenda for academic excellence and school-community connectedness, and a community agenda to enrich the lives of all children.
- Overall, the most successful programs were school-based, 12-month long programs that met the needs of special population groups (Oregon Council for Hispanic Advancement, Asian Youth Club). These had high attendance ratings, positive responses from the significant adult or family member, significant changes in student attitudes, and improved academic enhancement. The second most successful types of programs were those with a strong school link and coordination, focused on a special interest (Tears of Joy, OBC) and/or a school sponsored, school-year long program (the two middle schools). The least successful programs were those that lacked a strong school link, were not necessarily on-site at a school, and did not have a strong interest focus. In addition, these partners seemed to remain weak, even after they had additional experience as part of the initiative.
- Locating projects in schools with close involvement of school personnel dramatically reduced transportation issues and bolstered a sense of safety and well being for participants. Site coordination also seemed critical.
- A school link, including but not limited to direct school sponsorship, and a designated program coordinator were important to the success of a program or activity. A strong and observant coordinator (Parks and Recreation staff or staff from a community organization chosen in collaboration with the school principal) was able to identify gaps or different programming needs necessary to reach the diversity of children's interests and was in a good position to fill those gaps especially if a) financial resources were available and b) they were knowledgeable about community resources that might fit. They were also in a good position to bridge or link schools with potential partners.

- Non-profit agencies could be strong partners in school based after-school programming if they had a clear role and were accountable to a school site coordinator. Developing non-profit resources in a way that meets children's needs and is compatible with school environments and requirements, was a role for a liaison person between schools and potential partners. Neither then had to step out of their core mission.

Lessons Learned

Five main lessons were learned from the TFKI. They were: (i) difficulty in reconciling the missions of collaborative partners so they were consistent with TFKI's asset building goals; (ii) difficulty in getting some partners to think beyond their own narrow, specific focused contributions and, thus, contribute to planning of TFKI; (iii) challenges in operationalizing the desire for the program to be comprehensive, since this conveyed a different meaning to different people; (iv) underestimation of the time needed to launch TFKI; and (v) importance of focusing the program on a single middle school in each area.

An important organizational outcome for PP&R, beyond the immediate impact of TFKI, was its success in the role of "service broker." It brought a diversity of perspectives and partners who had not previously worked together, and facilitated the forging of new partnerships. However, the decision to give these partners equal status in the overall collaboration effort *failed to consider differences in their missions.* Some partners had a primary mission of youth development, while others had a message or subject area as their primary mission and wished to communicate it to youth. Thus, the most important lesson learned was the challenge of reconciling the different *missions* of the partner groups with the *mission* of the pilot project. Some partners' commitments to youth focused on "artistic expression," or "cleaning up the river." For example, Northwest Passage, which was a music group, was solely interested in getting flutes or other musical instruments in the hands of youth. They did not understand the broader issues of how the instruments and playing for parents at the end of a session, thus bringing parents and families into the school, had an effect on youth beyond learning to play "Twinkle, twinkle little star" or whatever. Similarly, the mission of the a.k.a. Science organization was to get science into the curriculum and classrooms of 3rd to 5th graders, and asset building was not part of their perceived mission.

The school districts, PP&R staff, and some of the partners were familiar with the Search Institute's study which had immediately preceded the TFKI program. They were well-acquainted with the notion of asset building, and subscribed to the broad mission of TFKI programs. However, others had no familiarity with the assets approach and despite initial training sessions, they had no real interest in it. The PP&R director of TFKI said, "If we were to do this over, I would pick partners based on their understanding of, and commitment to, the broader asset mission of youth development, rather than on their more parochial mission of involvement with an activity."

A second lesson learned was at the individual site and program level, where it became clear that *not all programs were structured so that every "partner" could be an equal partner*- -some organizations' contributions were limited to providing a specific service to a particular group of children. In hindsight it probably was not appropriate for them to be part of the decision-making for a site, since they had relatively little interest in investing effort into the overall planning and evaluation of the TFKI. As a result, planning, implementation and evaluation were not always bound together by a global outlook. It was probably too great an expectation for program oriented people, attached to a particular organization, to become overall advocates and planners for youth development.

The mandate was to develop a *comprehensive* after-school program and the third lesson learned was that *there are two ways of viewing the principle of comprehensiveness.* One perspective is to view comprehensiveness as referring to the whole multi-site TFKI, which included outreach programs at the elementary schools and other sites beyond the two middle schools that were its core. Thus, many partners looked at the list of funded programs and felt that it was comprehensive in that it offered art, music, academics, life skills, and community service.

From another, and perhaps more useful standpoint, programs often were not comprehensive when viewed from the perspective of a child or school. From the participants' perspective the most comprehensive programs typically were those located at the two middle schools. Other TFKI funded programs were "value-added" pieces, included as part of the commitment to provide comprehensive programming, but they seemed to have little connection with the school site. The independent consultants who evaluated the TFKI suggested that Oregon Building Congress classes at Tubman Elementary, and the Campfire program at George Elementary seemed to fit this category. They suggested that future comprehensive programming efforts should be examined site-by-site and customized site-by-site, based on the needs of children at that site.

Two other lessons were noted- -one negative and one positive. The negative lesson was that the *TFKI took much longer to organize, define and launch than anyone expected.* A positive lesson was the wisdom of the initial decision to *focus resources on a single middle school in each* area. This facilitated an in-depth, integrated effort which made positive outcomes more likely. The relationship between PP&R's site coordinator, the school faculty, and the non-profit program provider was crucial. In those TFKI programs that did well, the site coordinator invariably had a good relationship with the school faculty, who in turn trusted the site coordinator to bring in good non-profit programs. The consultants suggested that in the future for programs of this type, the site coordinator should be viewed as being in the best position to look at the overall needs of youth at that location and should play a central role in the programming. The non-profit programs could utilize the site coordinators both for helping develop the skills they need to work effectively with children and youth, and for establishing a strong relationship with school personnel. While some programs obviously succeeded without this liaison, they were the exception.

Conclusions

The evaluation of outcomes suggested that the TFKI program was successful. The independent consultants' report concluded:

> *Time for Kids was an important effort by Portland Parks and Recreation to redefine itself to meet the ever changing needs of Portland citizens. It was a very successful effort in establishing partnerships and meeting the needs of underserved youth.*

A key factor in the success of the TFKI was the leadership provided by both the PP&R's director and the elected Commissioner responsible for Parks and Recreation in Portland. This was a "top-down" driven program, characterized by strong political and administrative support and prioritization. The Commissioner ran on a platform of youth advocacy. It was both a personal passion and a high profile political priority for him. The PP&R director was similarly passionate about youth being at the top of the agenda. The Recreation Division staff were initially apprehensive about retreating from their broader focus of recreation-for-all in order to focus on youth. It took some time for them to buy into the mandate from the top that "Kids come first."

Many in the PP&R initially perceived after-school programs to be a school rather than a PP&R responsibility. However, PP&R's director viewed this as an opportunity for his department because the school district had no resources to invest in such a program. The director argued forcefully that "Yes, we are leisure professionals, but as part of that mission we are also 'the after-school professionals.' We can be instrumental in helping schools produce better students and build students' assets." The director's mandate to the Recreation Division was, "Your job is to make yourself indispensable to the school principals. Figure out how to help them do their job better." He recognized this was an excellent opportunity to reposition the PP&R's Recreation Division so it was responsive to a central concern of the city's voters and elected officials. Only when recreation services are perceived as contributing to alleviating problems which constitute the prevailing political concerns of policymakers who are responsible for allocating tax funds, can they expect to secure additional resources. Indeed, his coining of the term "After-school professionals" as describing PP&R's role is excellent positioning. It avoids connotations of competition with the schools; it moves PP&R away from connotations of "fun and games"; and it offers a platform which taxpayers and elected officials can support.

Like most departments, Portland Parks and Recreation has a wide array of traditional recreation programs for youth. However, the TFKI differed in that it was a youth development program rather than a recreation skill improvement program. Skill improvements in traditional programs are important and asset building *may* emerge from them. However, they are not designed specifically to foster specified assets, which is the characteristic feature of youth development programs. In the current context, recreation skill building is the only realistic outcome to which most agencies can aspire because budget limitations preclude the larger investments which genuine youth development programs require.

Thus, despite the evaluation evidence and political consensus that the TFKI was a success, expansion of the pilot program to a larger number of students remained problematic. The substantial investment of $600,000 over three years was targeted at a relatively small number of children. Participation at each of the two middle schools typically ranged from 60-80 students each term. This represented approximately 10-15% of the schools' enrollments. Thus, the cost per student of the program for the three years was between $3,750 and $5,000, i.e. $1,250 to $1,666 per year. It has long been argued in the parks and recreation field that the critical question is not "how many were there?" Rather it is, "What happened to Jose, Mary, Sam and Joan in this experience?" Programs like the TFKI which focus on effectiveness of outcomes require that considerable resources be invested in them to be successful. However, the political reality is that in terms of cost per person, the expenditure on programs like the TKIF is substantially greater than the costs associated with traditional recreation programs, so it is difficult to sell to a legislative body.

The potential magnitude of the on-going cost makes legislative bodies reluctant to make a commitment to support such programs out of general fund revenues on a city-wide basis. Approximately 54,000 children are registered in the Portland Independent School District (ISD) with another 30,000 in the Parkrose ISD and 20,000 in the David Douglas ISD, both of which are within the city of Portland. In the Portland ISD alone, 20,770 (38%) students qualify for free or reduced meals. If it is assumed that this 38% is a reasonable surrogate measure for "guesstimating" how many students are academically disadvantaged so they would qualify for the TKIF, then an extrapolation of the pilot program costs suggests the annual bill would be over $30 million. Even to extend the program to the 3,500 students most in need of it would require a budget increase to PP&R of over $5 million for students in the Portland ISD alone! Given that the total annual operating budget of PP&R is approximately $30 million, the political reality is that investments of this magnitude are not politically feasible from the city's general funds. Nor can such programs be funded by the ISD's. The school districts are 70% funded by the state, and legislators from outside the Portland area have shown little willingness to provide additional resources to the state's largest urban school systems to help them address the issues arising from the sudden influx of large numbers of students from different ethnic groups.

A reasonably strong case can be made that the annual cost of $30 million to extend TFKI to all those who meet the criteria for benefitting from it would be cost effective in the long-term, given the long-term costs to society of failing to provide youth with the assets and protective factors the program builds. However, there are "disconnects" between (1) the short and long term payers and beneficiaries, and (2) the geographical jurisdictions which pay for, and benefit from, such programs as TFKI.

The short-term actions of many elected officials are guided by their desire to be re-elected. The tax increases needed to fully fund TFKI are likely to be politically unpopular. The general public's decision horizon and perspective is notoriously short term, and elected officials have to be responsive to this. "Pay now or pay later" is not a convincing mantra to either group. Thus, elected officials perceive it to be advantageous to keep taxes low in the short term, recognizing that the societal, financial and political consequences of not providing youth with assets through TFKI will become the problem of their successors in the future. There appear to be few political advantages for those in elected positions to be proactive rather than reactive in the context of youth development. The political pressures are conducive to encouraging short-term rather than long-term action horizons.

A second disconnect discouraging local investment in youth development is that the primary economic beneficiary of such programs is often perceived to be state government. The costs associated with unemployment, welfare, incarceration, courts and other negative consequences emanating from maladjusted young people emerging into society are primarily borne by state agencies. Thus, local jurisdictions who invest in youth development programs see that most of the long-term economic savings that accrue from investing in them are captured by the state jurisdiction, which further reduces the incentive for local elected officials to accept the negative consequences likely to be associated with their support of a tax increase.

The Director of PP&R believes the funding problem is exacerbated because the targeted populations who would benefit from these programs have no political influence. He notes that the SAMs (shakers and movers!) in a community can make a call and get something done, but calls from those benefitting from programs like TFKI are likely to have relatively little impact on legislators even if the constituents had the confidence and knowledge to make them. Business associations downtown meet on a regular basis. They are organized, they have money, and they give major contributions and in-kind assistance to political campaigns, so they have influence. The TFKI clientele can offer an emotional appeal, but they are likely to receive only a pittance compared to what the business community is likely to receive for its favored projects. Even within the confines of PP&R's primary constituencies, the sports and athletic associations- -soccer, Little League and so on- -are typically middle class groups, which can organize and be relatively effective, but potential TFKI constituents are not organized. Thus, in the opinion of the PP&R Director, the long term prognosis for permanent on-going funding for such programs in Portland is not encouraging.

Although the TFKI was not extended beyond the three year pilot program period, it was succeeded by another program called Schools Uniting Neighborhoods (SUN). The demonstrated success of TFKI was an influential antecedent and precedent for the more comprehensive SUN initiative. Five elementary and three middle schools were designated SUN schools with a mission "to integrate the delivery of quality education with whatever health, social services, recreational activities and community involvement that is required in a community." Again, however, there is no long term commitment to funding since it does not come from the general fund or a designated revenue stream but relies primarily on foundation, state and federal grant programs; SUN operates in a limited number of schools; and it serves a relatively small number of people in the context of Portland's total population of 600,000.

SUN is a more ambitious program than the TFKI in that it embraces much more than after-school programs and seeks to respond to the needs of children, their parents and the community. SUN schools strive to be a hub in a community. They are modeled after national full-service schools. They are open before and after school, weekends, and during the summer. They partner with a non-profit agency at each site. Together they have a site manager to build, support and coordinate the network of services offered. Site advisory committees assure that community input guides development. Each SUN school looks different because it is tailored to the needs of its local neighborhood community. Examples of the types of services found in SUN schools are: homework help and tutoring; recreation and enrichment activities, such as art, cultural events and sports; health care, mental health and social services; parent and family involvement activities and skill building; adult education classes; and intergenerational and senior activities.

Sources

Mr. Charles Jordan, Director, Portland Parks and Recreation

Ms. Lisa Thomas Turpel, CTRS/CPRP, Recreation Manager, Portland Parks and Recreation

"Portland Parks and Recreation Out-of-School Hours Youth Pilot Program" Portland Parks and Recreation, February 5, 1998.

"An Evaluation of the Portland Parks and Recreation Time for KIDS Initiative. Final Report." Prepared by The Planning Group, Portland, Oregon with Forethought: Thinking for Success, Philadelphia, Pennsylvania. August, 2000.

Shelley Kowalski. "Schools Uniting Neighborhoods: Baseline Report"

Multnomah County Evaluation Research Unit, 2001.

Katie Swartz. Oregon Mentoring Institute. ormentoring@hotmail.com

Northwest Regional Education Laboratory. www.nwrel.org

The Mentoring Partnership. www.mentoring.org

CHAPTER 15

CONCORD/BAY POINT AFTER-SCHOOL LEARNING AND SAFE NEIGBORHOODS PROGRAM

The communities of Concord and Bay Point are both located in the Mt. Diablo Unified School District (MDUSD) which serves over 36,000 students in Contra Costa County, California. At first glance, the two communities appear to be dissimilar. Bay Point is an unincorporated semi-rural community located on the Sacramento River 40 miles upstream from the San Francisco Bay. In contrast, Concord is a city of 122,000 population, but the program described in this case is limited to the city's Monument Corridor area. This is a high density pocket of low income, multiethnic families, with many new arrivals from other countries, all living within a few blocks of Monument Boulevard in Concord.

Although one community may be characterized as "semi-rural" and the other as "inner-city," both have common issues, including poverty, non-English speaking families, crime, teen pregnancy, truancy, and public safety fears. These commonalities and their location in the same school district caused the two communities to collaborate in the development of this program.

The Genesis

The program's genesis was the City of Concord's initial collaboration with MDUSD in the Healthy Start Program. The city engaged in this collaboration to further one of the Council's primary goals which was "neighborhood improvement and youth education and enrichment activities." As a collaborative partner in the Healthy Start Program, the city established after-school programs at Cambridge and Meadow Homes Elementary Schools, which both served high density and culturally diverse neighborhoods. The objective of the after-school program was to provide supervised youth activities at each school and achieve measurable improvement in skills that promoted positive behavior. Working closely with administrators and teachers at each school, the city and the district measured the academic performance of the students involved in the after-school program by evaluating classroom homework logs, physical fitness scores and attendance records.

The results generated by the program showed that participating students were achieving measurable improvement. However, funding constraints limited the participation of students to approximately 200 students. The programs were limited to 3 days a week until 5 p.m. They were each staffed with a site coordinator, 4 teachers and 4-5 Concord Leisure Services (CLS) Department assistants. The teachers taught literacy, math and other academic and education activities, while CLS provided programs and staff for enrichment and recreation. The maximum enrollment of 100 students per school for each six-week sequence filled up in one day, and waiting lists of up to 100 students were generated within 24 hours of the announcement dates. In order to expand and enhance the program in a manner that could involve more students and increase the performance standards, the district and the city needed to identify additional funding sources and revise the program model.

In 1998, the California Legislature and United States Congress enacted legislation intended to increase the level of organized after-school programs available through local communities. The legislation resulted in the availability of grants administered by both the State and Federal Departments of Education. The grant program is termed "The 21st Century After-School Community Learning Centers" fund. Its stated purpose is "To provide enrichment, academic, and support service in a safe environment for children and their families through collaborative partnerships." Grant funds are targeted at low income areas within school districts. In Concord, both of the existing elementary school sites qualified, as did a third site, Ygnacio Valley Elementary School.

All four schools within the neighboring community of Bay Point (three elementary and one middle school) were also eligible for the grants. Thus, a collaborative group led by the School District, City of Concord, Ambrose Park and Recreation District (serving the Bay Point community) and the Contra Costa County Employment and Human Services Department completed the grant applications based on the need to expand and enhance the programs that had been implemented at the Concord schools. They were successful in receiving a three-year renewable grant from the state and federal programs which provided most of the $1.5 million annually it needed to serve approximately 800 students in the program.

Goals

The program has five goals which are listed in Exhibit 15-1. The exhibit also shows the specific objectives which operationalized these goals, and the assignment of responsibilities for attaining them. The seven schools had an aggregated enrollment of 4,700 students and approximately 800 students were served by this program at the seven sites. Students in these schools scored substantially below average on California's STAR testing system and experienced high levels of truancy. Each after-school program operates for three to four hours a day, five days a week, throughout the school year and summer session. The array of programs is shown in Exhibit 15-2.

The highest priority for participation was given to students who met the following criteria (not listed in priority order):

- Testing results in the 40th percentile and lower on the California Standard Testing and Report (STAR) scores in reading, math or English language
- Identified as "high need"
- Teacher recommendation
- Previous enrollment in the program
- Parent participation in Adult Education classes
- School referral from a Student Study Team or Family Study Team

Exhibit 15-1

PROGRAM GOALS AND OBJECTIVES

1. Participating students will increase their reading, writing and math skills to levels consistent with national and district averages.
   - By June 2001, for each year of participation in the ASP, at-risk students will increase their reading, writing and math proficiency to at least grade level or by at least 1.25 academic years. *MDUSD and school site staff have primary responsibility, but all partners will participate.*
   - By June 2000, participating students will complete and turn in at least 90% of all homework assignments during the year, as measured by classroom logs. *All partners working with students at the school sites.*

2. Participating students will develop critical thinking skills and participate in enriched learning experiences.
   - By June 2001, students who have participated in the program for at least one year will have completed at least one enrichment activity and will have enrolled in at least one additional enrichment activity. *Recreation/Leisure Service Agencies, school site staff.*
   - By June 2001, students who have participated in enrichment activities will report an increase in their understanding of the field in which the activity occurs, (e.g., music, visual arts), as measured by a survey instrument. *Recreation/Leisure Service Agencies, school site staff, External Evaluator.*

3. Participating students will increase their physical fitness and teamwork skills through recreational and related activities.
   - By June 2000, participating students will develop a sense of team play, sportsmanship and social skills through participation in intramural activities demonstrated by at least a 50% decrease in the number of adult interventions required per activity. *Recreation/Leisure Service Agencies, school site staff.*

4. Students will increase their life skills, including self-esteem, conflict resolution and respect for others and property.
   - By June 2001, school attendance for students who have participated in the program for at least one year will improve at least 20%. *MDUSD, site staff, counseling/life skill partners.*
   - By June 2000, the number of suspensions and expulsions for students who have participated in the program for at least one year will decrease by at least 10%. *MDUSD, site staff, counseling/life skill partners.*
   - By June 2002, crime statistics for crimes committed by juveniles during the hours of 3:00-6:00 p.m. will decrease by at least 15% based on statistics prepared by Concord Police Department and Contra Costa County Sheriff Department and by community business surveys. *MDUSD, site staff, counseling/life skill partners.*

5. The centers will become the focus of community learning and related adult and family service activities for the surrounding communities.
   - By June 2000, training for staff, volunteers and parents will be implemented at the centers, and at least 25 CalWorks participants, parents and other community members will have completed the training and begun working at the centers. *MDUSD Adult Education, CalWorks, community based agencies.*
   - By June 2001, each center will provide a variety of training and learning opportunities for community members, and at least 30 adults will have completed at least one course at each center. *MDUSD Adult Education.*
   - By June 2000, at least 15 families will meet with Family Resource Workers at each center, and at least 75% of these families will receive referrals to other community services, as measured by visitations and referral logs. *Family Resource Workers, referral agencies.*

Exhibit 15-2

The Programs Included in the After-School Programs

- Homework Club
- Reading and Math Tutorial
- Interest-based Classes
- Sports and Games
- Cooking
- Dance
- Drama
- Arts & Crafts
- Music
- Science
- Gardening
- Expanded Learning Opportunities
- Jr. Achievement Activities
- Violence Prevention Curriculum
- Teambuilding
- Conflict Mediation
- Counseling
- Parent Education/Service
- Family Nights/Events

- Positive behavior during the regular school day
- Parent request
- Open enrollment

It was required that the after-school program student population be reflective of the regular school day student population. Program managers made every effort to ensure that student participants were a heterogeneous group that was equally representative of all grade levels. They were also instructed to take into consideration the siblings of students being referred.

In cases where student interest exceeded program capacity, a wait list was maintained. As space became available, students on the wait list were considered for enrollment and program managers contacted the home to see if the student was still interested in attending the program.

Organization

The lead partners in the collaboration were MDUSD, CLS and Ambrose Park and Recreation District (PARD) which served the Bay Point Community. CLS served in a mentoring capacity for the Ambrose PARD in the first year of the program. Thus, CLS operated the Bay Point sites for the first year while preparing Ambrose staff through joint program planning, implementation and evaluation processes. Ambrose PARD assumed full operation in the second year. The detailed formal contract agreement between the parties required MDUSD to provide 17% of the total staff comprised of:

- An After-School Administrator
- 7 Site Teacher Leaders - - one at each site. These individuals were the site managers. They were full-time, credentialed teachers who work with the recreation staff to conduct the academic enrichment and recreation activities, set behavior standards, and report data necessary to evaluate the outcomes.
- Interest Class Teachers and Resource Persons

- Homework Help Teachers
- Tutoring/Intervention Teachers

CLS and Ambrose PARD provided 83% of the total staff comprised of:

- 2 Recreational Supervisors/Coordinators (one for Bay Point and one for Concord)
- 8 Recreational Specialists at each site (7 adults, 1 teen). They are selected to reflect the demographics of the surrounding school community, including racial and ethnic backgrounds and income levels; approximately 50% of them are Cal-Works participants.

The three lead collaborators developed job descriptions which identified the specific roles and responsibilities associated with all of these part-time positions, together with a Staff Manual given to each employee and a Parent Handbook given to each parent. The number of staff was designed to maintain a student to staff ratio of 20 to 1.

In addition to the three lead collaborators, 10 other organizations and agencies were involved in developing the program and committing resources to it.

Contra Costa County Employment and Human Services Department provided the employment and training services associated with the Cal-Works Program (Welfare to Work) for the part-time staff employed in the program and assisted in the coordination of the Steering and Advisory Committees. It also agreed to underwrite the costs of eligible children of Cal-Works participants who were in the program. In the first year, 15% of all staff/students were Cal-Works participants.

Concord Police Department provided drug and violence prevention education and conducted safety assessments for the Concord sites.

Contra Costa County Sheriff's Office provided drug and violence prevention education and conducted safety assessments for the Bay Point sites.

Kaiser-Permanente Community Health Partnerships provided staff training in classroom management and discipline techniques.

John Muir/Mt. Diablo Health System provided health care education and referral resources.

Diablo Valley College provided student volunteers for the tutorial and homework assistance activities.

Concord Healthy Start provided resource teachers who assisted parents in addressing family and personal issues.

Teenage Assistance Program provided volunteers to train and support the part-time Recreation Specialists.

Bay Area Junior Achievement supplied a civic/community/career development curriculum as part of the enrichment component.

Chapman College provided volunteers for the tutorial and homework components and training for Teachers/Leaders interested in pursuing a school administrator career path.

These organizations and agencies, together with individual volunteers provided:

- enrichment and educational services;
- resources and materials directly to students either one-to-one or in small groups
- staffing and volunteer pools;
- linkages to outside resources and services for students and their families, during and after school hours; and
- ongoing partnerships and services between the school, families and the community.

Performance Measures

The City of Concord uses a Performance Based Budget which requires city management staff to establish goals and objectives for each program and evaluate the outcomes against these measurable goals. Exhibit 15-3 offers illustrations of the type of Performance Indicators used in the CLS budget process. An overall program objective is specified. Performance Indicators are the measures that will be used to ascertain if the Program Objective has been met. The "Target Percent" column relates to the desired objective the program seeks to attain, while the "Actual Percent" column shows what the measures reported was actually achieved.

CLS managers sought to measure both the program's efficiency and its effectiveness. The effectiveness measures selected were the students' academic performance and changes in student behavior and attitudes. An independent consultant was selected to undertake both these effectiveness measures.

Academic performance outcomes were measured by comparing changes in California Standard Testing and Report (STAR) scores in reading, math and English language from the previous school year to the current school year.

School attendance outcomes were measured by comparing the change in student absences as a percentage of days enrolled for the previous and current school years.

For both these measures, students enrolled in the after-school program (ASP group) are compared to a matched group of non-ASP students (match group). Students in the match group were selected on the basis of having five demographic dimensions matched as closely as possible with those of ASP students. These dimensions were race/ethnicity, sex, grade level, school attended, and previous year's average STAR test score.

Changes in student behavior and attitudes were measured by response data collected through surveys administered to parents and ASP students, interviews with school administrators and staff, and an ASP Teacher Leader focus group. The specific sources of data collected were:

- Individual interviews with representatives of Concord Leisure Services and Ambrose Recreation and Parks, two key collaborating community agencies in the ASP.
- Individual interviews with school principals of each of seven ASP sites.
- Individual interviews with head custodians at each of seven ASP sites.

Exhibit 15-3

Illustrative Performance Indicators Used to Evaluate the Project

Program Objective	Performance Indicator	Target Percent who Achieved the Objective	Actual Percent who Achieved the Objective
Provide supervised program activities for elementary age youth in targeted neighborhoods and achieve measurable improvements in skills which promote positive behavior in 50% of participants.	1. Percent of After-School participants who improve or maintain their school attendance	50%	52%
	2. Percentage increase in After-School participants in their State Standardized achievement test scores for Reading, Math and Language	50%	62%
	3. Percent of children and parents who rate the program good or excellent	80%	84%
(Number in After-School program = 460)	4. Number and percent of students with improved physical fitness as evaluated by the Presidential Fitness Test	50%	93%
	5. Number and percent of students completing homework assignments as measured by classroom logs	50%	92%

* The indicators are based on those used by Concord Leisure Services as part of their budget process, but have been adapted here for illustrative purposes. The authors have omitted and changed some details in order to facilitate an easier understanding of the general process that was used.

- An ASP teacher leader focus group attended by teacher leaders of each of seven ASP sites.
- A parent satisfaction survey instrument (in both English and Spanish) mailed to 730 families of students enrolled in the ASP, with a survey response rate of 18.6% (136 families).
- A survey instrument administered to elementary and middle school students enrolled in the ASP. A total of 248 students responded to the survey.
- A survey instrument administered to teachers of interest classes in the ASP. Nineteen teachers responded to the survey.

Evaluation Results

In terms of Academic Performance prior to the initiation of the program, a significant gap existed between the ASP students and the match group based on STAR test results. Following the initiation of the program, the ASP students achieved near parity in test scores for two out of the three subjects after one-year participation. The points below illustrate the results:

- The point spread prior to the program in reading rank between the ASP group and the match group was <u>three</u> points. After a year of the program, the point spread was also <u>three</u> points.

- The prior point spread in math rank between the ASP and the match group was four points. The post program point spread decreased to one point.
- The prior point spread in language rank between the ASP group and the match group was six points. The post program point spread decreased to two points.

Thus, the academic performance objective at the end of the first year was evaluated as having been achieved since two of the three areas showed significant improvement for the ASP group. However, there were no further gains in these scores in the second year of the program, which caused the partners to search for reasons accounting for this. A primary reason was attributed to staff turnover due (i) to burn-out caused by the great demands placed on them by the program; and (ii) the difficulty of recruiting, training and retaining people to the recreation staff positions because of low pay and inconvenient work schedules.

The comparison of *average attendance* rates of ASP and match group students revealed there were no significant differences between them in terms of excused absences, unexcused absences, or truancy rates. In the second year, ASP participants improved their attendance by 5.5% relative to the match group. The evaluators suggested that a better performance indicator in the future would be to focus only on those students who had the highest absence rates since they are most at-risk of doing poorly in school.

The measures of students' *behavior and attitude* revealed:

- 90% of the students and parents evaluated the program as good or excellent and felt it was a valuable experience.
- While academic performance measures focused on reading, language and math, students enjoyed these classes the least, and preferred enrichment classes, recreation activities and sports more. Parents were more interested in their child's participation in academic subjects than in the enrichment curriculum.
- Students and parents felt that the program was respectful of them and their cultures, although students felt less strongly than their parents did that the program taught them about other cultures.
- Students and parents felt that the program provided a safe place for students. However, many students still worried about their safety going home from the program.

Three measures were used to assess efficiency. The total number of participant hours (number of participants multiplied by the number of activity hours) was 162,666. Units per hour (number of participants engaged in the program for each staff work hour) were 13.8. The unit cost (cost to provide the service to each participant) was 61 cents. These provided baseline measures against which the program's efficiency in future years could be assessed. However, they compared favorably with similar efficiency measures which CLS reported for its other programs.

Lessons Learned

The major lesson learned was the importance of having well qualified, enthusiastic staff in leadership roles on the sites. Despite the tireless work of a few School District employees, many site teachers did not support the program with their time and resources. To fill this void, part-time recreation staff were assigned to lead academic and enrichment activities. Unfortunately, however, while expectations and responsibilities of these recreation staff have increased, their compensation has not increased. Four strategies were suggested by CLS to address this inequity:

- Continue the teacher-leader position.
- Establish a "para-professional" lead recreation specialist position who would act as a "co-director" of each site by leading assigned academic and enrichment activities, supervising/training the recreation specialists and resolving facility issues. Qualifications for this position should include an undergraduate degree or an acceptable level of experience as a substitute; compensation of $18 - $20 per hour as a permanent part-time employee with retirement benefits should be considered.
- Establish higher standards for the recreation specialists and develop additional training programs to enhance their ability to utilize educational resources for the academic and enrichment components of the program. Compensation for the specialists of $10 - $12 per hour should be considered.
- Continue to be flexible in the assignment of responsibilities, filling of teacher-leader positions and development of programs at each site.

It was noted in the evaluation discussion that the lack of a uniformly well-trained, enthusiastic staff was perceived to explain why the academic goals of the program did not progress in the second year. A key recommendation in the consultant's second year evaluation report was "Ensure that recreation specialists and teacher-leaders have ongoing training in how to provide enriched learning experiences to develop the critical thinking skills of participating students. Such experiences should include classes in science, social studies, computing, art, and music and field trips in an effort to promote academic achievement and appreciation for learning." The existing part-time recreation staff were being expected to fulfill this role without being equipped to do it.

Source

Mark G. Deven, Director of Leisure Services, City of Concord, California.

CHAPTER 16

SAN ANTONIO'S AFTER-SCHOOL CHALLENGE PROGRAM

This case study discusses the issues involved in developing and maintaining a large-scale, citywide after-school program. It offers a good model of how a city and several school districts can achieve their complementary goals by working together to deliver quality after-school programs. Within the San Antonio city boundaries, there are 251 elementary and middle schools which are under the jurisdiction of ten different independent school districts. Only ten of these schools currently do not offer some type of after-school program, and most of these are middle schools. The city council's goal is that an after-school program be available at every elementary and middle school in the city.

At 155 of these sites (118 elementary and 37 middle schools), the San Antonio PARD cooperates with eight school districts to offer the After-School Challenge Program (ASCP). The program is scheduled for three hours per day, five days per week, and is free to participants. Future expansion of the program is likely to include extending it through school vacation periods.

The 86 schools offering after-school programs that are not supported through ASCP funds, operate either from grants or through partnerships with others such as the YMCA or YWCA. If additional ASCP funding becomes available, the sites without programs and those reliant on grants or tenuous partnerships could be incorporated.

ASCP was originally initiated at three middle school sites when PARD and elected officials saw a need to provide after-school activities for children not being served at one of the city's 27 community recreation centers. Officials approached the San Antonio Independent School District (SAISD). SAISD welcomed the opportunity to host programs since it was also considering developing after-school educational opportunities to help academically struggling students and those seeking additional opportunities for reading, math, science, and physical fitness.

From the beginning, two local community advocacy organizations, COPS (Communities Organized for Public Service) and the Metro Alliance, supported the program by organizing volunteers at the schools, getting parents involved, and vociferously advocating the program before City Council during the budget process. The successful collaboration of the City, SAISD and these community organizations, resulted in the program steadily growing each year and expanding to include an additional seven of the other nine school districts in the city. Both the PARD and the school districts contribute resources, and by pooling them they are able to provide a service that would be too costly for either entity to deliver alone.

The purpose of ASCP is to provide children with homework assistance and tutoring in a safe environment, together with the opportunity to participate in recreation activities and enhance their social interaction skills. The objectives of the program are to:

- enhance social skills by encouraging children to interact with their peers rather than going home to an empty house;
- improve their grades through tutoring and enrichment activities; and
- develop physical fitness skills and habits, through participation in recreation activities.

Enabling children to remain in a safe, nurturing environment after school gives parents peace of mind. ASCP's policy has been to operate the program from the first to the last day of school, so as to provide working parents with a consistent, reliable service. This facilitates employment retention, the pursuit of career opportunities, and perhaps greater productivity in their jobs.ASCP has been identified as a focus area in the city's Better Jobs Initiative (BJI). The City of San Antonio developed the BJI to provide training and education that would improve the employability of youth and develop a more skilled work force. The initiative includes efforts to strengthen education processes and outcomes from early childhood through high school education. After-school programs are perceived to be a vehicle for accomplishing this goal. Elected officials in San Antonio have consistently supported after-school opportunities that provide positive social interaction and learning environments as well as contribute to lower rates of delinquency, teen parenthood and substance abuse.

Program Design

The school districts identify schools that would like to be involved. Campus administrators at each site tailor programming to the campus's needs based on input from teachers, students and parents. The program must include the core elements of homework assistance, recreational activities, activities that promote social skills and a snack, but may also include music, dance, drama, computers, arts and crafts and a myriad of other activities. Program spaces vary depending on the amenities available at each campus, but are likely to include gymnasiums, cafeterias, libraries, computer labs, art rooms, playgrounds and classrooms.

Through the organizing efforts of COPS and the Metro Alliance, more parents have become involved in their children's schools. They participate in the process of designing curricula and volunteer at the sites their children attend. This has led to more parent participation in the overall educational process. Exhibits 16-1 and 16-2 provide examples of after-school programs at an elementary and a middle school site.

Exhibit 16-1

Pecan Valley Elementary's After-School Challenge Program

At Pecan Valley Elementary, the After-School Challenge Program (PVASCP) operates out of the gymnasium. Different centers are set-up throughout the gym and participants visit each center on a rotating basis. The participants attend all the activity centers every day. The program has an average daily attendance of approximately 120 students.

The Quiet Time/Reading Center is set up on a blanket in the corner. Here students enjoy quiet time to read books or rest until they go to the next station. The Strategic Games area has games like Battleship and Connect Four to help children develop strategies and learn problem solving and analysis skills. At the Chill Time center, participants quietly talk to each other and to the instructor about anything: the weather, other friends, what happened at school that day, vacation plans, etc. The Building Center offers a variety of building manipulatives including blocks, Legos, Don't Break the Ice and Jenga. These activities are designed to help participants increase mobile skills, experiment with balance and understand sizes and shapes. At the Homework Center teachers help children finish homework and practice academic skills with flash cards or other materials. Finally, there is a Crafts Center that offers a different craft project each day. Some projects may be worked on over the course of several days. Coloring books and crayons are also available.

In addition to the daily centers, PVASCP offers some special activities, usually on a weekly basis. These include arts and crafts projects such as painting or holiday theme projects. There are visits to the computer lab where participants play educational games such as math or spelling. No internet use is allowed. Also, participants enjoy trips to the game room where games like Mancala, Chutes & Ladders, and Candyland can be found. This program has also developed a garden that students are responsible for taking care of with assistance from staff.

PVASCP staff plan family days strictly for program participants and their families. The staff have been able to solicit donations for hotdogs and other snacks for the families. In addition, the staff plan a variety of family games and entertainment for everyone to enjoy. The family days are sometimes focused around holidays such as Cinco de Mayo. These family days help encourage parent participation and have been well attended.

The PTA helped the PVASCP by purchasing radios to aid staff communication for sign-out and picking up participants.

The staff is comprised mostly of professionals who plan the program and they seem to enjoy working with the participants. The staff includes a coach, a special education assistant, and other members with complementary skills. The diversity of skills among the staff is one of the reasons the program has been successful at this site.

Exhibit 16-2

Cooper Middle School's After-School Challenge Program

Cooper Middle School operates like most other programs with time for homework, socialization, snack and recreational activities. But that's where the similarities end. Staff members at Cooper have created an environment that encourages individual expression. On average 63 students attend the program each day.

One staff member, who is a paraprofessional teacher's aid and substitute, is a talented artist. He teaches students about different art media, including water colors and tempra paints. The students participate in a number of art projects including sketching, painting and some cartooning. When a participant is having a "bad day," his or her artwork can be used to express those feelings in a positive manner. Participants put on an art show in October to exhibit some of the work they have created.

The students have a talent show at the end of the spring semester. Talents include singing, dancing, cheers and gymnastics, rapping, juggling, etc. The participants work with each other and with staff to prepare their routines for the show. The staff involves students in designing and creating the show's backdrops and props. Considerable drawing, painting, glitter, cutting, fastening, etc. goes into this project. Students from nearby Barkley Elementary are invited to the show as participants and spectators.

Another staff member shares her talents in creating crafts. She has taught the students to make needlepoint crafts, bookmarks and friendship bracelets. She lets participants tell her what they want to create and works to get additional supplies as needed.

The program facilitator teaches dance. Participants learn a variety of dances, including 50/60s dances, technodance, salsa, cumbia, and line dancing. The dance instructor discusses costumes and appropriate dress. One participant commented that when she went to a party, she knew how to dance cumbia when others did not. She wondered where other kids learn to dance if they do not have someone to teach them.

Cooper Middle School offers athletics and a chess club to students separate from the ASCP. Participants from these programs often join ASCP when the other activities have concluded. The staff at Cooper Middle School's ASCP have been counselors, mothers, fathers, and friends. They are a reliable and consistent presence in the lives of participants in the program. Some kids don't want to go home because of situations in their own lives, so they stay at Challenge as long as they can.

Each school recommends teachers and para-professionals from its site whom PARD hires as instructors. This means that staff have an investment in respecting the equipment and facilities used at the site, and are familiar with the students' needs and interests. Similarly, students are familiar with these adults and are likely to feel comfortable interacting with them. These staff members are able to provide informed assistance with homework, since they are likely to have strong links with other teachers in the school. Staff members are required to plan activities in advance and provide a weekly schedule of activities to their area supervisor. The 20 Area Supervisors provide program staff with assistance in program development and monitor site activities.

Approximately 28,600 students are registered in the program, with an average of 17,700 attending daily, an average of 114 participants per site. ASCP maintains a student-teacher ratio of approximately 25 to 1. A pilot program operating at 17 sites currently is evaluating the impact of reducing this ratio to 15 to 1. Survey results from parents, students and staff have shown slightly higher satisfaction with ASCP at these sites than the others. Staff who previously worked at sites with a 25:1 ratio and now work at those with a 15:1 ratio report that there is a difference in the amount of attention they give to each participant.

Employing parents and college students helps reduce staff burn-out. Staff members are able to work flexible times when more staff are available. Parents and college students are trained with other staff, and are included in the 1:25 staff to student ratio. Parents are able to learn more about campus activities, while college students gain hands-on training to prepare them for their future roles in the labor force.

To enrich the program, ASCP hires mural artists, musicians and dance instructors, who rotate among sites that do not have access to these resources. However, limited budget resources means that not all sites receive an enrichment instructor. Some schools have used funds from the Federal 21st Century Community Learning Center program to provide enrichment staff who offer such programs as dance, music, fine arts, specialty sports (badminton, ping pong, etc.), puppetry, conflict resolution and photography.

ACSP has collaborative relationships with multiple organizations, including the Bienestar Program (in which participating health clubs focus on diabetes prevention among elementary students); Y-teens (YMCA program focusing on middle school youth development); San Antonio Fighting Back (a grass roots program developed to reduce crime and violence by reducing substance abuse); State of Texas 78207 Grant (a Community Youth Development Program providing mentoring, recreation and family support); San Antonio Youth Literacy Program (which recruits volunteers to tutor children in reading in order to increase reading skills and literacy rates); Girl Scouts (with Americorps volunteer leaders); Alamo Area Boy Scouts (provides programs that build character, teach citizenship and encourage physical fitness); and Urban smARTS (a city funded after-school arts enrichment program). The YMCA, Bethel Childcare Center, Inc., Madonna Neighborhood Center and Positive Beginnings, Inc., take full responsibility for ASCP at ten of the school sites.

Several other mechanisms have been used to incorporate enrichment activities into a given program. For example, if one of the teachers has art skills, additional supplies may be provided so that teacher can offer more fine art activities. ASCP has used an art teacher who is on staff at one school to travel to a neighboring school one day a week to conduct art projects. In another case, one site had Mariachi guitars, while another site had a guitar instructor. Arrangements were made for the instructor to travel to the campus with the guitars to teach participants and then transport the guitars back to the instructor's home campus to teach participants there.

Middle Schools

Middle school programs focus on positive socialization, constructive competition and academic achievement. In contrast to the elementary schools, it has been difficult to attract and to retain students at the middle school sites. Efforts have been made to create clubs which offer different activities (e.g., chess club, ping-pong club, choir club). Clubs are offered for a specified length of time (e.g., monthly, or the 9-week grading period) and students are free to participate in whichever offerings they wish. Finding staff, who are able and willing to share their talents and interests with participants in these clubs, is a challenge. Thus, area college students have been recruited to work at some of the sites and to participate in the "Do It" Program (a volunteer program that provides mentors to program participants).

ASCP received a grant from Mervyn's Department Store in San Antonio to create more community awareness of the middle school program. As a result, "El Dia de la Familia," which were one-time promotional events were offered at six middle school sites. Each school offered a variety of entertainment for participants and parents, and provided information about the after-school program. Local businesses donated supplies for the program and the promotional event. The events were successful in raising awareness of the program; however, they require additional funding and a significant amount of planning and coordination, which makes their on-going use problematic.

Several other promotional approaches to attract middle school students have been tried. Flyers and registration forms have been passed out during school and a pizza party held for all who return a signed registration form by a given day. Door prizes have been awarded to participants during the first weeks of the program to encourage them to enroll. School staff encourage registration and participation, and they periodically stop by the program to observe which students are attending. Some campuses offer students the option of getting involved in ASCP in lieu of detention. This opportunity is only offered once, but does give additional exposure to the program.

At one time, ASCP served six high schools, but these programs have been discontinued due to lack of participation. High school students have other extracurricular activities in which to participate, and they have access to cars that enable them to attend other activities away from school.

Self-Monitoring Standards

In accordance with Texas state childcare laws, ASCP has developed Self-Monitoring Standards to ensure quality programming. These standards address such areas as staff training, program planning and implementation, participant to staff ratios and health and safety measures. The standards were developed in lieu of complying with Texas Child Protective and Regulatory Service childcare facility license requirements. Texas law allows PARDs to develop their own standards and have them approved by the City Council as minimum standards for program operation. Representatives from the PARD are responsible to the City Council for quarterly and annual evaluations of program sites to ensure compliance with the standards. Standards have been developed in the following areas:

- Governing body responsibilities.
- Notifications of program changes between partners and program issues within program management.
- Posting requirements (e.g., notices, standards, emergency evacuation, contact phone numbers).
- Enrollment information and other records (file information to be maintained for each participant).
- Communication with parents.
- Staff qualifications.
- Program staff responsibilities (director, program coordinator, area supervisor, site supervisor, program staff).
- Staff Training (including safety, health, fire safety, emergency precautions, injury and illness).
- Monitoring of compliance with standards and enforcement.

Staff Training

The training budget is approximately $50,000 per year. This provides instructors and pays training fees, but does not include the cost of paying staff salaries to attend training. ASCP is currently seeking a grant to cover the cost of staff salaries for training hours. ASCP offers in-house training, but supplements this by partnering with other agencies. Exhibit 16-3 provides examples of staff and supervisor training opportunities that are offered. In addition, staff can earn credits towards their eight hours of required training by attending training sessions offered by individual school districts when the training subject matter applies to ASCP. San Antonio's Department of Community Initiatives provides most of the training through a Federal childcare development grant. Training covers such topics as conflict resolution, nutrition, safety, curriculum planning, customer service, risk management, recognition of child abuse, neglect and sexual abuse, cultural diversity, CPR and First Aid, life skills and age appropriate activities. Training materials are available from several sources including: http://www.afterschoolalliance.com/, http://www.wellesley.edu/WCW/CRW/SAC/, and http://www.nsaca.org/.

Exhibit 16-3

Staff Training

ASCP holds an annual staff development conference. The topics at a recent conference included:

- Facilitating activities
- Thematic planning: (assistance in planning activities involving the children's suggestions)
- Communication with parents, school employers and co-workers (tips on communicating with everyone from children to principals)
- Clubs for middle school (development of clubs of interest for middle school children)
- Dealing with violence in children's lives (development of caregiver skills to help children cope with the violence they are confronted with in their daily lives)
- Behavior management for special needs (help caregivers improve communication and behavior management skills when working with special needs children)

An annual site director's symposium is held to promote professional development. A number of organizations sponsor the effort, including the San Antonio Department of Community Initiatives, Family Service Association, San Antonio Association for the Education of Youth and Children, and Texas Department of Protective and Regulatory Services. Recent workshops have included:

- Problem solving and techniques to improve participant's ability to manage stress
- Excellence in customer service
- The role of the director in building and supporting community
- Team building through successful staff meetings
- Developing a caring employee
- Staff evaluation
- Staff motivation

Funding

The City of San Antonio pays for two teachers at each site from the General Fund, while the school districts pay for one teacher. For sites that have more than 75 participants, the city provides the additional staff needed to stay within the 25:1 ratio. Recreation supplies (such as table games and recreational sports equipment) for the program also are paid for out of the city's General Fund. The city currently allocates over $4.2 million to the program, with $3.6 million funding 1,011 part-time staff, and the remainder being used to fund seven full-time administrative positions, supplies, mileage, insurance and other costs. Snacks are paid for through United States Department of Agriculture grants (approximately $500,000), which are available to the school districts. At the two sites that do not qualify for these funds, the snack costs are paid out of the city's General Fund. In the most recent budget year, the school districts contributed $1.75 million to fund one staff member at each site. In addition, the school districts provide in-kind services in the form of utilities, facility maintenance, and custodial services and supplies.

A proposition to establish a 1/8-cent sale tax in San Antonio will be voted on in a future referendum. The estimated $15 million generated will be used to fund a variety of initiatives, including early childhood development programs, and ASCP could potentially be considered for a portion of this funding.

Funding for the program reflects a commitment on the part of the City Council to provide the city's children with safe havens each day after school throughout the school year. As the city goes through the yearly budget process, the Council prioritize programs and allocate funding for them. This is challenging especially in economic downturns. For example, one year when the city was faced with a $13 million deficit, all departments were asked to identify priority areas for service reductions. Because, youth and public safety were key priorities for the council, ASCP funding was ranked as a high priority and not considered as a primary area when reductions in the PARD budget were identified.

During the first year of the program all staff members were volunteers, but for the program to expand and achieve higher quality, paid staff had to be hired. Pay for most positions was $10.00 per hour. To attract and retain staff, the Metro Alliance lobbied the city to pay higher pay rates for professionals. As a consequence, the city pays certified teachers, counselors, librarians or other ISD professionals $11.50 per hour while, para-professionals (classroom aides, secretaries, cafeteria attendants and other district employees) receive $10.00 per hour; and non-district employees (parents, college students, etc.) $9.00 per hour. The districts pay employees based on their standard hourly rate, which is usually $18.00 - $25.00 per hour plus any benefits required. San Antonio instituted a livable wage policy that requires all salaries must exceed its minimum requirement of $8.50 per hour.

Program Outcomes

There have been recent decreases in the city's juvenile crime and juvenile victims numbers. While no one program or policy can be cited as the sole cause of this, there is widespread belief that ASCP has been a contributing factor. In addition, program providers feel that children are learning recreation skills that improve their physical fitness, and that enrichment activities and homework assistance is leading to improved grades. Children also appear to be interacting better with others, suggesting there has been improvement in their pro-social skills.

The data that have been collected have been confined to output measures (e.g., percent of school days ASCP operates; per site average attendance; percent of eligible children regularly participating in ASCP) and satisfaction measures (e.g., percent of ASCP parents satisfied with the program). The PARD annually surveys participants, parents and staff separately to determine their satisfaction and solicit suggestions for program improvements. This is a comprehensive exercise. During a typical school year, 13,699 surveys (9,279 participants, 3,894 parents, and 496 staff) are completed and analyzed. Survey results showed a high level of satisfaction (over 82%-98% responded "agree" or "strongly agree" on individual items) for both program inputs (provision of a safe environment, staff, variety of activities provided, children encouraged to attend school, and academic assistance provided), and achievement of desired outcomes (grades have improved, school attendance has been improved, social skills have increased, and behavior has been improved).

In addition, focus groups are held with ASCP staff at each school midway through the program year to discuss suggestions for improvements, increasing participation, promotion ideas, etc. In general, school staff are supportive of the program. Outcome measures have been difficult to obtain. Parents report that their children's grades and standardized test scores have increased as a result of the program, but this is only a surrogate proxy measure used in lieu of measures of changes based on school record data. The percentage of eligible children regularly participating in the program who improve their grades would be a useful outcome measures if the program was permitted to track grades of program participants. However, because of confidentiality concerns, school districts have not been willing to release these data.

Lessons Learned

Partnering is essential to the success of this type of after-school program. Each partner brings to the table what it does best and its own resources. In the current case, the school districts provide the sites and recommend teachers to be hired; teachers, parents and administrators select the curricula; the PARD provides the recreational component; and funding is provided from the City of San Antonio General Fund and the school districts. Partners also contribute monies for training, snacks and other program amenities. Putting a dollar amount on the value of all of these partnerships is difficult, but estimates indicate that ASCP would have to find an additional $750,000 to fund all the different elements that partners currently bring to the program.

Involving the community stakeholders is critical to long-term program sustainability and success. Continued community involvement through planning and feedback increases citizens' awareness and knowledge of the program and provides ASCP with valuable suggestions for program improvements. Citizens' voices resonate with elected officials and their advocacy for program needs invariably carries more weight than staff generated outcome measures. Through meetings with political officials, advocacy groups have the ability to raise the priority of after-school funding. This role is particularly critical in periods of economic downturn when city budgets are tight and ways are sought to cut expenditures.

Evaluating program outcomes is essential but also problematic. Evaluation should be sensitive to the goals various stakeholders hope the program will achieve. In the current educational environment, schools are under pressure to increase standardized test scores and after-school programs are seen as a vehicle for doing so. Until recently, ASCP has only evaluated academic achievement through asking parents and teachers whether they thought their children were improving academically as a result of their participation in the after-school program. While these results are positive, having numeric data about changes in scores on the state mandated achievement tests would be more useful. To conduct a successful analysis of test score changes attributable to after-school program participation, comparing program participants to non-participants at each school is necessary. Analyzing campus-wide changes in scores from one year to the next can be misleading and insufficient. Unfortunately, collecting student ID numbers, gaining parental permission to access scores, and obtaining the resources to analyze and interpret the data are all obstacles to generating test score change data. In the current case, one of the partner school districts recently indicated a willingness to devote the necessary resources to collect and analyze data. Hopefully, this will lead to wider involvement among the districts and the results will demonstrate the academic enhancement value of the program to the school district partners in the program.

A related issue is that if academic enhancement is a component of the after-school program, programs must contain enough academic enrichment content to actually influence academic improvement in the classroom. Simply offering a "fun and games" program designed for participants to have fun and keep them out of trouble will not lead to academic improvement. On the other hand, using the after-school program simply as a means to extend the school day ignores the physical, recreational and social development needs of children. An advantage of the ASCP program is that the schools and PARD are partners in designing and carrying out the program, which makes a balanced approach likely.

Efforts need to be made to create consistency in offerings across sites. While some sites offer a wide variety of activities, other sites have more limited offerings. In recent years, additional training has been available to staff members to assist with generating ideas for activities. ASCP is currently trying to create a curriculum of enrichment, social development and physical activities that could be used program-wide.

Developing program standards is critical, but must be thoughtfully undertaken. Many PARDs have found that state child protective service standards are too restrictive, and inhibit their ability to offer after-school programs. This has led to statutes being enacted that allow cities like San Antonio to develop and administer their own standards for city operated programs. On the other hand, many for-profit after-school program providers must adhere to the state standards which they argue places them at an unfair competitive disadvantage. In San Antonio, this has led to efforts to develop common standards that would apply to all after-school program providers. This may help diffuse for-profit provider concerns that they are required to operate in a more regulated environment, while at the same time enabling PARDs to avoid more cumbersome state regulations. Another possibility is to have programs accredited by the National School-Aged Care Alliance (NSACA), which has the potential to align local programs with accepted best practices at the national level.

Area supervisors are critical to maintaining program oversight, consistency and quality. Currently, each area supervisor has between six and nine sites. The more schools they have, the less time that they can spend at each school to assist with program development and evaluation. Five to six sites per supervisor would be ideal and give maximum opportunities for observation, trouble-shooting and training.

CHAPTER 17

CONTINUOUS EVALUATION:
THE KEY TO DEVELOPING HIGH QUALITY SUMMER YOUTH CAMPS

Background

The Fairfax County Board of Supervisors established the Fairfax County Park Authority (FCPA) in 1950 under the auspices of the state of Virginia's newly created 'Park Authorities Act,' which gave counties the right to establish park authorities to preserve open space, acquire parkland and develop park facilities. The agency has a two-pronged mission to both "set aside public spaces for...the protection and enhancement of environmental values, diversity of natural habitats and cultural heritage" as well as "to create and sustain quality facilities and services that offer citizens opportunities for recreation...physical and mental well-being and enhancement of their quality of life."

FCPA is one of several providers of recreation services in Fairfax County. Because it was created as an authority, the FCPA is quasi-independent from County government administration. A 12-member Park Authority Board appointed by the County Board of Supervisors sets FCPA policy and priorities. The FCPA's Director reports to this board rather than county administration, which also operates a separate Department of Community and Recreation Services (DCRS). Among DCRS' historic responsibilities were the provision of recreational classes, camps and tours in county school facilities, though this responsibility was recently transferred to the FCPA. One incorporated city and three towns located within Fairfax County also provide local recreation services to about 6% of the population residing within the county.

From its humble beginnings when the park system consisted of one 15-acre park, the FCPA has grown to encompass 387 parks containing nearly 21,500 acres of parkland. The majority of the authority's holdings are in stream valley parks and unstaffed neighborhood and community parks. Twenty-six sites are staffed and contain a variety of recreational amenities including historic sites, nature centers, lakes and marinas, campgrounds, a water park, an ice rink, a working farm and equestrian facility, a horticultural center, golf courses, and recreation centers.

Fairfax County has evolved from a sleepy farming community providing dairy products to the nation's capital to the most populous jurisdiction in the Washington, D.C. metropolitan area. Current population is nearly one million. Population growth was dramatic during the last two decades when the county was among the fastest growing communities in the nation. During that time Fairfax evolved a burgeoning technology sector, billing itself as the Silicon Valley of the east. As a result, low unemployment, a rate of two career families that is well above the national average and a median household income that ranks among the highest in the nation characterize the area.

With population growth has come an evolution in how FCPA approaches the recreation service provision aspect of its mission. During most of the first three decades of its existence, the FCPA focused on land acquisition and the provision of outdoor recreation opportunities. This emphasis began to change when the FCPA opened its first indoor recreation center in 1977, initiating its venture into recreation programming. Seven other recreation centers followed this initial 76,000 square foot facility over the next decade. In addition to embracing its outdoor recreation heritage, the FCPA grew to become the county's largest provider of recreational programs as well. A recent quarterly program guide listed approximately 3,700 different recreational program offerings and the authority now enrolls nearly 100,000 registrants annually in a variety of recreational class, camp and tour offerings. An important component of the FCPA's recreational programming is its summer youth camp program (SYCP), which has grown steadily over the years based on the FCPA's ability to continually monitor parent feedback and improve program quality to meet customer needs.

A key aspect of recreation center service provision that differentiates the FCPA from many other service providers is its operational funding structure. Development of recreation centers in Fairfax County has historically been tax supported, but it was decided at the outset that their annual operations must be self-supporting through user fees. Therefore, recreational programming at these facilities is funded entirely within the FCPA's Park Revenue Fund.

Thus, unlike the other cases presented in this book, the goals of the FCPA summer youth camp program were not developed to address youth development and the assets or protective factors models. Rather, the program has been developed to fill the summer daycare needs of two career families who generally desire quality sports and recreational experiences for their children. FCPA's Deputy Director stated: "The camp program design is driven by what we hear from our clients. We want to provide what they are looking for." This case focuses on the FCPA's approach to meeting customer needs and has been included because it offers a good illustration of how a continuous improvement process uses evaluation to revise, expand and improve program delivery.

The Summer Youth Camp Program

A centralized SYCP was launched in 1990. Prior to that time site programmers at individual recreation center locations developed and administered summer camp programs. A centralized position was created in 1990 to manage the entire program and better enable the FCPA to make strategic decisions that would facilitate growth of the program over the long term. The year before a centralized program was created, FCPA summer camp enrollment was approximately 1,800. By 1995, enrollment in the various camps had reached about 4,600 and by 2001 this had increased to over 9,000. Camp program gross revenue grew from $836,000 to nearly $1.8 million between 1995 and 2001; and the program was fully self-sufficient.

Today the SYCP consists of over 100 different camp titles offered at 17 different park locations.

The program consists of camps directly operated by the FCPA and those that are contracted out to other individuals or organizations to operate. The FCPA's traditional camp offerings, which form the core of the customer base, are typically self-operated at FCPA's recreation centers, golf courses, lake parks and other outdoor park sites, and seasonal staff are hired to lead these programs. Over the years, expansion in camp offerings has been achieved largely through contracted-out camps. These typically involve more specialized camp experiences, challenging or advanced activities in a variety of sports, outdoor adventure, and the performing arts. In these cases, FCPA typically negotiates with the contractor that the agency receives 25% - 40% of gross revenues to compensate FCPA for registration, promotion, administration, training and evaluation costs. Camps are run in one and two-week sessions from the time school ends until the end of August.

The SYCP is managed centrally by a Youth Services Coordinator with assistance from program staff at the FCPA's recreation centers. The Youth Services Coordinator is responsible for overall program development, staff training and evaluation, as well as direct administration of contracted-out camps and those held at parks without full-time staff. Recreation center program staff administer camps held at their centers, under the oversight of the Youth Services Coordinator.

Recruitment of frontline camp counselor staff starts in January and all positions are typically assigned and filled by the end of March. All camps are required by the State of Virginia to be licensed daycare sites. As a part of the state licensure requirements, camp counselors are required to have eight hours of training and there must be a minimum ratio of one councilor for every 20 children in each camp program. Training is guided by an extraordinarily detailed, thorough and comprehensive 145 page *Camp Counselor Handbook*. Training topics include: program planning/camp themeing, licensing standards, administrative caring for children's health needs, safety/handling emergency situations, diversity/sensitivity training, communication with parents and time management, spotting child abuse and neglect. The quality of the camp training materials has been recognized nationally by peers. Camp training materials have been placed on CD-ROM and have been requested by several hundred park and recreation organizations throughout the U.S.

The Role of Evaluation

The SYCP's evolution and growth has been consistently guided by customer feedback and the FCPA's ability to act on that feedback to make improvements in the camp program. The Deputy Director noted: "This forces us to continually readjust and it ensures that the customer is the focus of everything we do." This process was started in 1992 and was stimulated by a suspicion that the camps were failing to retain a large proportion of repeat participants. The current customer satisfaction system used to manage camp quality is shown in Exhibit 17-1

Exhibit 17-1

FCPA Summer Camp Satisfaction System

It contains both customer listening posts and opportunities for staff feedback. These data are analyzed and then presented for discussion to all full-time programming staff who are involved with the development of the SYCP. Strengths and weaknesses of the camp program performance for that year are discussed, as are potential opportunities for improving and expanding the camp program for the upcoming year. Based on the information presented in this meeting and the subsequent discussion from program staff, the Youth Services Coordinator then develops the program and service strategy for the coming year.

Customer feedback is obtained from two sources. Information packets that are received by parents after they register for a summer camp contain a parent feedback form. Parents are advised that this form can be used to communicate "...comments, suggestions, compliments or concerns" while a camp is in session. This gives the Youth Services Coordinator an opportunity to hear, respond to and resolve parental concerns about camps while the programs are still in progress. Parent feedback comments that require a response are acted on within 24 hours of their receipt by the Youth Services Coordinator.

Customer surveys are administered at the end of every camp session throughout the summer. Several procedures have been used to distribute surveys over the years. In the early years, a sample of campers were mailed surveys and they were returned via postage paid envelopes included in the mailing. One follow-up attempt was made to non-respondents after one week. Response rates were high for this method (over 50%), but it was discontinued both to reduce costs and to find an alternative method that would provide more data to and, hence, allow more detailed levels of analysis. The next procedure that was attempted consisted of distributing questionnaires to all parents at the end of each camp session with no postage-paid return envelope. This procedure was certainly cost effective, but resulted in a low survey response rate (15%) and so also was discontinued. The current procedure still involves handing questionnaires to parents when they collect their children at the end of each camp session, but the postage-paid envelope feature has been re-established. An incentive of a drawing for a free camp session for the following year was also added to the procedure to encourage response. The incentive is substantive – several free camp sessions are given away at the end of the summer valued between $100 - $300 each. Adding an incentive to the survey distribution procedure has increased response rates to an acceptable level of 40 to 45%.

The standard survey questionnaire that is used is included as an Exhibit 17-2. At the core of the questionnaire are three components that are used to evaluate customer satisfaction.

- Overall ratings. These include overall satisfaction (the last item in #10), as well as perceptions of value (item #11) and two items (#12 and #13) that serve as surrogate measures of customer loyalty – the likelihood of future enrollment and the likelihood of recommending the camp to others.
- Evaluation of the camp on specific features (items #9 and #10).
- And written comments highlighting areas for improvement (#14).

Exhibit 17-2

The Survey Questionnaire

4. Was this the first year your child was enrolled in an FCPA summer camp?
   1 Yes 2 No

5. How did you find out about this camp?
   CHECK ALL THAT APPLY
   1 Parktakes
   2 Parent Resource Guide Magazine
   3 Connection Newspaper
   4 Journal Newspaper
   5 Other Newspaper
   6 Picked Up Info At Park
   7 Friend
   8 Other (Write-in)

---

6. Did you receive...
   A. a notice confirming enrollment?
   1 Yes 2 No 3 Don't know
   B. a calendar at the start of the sessions describing all activities your child would do during the camp session?
   1 Yes 2 No 3 Don't know
   C. Either oral or written feedback from your child's counselor during the camp session?
   1 Yes 2 No 3 Don't know

7. How important is receiving oral or written feedback about your child during the camp session?
   1 Essential feature of camp
   2 Not an essential feature of camp

8. Did you use extended care service for this camp?
   1 Yes 2 No

Please rate the following features on this summer camp using the scale below. Put the number in the space provided or mark an "X" next to any aspect of the service.that was not experienced either by you or your child.

Not at all Satisfied 1__2__3__4__5__6__7__ Completely Satisfied

9. First, your ratings for aspects of service that occurred before the start of camp....
   Place yourRating Here
   __ Usefulness of camp descriptions in Parktakes
   __ Convenience of the registration process
   __ Variety of camps to choose from
   __ Variety of locations offered for different camps
   __ Staff's ability to answer my questions
   __ Prompt answers to my questions

10. Next, rate the features of the camp...
    Place yourRating Here
    __ Variety of activities
    __ Activities appropriate for child's age
    __ Cleanliness/appearance of camp facility
    __ Ratio of counselors to children
    __ Teaching ability of counselors
    __ Counselors' ability of get along well with children
    __ Counselors' enthusiasm
    __ Overall satisfaction with child's counselors
    __ Safety of camp environment
    __ Procedures for picking up children at end of day
    __ Staff's communication with parent/guardian
    __ Extended care
    __ OVERALL CAMP RATING

11. Considering your child's experience with this camp, how would you rate the value that you got for the money? The value of this camp was
    1 Excellent 3 Fair
    2 Good 4 Poor

12. How likely is it that you will enroll your child in the FCPA summer camp program next year?
    1 Very Likely
    2 Somewhat Likely
    3 Not Likely

13. How likely would you be to recommend this camp to a friend who is looking for such a program?
    1 Very Likely
    2 Somewhat Likely
    3 Not Likely

14. Any additional comments to help us improve service in the areas you rated in question 10? (We are particularly interested in your comments about areas in which you were not COMPLETELY satisfied.)

Please Continue

The overall ratings – especially overall satisfaction – serve as the principal barometer of customer satisfaction with the summer camp program. These measures are monitored over time (between sessions and from one year to the next) to determine whether customer satisfaction with the camp program is stable, improving or declining over time. The overall measures are not sufficient in and of themselves, however. They indicate how customers perceive the program, but do not generally indicate why they feel as they do. This is the function of the more detailed feature ratings, which are used as diagnostic clues to uncover why overall perceptions are what they are. Written comments – much like those received on the parent feedback form – are then used to provide real world examples of strengths or weaknesses shown by the numerical ratings.

Typically the survey contains several other questions that vary from one year to the next depending on specific information needs in a particular year. One additional survey question that is a constant fixture is an item that asks parents to indicate whether this is the first year their child has been enrolled in an FCPA camp. First time and repeat enrollment are tracked over time as a measure of program maturity.

Completed surveys are returned first to the Youth Services Coordinator who is then able to respond immediately to resolve any site specific issues that are identified in any written comments. While not as timely as the parent feedback form, comments received on the surveys from early camp sessions can be used to resolve problems that improve staff performance later in the summer. Once the Youth Services Coordinator has reviewed the returned surveys for comments that require action, the questionnaires are forwarded to the FCPA's Market Research and Planning Section where the quantitative portions of the questionnaire are analyzed.

Lessons Learned

Park and recreation agencies and the communities they serve are highly variable. What is effective for one may not always be effective for another. Yet, there are several lessons learned from the FCPA experience in evaluating its summer camp program that may help other agencies seeking to improve their evaluation and continuous improvement processes.

1. *Use multiple listening posts to capture customer feedback and gauge customer satisfaction.* Employing more than one customer feedback mechanism has improved the robustness of customer feedback about camp performance that comes to the Youth Services Coordinator, allowing her to resolve problems at multiple points in the service cycle – while children are experiencing a camp, between camp sessions and from one summer's program to the next. It has also reinforced the notion among parents that the FCPA is responsive and actively seeks customer feedback to improve service delivery.

2. *How much satisfaction is enough? Hold a high standard.* Inexperienced users of satisfaction research are often perplexed by how to determine whether the ratings they receive from users indicate satisfaction with their programs or not. It is not uncommon for managers to overestimate the level of performance implied by ratings in the middle of a scale, for example, considering ratings of 5 or above on a 7-point scale to be "pretty good." The FCPA uses a 7-point scale to measure feature performance and overall satisfaction where 1 is 'not at all satisfied' and 7 is 'completely satisfied. Ratings are obtained on a 7-point rating scale in order to improve the explanatory power of the data. During analysis, however, a distinction is made between ratings of 6 or 7 and those of 5 or below. Satisfaction is defined as a rating of 6 or 7 as the FCPA's analysis over the years has consistently shown that these ratings are associated with higher rates of likely repeat enrollment in future camp programs, while ratings below 6 tend to be associated with rates of likely repeat purchase that are considerably lower. Therefore, analyses monitor the proportion of customers rating camps a 6 or 7 and consider anything below that indicative of unsatisfactory performance.
3. *Identify the key drivers of customer satisfaction.* Analysis has shown that not all aspects of summer camp service delivery contribute equally to overall customer satisfaction. This is not an uncommon occurrence in the management of services – whether public or private. The trick is to understand the degree to which various aspects of service delivery impact customer satisfaction as this has implications for prioritizing potential service quality improvements. Statistical analysis has revealed that the 17 individual features of summer camp service delivery that parents evaluate on the survey actually can be grouped into five more general dimensions of summer camp service delivery as shown in Exhibit 17-3. These are the aspects of service delivery that parents consider when evaluating their satisfaction with FCPA summer camps. Performance in all five of these areas influences perceptions of overall satisfaction with summer camps. That is, they are all drivers of customer satisfaction. However, analysis has shown that some of these aspects of service delivery are more influential satisfaction drivers than others. The most important drivers of the satisfaction with FCPA camps have consistently been staff performance and the activities/communication dimension. The other factors are still important, but have less impact on customers' bottom line judgements of service quality.

Because of its top billing as a driver of camp satisfaction, staff performance and development has received a considerable amount of attention in continuous improvement efforts over the years. Since the mid-1990s, numerous staff-related enhancements have been incorporated into the summer camp program in response to customer and staff feedback received from the camp satisfaction system. Examples include the following:

Exhibit 17-3

Drivers of FCPA Camp Satisfaction

HIGH

Influence on Overall Satisfaction

Camp Counselor Performance
Camp Activities & Communication With Parent
Customer Responsiveness
Registration Process & Camp Selection Process

LOW

1. The number of hours of training devoted to first year counselors was increased from 8 to 12 in response to survey feedback that indicated lower than average staff performance ratings in a Summer Fun Camp and Kiddie Camp-two introductory summer camp experiences that are frequently led by first year counselors.
2. The ratio of campers to counselors was reduced from 1:20 to 1:10 when survey ratings and comments indicated that parents felt their children were not receiving enough individual attention.
3. Communicating with parents and time management were added as standard training modules in response to data indicating that parents were not satisfied with the degree of communication they were receiving from counselors regarding their child's camp experiences and counselors felt they didn't have the basic skills necessary to juggle daily camp activities and contacts with parents at the same time. Over the past few years, the training curriculum has remained standard, but the degree of emphasis placed on one topic or another has varied based on the nature of parent and staff feedback received the previous year.
4. *Build relationships with parents.* One of the more surprising revelations of the FCPA summer camp survey over time has been the realization that providing quality service to parents is just as important as providing a satisfactory camp experience to their children. Early findings indicated that parents expected more communication from camp staff regarding what activities their child was doing in camp and how they were progressing. Parents wanted to feel more connected to their child's camp experience. And rather than being a time of pure diversion, parents expected that their child was "accomplishing" something. Through analysis, the FCPA discovered that evaluating camp activities and parental communication were related in parents' minds and formed the second most important driver of customer satisfaction with summer camps. The FCPA's initial response to its weakness

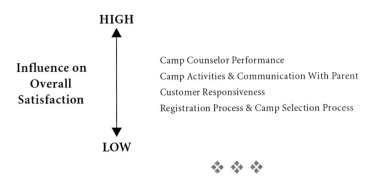

in this area was to include a camp activity calendar at the time of registration that described all of the activities included in the camp session. Subsequent communication ratings indicated that parents were looking for more. Later efforts evolved to the point that today's relationship building and communication efforts with parents include:

- a *pre-camp phone call* explaining what parents need to do to prepare their children for the first day of camp;
- a *follow-up telephone call* while camp is in session providing feedback about the child's activities and how they are assimilating into the camp routine;
- the *parent feedback form* provided in the materials received after registration that allows parents to communicate concerns about the camp if they desire;
- an *activity summary* provided at the end of the camp session, describing what the child accomplished.

The relationship building program now in place allows parents to feel more connected to their child's camp experience, provides an opportunity for two-way communication about service delivery between parents and staff, and gives the FCPA chances to communicate the value of its services to parents.

5. *Track first time and repeat enrollment.* In addition to the performance measures that were described above, the FCPA summer camp questionnaire also asks respondents whether they are first year or repeat summer camp customers. Experience has shown that first year customers, by nature, exhibit less program loyalty. As a group, they are less likely to recommend the program to others or say they will enroll again in the future. Therefore, the FCPA monitors first year customers in the survey analysis to identify any indicators of dissatisfaction that may be unique to them.

   The proportion of first year versus repeat use is also monitored for each camp type as a measure of program maturity. When a camp's percentage of first time use drops over time it is an indication that the program is in a mature stage of its life cycle and, therefore, susceptible to future declines in enrollment. At one point, the FCPA's core summer camp offerings – Summer Fun and Kiddie camps – showed drop-offs in the proportion of first time users, combined with lower than average activity variety scores compared with summer camps overall. The FCPA reacted on several fronts. First, the activities within these camps were re-tooled to improve activity interest and variation from what had been offered previously. A program development guide called "*Fun Camp Theme Days*" was developed containing over 370 activities and more than 20 camp themes. These camps now contain program themes and a customized set of activities that relate to the theme to complement and add interest to the general camp program. Sample themes include Wild, Wild West; Retromania; H2O Extravaganza; Island Shipwreck; Fitness Frenzy; Wacky Olympics and others. Camp counselors use the program development guide to select a theme and related activities prior to the start of camp. The Youth Services Coordinator observes, "themes have re-energized our core camp offerings by adding interest and excitement. They make camps fun!"

At the same time, a decision was made to diversify the summer camp program product line over several years as a growth strategy and to promote customer retention. Many children were attending multiple camp sessions throughout the summer – often experiencing the same camp over and over. The survey data and parent comments indicated that a significant number of children were becoming bored with the existing set of offerings or were just aging-out of the program (most offerings were targeted at children age 5 to 9). A multi-year program was set in place to expand the number of camp titles and to target camp expansion primary at an underserved target market (10 to 15 year olds) that demographic analysis showed would have a higher rate of growth in the near term than the existing core market of 9 and under. Most of the expansion occurred in single focus, specialty camps in sports (soccer, lacrosse, football, tennis, basketball, in-line hockey, etc.), adventure activities (mountain biking, skateboarding and in-line skating, kayaking, rock climbing) and performing arts. In order to facilitate the expansion, the Youth Services Coordinator sought out the use of outdoor park sites that had previously not been used for summer camps and contracted with private camp providers to obtain the needed expertise in specialty camp areas. Over the next four years, the number of camp titles in the product line grew 40% (contracted camps grew 150%), camp enrollment expanded by 48% and gross revenues grew by 56%.

6. *In monitoring satisfaction, couple front-line staff feedback with customer feedback.* The FCPA's camp satisfaction program includes a separate camp counselor evaluation at the end of every summer. At its essence, the staff evaluation asks counselors to provide suggestions for improving the program and also asks how the FCPA can improve counselor satisfaction with their jobs. "Since we know they are the number one driver of customer satisfaction, if staff's not happy, the kids aren't happy," says the FCPA's Youth Services Coordinator. Staff feedback engenders seasonal staff buy-in and loyalty, and helps to retain staff from one year to the next. Suggestions that have been implemented from this mechanism include minimizing the training time of returning staff relative to newcomers, providing step pay increases for each successive year of summer camp work, and providing a mid-summer tail gate party for camp counselors to allow them to share war stories and release tension.
7. *Anticipate that satisfaction ratings will vary over time and constantly search for variations in performance.* Because the core offering is essentially a human performance, camp programs like other services are subject to variability in service delivery and, therefore, variability in customer satisfaction levels. This is not unique to the recreation setting, but is true of all services. For example, airline industry satisfaction ratings reported in the American

Customer Satisfaction Index monitored by the University of Michigan varied 15% between 1995 and 2000 and long-distance telecommunications industry ratings fluctuated 7% over the same time period. Between 1995 and 1997 FCPA summer camp satisfaction ratings declined about 8%, before rebounding. The decline occurred despite setting in place several strategies it was felt would improve satisfaction. The culprit turned out to be aggressive expansion in the number of camps offered, which made it difficult for the Youth Services Coordinator to monitor the quality of service delivery in individual camps as closely as she had previously. It was at this point that survey data started to be scrutinized more closely for variations in ratings that would indicate satisfaction 'hot spots.' Standard procedure now is to analyze and compare ratings in the following ways:

- in-house camps versus contracted camps;
- site-by-site comparisons; and
- comparisons by camp title.

The ultimate objective is to decrease the amount of service variability in the camp program over time by improving the performance of camps exhibiting low satisfaction ratings. The process for doing this starts with making the satisfaction rating comparison shown above and identifing below-average performers. Best practice camps – those with above average satisfaction ratings – are identified at the same time. Feature ratings and written comments for the below-average performers are then analyzed for contributing factors. The quantitative data is shared at the camp program summit in the fall. Programmers then discuss what they feel are the differences between best practice and below average performers, relying on the quantitative data and their own observations to develop improvement strategies for camps that reported below average satisfaction ratings. The FCPA feels this approach is crucial to the successful application of customer satisfaction data in program management. Rather than presenting survey results in a punitive way and dictating actions for improvement, the data are presented as a diagnostic tool that staff can meld with its own observations and experience to devise actions for continuously improving camp service delivery over time. This approach has engendered a sense of support and commitment among staff to a process of continuous improvement for FCPA summer camps.

Sources

Nick Duray, Marketing Research and Planning Manager, Fairfax County Park Authority

Ellen Greenberg, Youth Services Coordinator, Fairfax County Park Authority.

Mike Kane, Deputy Director, Fairfax County Park Authority

CHAPTER 18

ACTIVITIES IN MOTION (AIM):
A YOUTH PARTICIPATION INCENTIVE PROGRAM

Activities in Motion (AIM) is a year-round program designed for and with teens to enable them to find out about, and be involved in, recreation activities, community service, and other growth and learning opportunities. Participants earn points for engaging in activities. Earned points are redeemable to offset costs of participating in field trips or other activities. Using incentives is a way to encourage teens to become aware of and access existing opportunities.

AIM evolved from an Arlington County (Virginia) Department of Parks, Recreation and Community Resources (DPRCR) initiative. In the summer of 2000, teen programmers in the DPRCR designed and implemented Mission Impossible Teens (MIT). The purpose of the initiative was to provide greater opportunities for teens from various parts of the county to meet and engage in activities together, and for staff to design and implement programs so they are better integrated. Teen programmers from various units in the Recreation Division of DPRCR met to discuss programming and ways to increase teen involvement as participants and/or leaders in year-round programs. The meeting was initiated by DPRCR's Office for Teenagers and teen programmers from the four recreation neighborhood service areas.

The group determined that there was little opportunity for teens to be involved in county-wide activities and no initiative to motivate teens to participate or assist with planning and implementation of year-round programming. The MIT format involved teens being able to earn points through participation in various special events identified as "Missions" including an Olympic Challenge, Battle of the Bands, Hoop It Up and Leadership Retreat. The points would be used to defray the costs of a day trip to Virginia Beach. Teens could also earn points through participation in "Bonus Missions," including car washes, neighborhood teen programs (drop-in programs at DPRCR's recreation centers), the Volunteer Internship Program (a two week service and leadership development camp designed to enhance teens' leadership skills and put these skills to use through program facilitation with younger children during the second week of the camp), or Teen Options (a drop-in program at a county-wide recreation facility). Participants earned 25 points for attending each of the first three missions, 50 points for volunteering to assist in staffing a mission, and 100 points for participating in the Leadership Retreat. Bonus mission participants earned 75 points for car washes, 25 for neighborhood teen programs and 10 for Teen Options. For those who earned 400 or more points, $20 was subtracted from the cost of the Virginia Beach trip. Those with 300-399 points subtracted $15.00; 200 –299 points $10; and 100-199 points $5.

One hundred-sixty (160) teens registered for MIT during the summer. Seventy participated in the beach trip. Twenty-five percent (25%) redeemed $5 in points,

50% of the participants redeemed $10 in points, 20% of the participants redeemed $15 in points, and 5% of the participants redeemed $20 in points. Ninety teens did not participate in the trip, but participated in at least one mission or bonus mission activities.

The MIT initiative responded to one of the three goals of the Arlington Partnership for Children, Youth, and Families, a county-wide effort to bring together agencies and community representatives to develop an agenda for meeting the needs of Arlington County's youth. The partnership's goals were to (i) provide a wide range of opportunities for youth, (ii) ensure school success and (iii) provide access to health and mental health services. The required coordination and regular communication between neighborhood recreation staff and other youth service providers was consistent with the Department's efforts to become an asset building organization, in conjunction with Benefits Based Programming. For example, the Therapeutic Recreation Prevention Intervention Unit has a Juvenile Justice Title V grant for Bullying Prevention and Reduction that is based on the asset framework. The Rites of Passage program (designed to help teens make the transition to adulthood) also uses the assets framework. All summer programs have goals, objectives and expected outcomes that support the asset philosophy.

Development of AIM

As a result of the success of the summer MIT initiative, a workgroup was created to look at issues of coordination, motivation and participation on a year-round basis. The workgroup was made up of several DPRCR staff (Teen Specialist, Teen Programmers, Community Services Supervisor), and representatives from the American Red Cross, 4-H, Arlington Housing Corporation, Arlington Community Action Program, Virginia Cooperative Extension and a community member. Other organizations subsequently joined the initiative including Arlington County Libraries, Arlington Police Department and Arlington, Public Schools. The work group created AIM, a year-round incentive-based program.

Teens were involved in evaluating the MIT concept as well as its point system and missions. Several focus groups were held with county-wide and neighborhood teen clubs regarding motivation and participation. Teen club and county-wide teen council representatives provided input regarding program design and implementation.

Teen clubs have been organized at each middle school. The clubs meet each week and participants take part in leadership development activities and make plans for other activities in which they want to participate. A departmental teen staff member serves as leader for each club. One of the goals of the clubs is to groom middle students to become members of the teen council when they reach high school. The council has 15 members and is also focused on leadership development. Members help plan teen activities and recruit other teens to provide input or assistance. Council members are also called upon to provide input to DPRCR staff and community groups concerning teen issues and needed services.

AIM's goal is to provide Arlington teens with positive alternatives that will assist them in making healthy life choices. AIM provides a means for young people in middle and high school to earn points through their participation in education, skill development, service, leadership, arts and cultural activities. AIM activities are based on selected elements of the Search Institute's Developmental Assets Model. Currently, points can be redeemed only for asset-building opportunities offered by the DPRCR and the American Red Cross (e.g., AIM members participate in the Red Cross baby sitting classes at a reduced price). However, other partners are being sought who would be willing to redeem AIM points in lieu of some proportion of fees for activities. The objectives of AIM are to:

- increase awareness of and access to existing opportunities by identifying enriching and age-appropriate programs and promoting alternative forms of transportation and assistance;
- increase teen participation in citizenship, cultural and educational activities;
- increase interaction and socialization among peers, family and adults by fostering environments to build relationships; and
- develop a consistent mode of communication by the creation of a youth service provider network.

The AIM workgroup is responsible for:

- implementing needs assessments and evaluations (both surveys and interviews), including identification of recommendations and options based on documentation, feedback and data;
- devising strategies to increase youth participation and coordination of activities;
- strengthening communication and coordination of neighborhood and division-wide programs and services to decrease duplication and maximize resources;
- designing, updating and implementing AIM operational procedures and developing an operations manual (in process);
- coordinating and staffing AIM events;
- serving as school representatives to develop and maintain relationships with teens;
- developing means to create an image for the teen programs such as using common language and logo on all teen fliers; and
- serving as a forum for dialogue about asset building, after school activities, information sharing and creating other opportunities and resources to engage youth (e.g., Recreation Days, AIM events, Teen Council, Teen Review – a teen staffed newsletter, etc).

School Visits

Representatives from the AIM workgroup bi-weekly visit five middle schools, one combined middle and high school, and three high schools in the county to recruit and register teens for AIM. They also distribute activity verification forms, membership cards, collect a $1 registration fee, and share information on activities and opportunities to redeem points.

Participants earn points through their regular, positive involvement in designated activities. To be credited with points, teens submit an activity verification form as proof of participation. On the form, students supply information about their activity involvements and the club leader, event organizer or activity coordinator signs to verify that participation has taken place. The completed form is submitted to the AIM school representative who stamps the participant's membership card with the AIM logo for each point earned. Teens present their stamped card at events to redeem their points and a hole is punched through the membership card for each point used.

Teens earn one point per activity with the exception of grades and community service, where one point is earned for every two hours of community service (maximum of eight hours or four points), and one point is earned for every grade of A or B, and every improved grade of C or higher (maximum of four points). A participant may earn ten points in each of three categories with a maximum of thirty points per session. There are three point-earning sessions per year (January-June, June-September, October-January).

The three activity categories are:

- AIMING UP, which focuses on education and skill development activities such as making the honor roll, grade improvement, college preparation, skill development or career seminars
- AIMING OUT, which focuses on citizenship/leadership activities such as school clubs, leadership/youth groups, organized sports, service projects and volunteering.
- AIMING AROUND, which focuses on arts and cultural awareness activities such as ethnic festivals, theatrical productions, Rites of Passage, cultural programs and art exhibitions.

Event and activity fees are reduced based on the number of points earned (one point = $1 in reduced fees). Points are not redeemable for cash. For example, a trip to Six Flags, which normally would cost $25, would be reduced to $10 in exchange for 15 points. The department subsidizes rewards through the general budget and fundraisers. Approximately $2000 was subsidized during the initial year and is likely to double as the program expands.

Currently, there are 250 teens registered in AIM, with the majority being in middle school. High school students seem to be more involved in employment, exercising driving privileges and traveling outside the county. To date, teens have engaged in the following AIM point earning and redeeming activities: Kickoff party, Summer Olympics, Battle of the Bands, Success Retreat, field trips and fundraisers.

As part of the AIM project, DPRCR has also funded a shuttle program that brings AIM members from three of the middle schools to county-wide recreation facilities. Transportation was cited as a major barrier to participation by many of the middle school students.

Exhibit 18-1

AIM Point Earning Opportunities

	Aiming Up	Aiming Out	Aiming Around
Focus	Education and skill development activities (I am successful)	Citizenship/leadership activities (I am giving to my community)	Arts and cultural awareness activities (I am broadenting my horizons)
Activity Types	Honor roll Grade improvement College preparation Skill development Career seminars	School clubs Leadership/youth groups Organized sports Service projects Volunteering	Ethnic festivals Theatrical productions Rites of Passage Cultural programs Art exhibitions
Upcoming Events	College tour Camping/horseback riding Health, safety disaster classes Artswork job training program	Teen Council (meets weekly) Red Cross National Youth Service Day Community Car Wash State Golden Gloves Boxing competition Columbia Heights West Pride	Art series Kennedy Center performances Poetry reading Artswork job training program Salsa dancing

Future Plans

Plans for the future include

- increasing the frequency and amount of communication in schools, with other county departments and services (e.g., Human Services, Court Services, Fire Department), and with community non-profits and businesses;
- increasing teen involvement in program design and direction (e.g., additional input from Teen Clubs and Councils);
- continuing evaluation of program design;
- incorporating tenets of the bullying prevention and reduction program into AIM activities. (Parks and Recreation staff in Arlington County in collaboration with Arlington Public Schools, Department of Human Services and Juvenile Courts implement the Positive Attitudes in Learning and Leisure [PALL] project. This program is implemented at one school site and four after-school programs serving elementary children. PALL focuses on promoting healthy and constructive ways to socially interact and maintain friendships. Opportunities are provided to develop skills and strategies to effectively prevent bullying behavior and encourage healthy attitudes that promote positive interactions).
- developing a comprehensive marketing and community outreach plan involving the use of technology, activity fairs and resource centers and hosting talent showcase events;

- implementing an awareness campaign on transportation and access. For example, DPRCR and the Commuter Assistance Program sponsored by the county have co-designed and proposed a summer discount program that would allow AIM members to visit commuter stores and purchase bus and rail passes at discounted rates. Students will show their AIM cards at commuter stores or the Mobile Commuter store. Commuter assistance will offer teens up to $20 (retail value) in both Metrorail and Metrobus/ ART purchases per month. A brochure is being developed to provide information about places teens might go using the available transportation.
- Developing a youth employment program as part of AIM. The goal is to employ young people to work at community centers and departmental offices, expand the roles and responsibilities teens currently undertake and provide useful roles in the community. This effort will help to build linkages with neighborhoods to allow a greater flow of information between community youth and teen programmers. This also will assist in the integration of the Community Recreation Division and ultimately include the Administrative Unit, Parks and Natural Resources, Planning and Design, Cultural Affairs, Sports, Planning and Design and Special Programs Unit of DPRCR.

Lessons Learned

Developing partnerships and collaborations requires patience and commitment. Weaving together different service philosophies and structure agreements about who will do what to achieve objectives takes time and effort. Initially, time must be spent in dialogue about philosophy, framework, mission commonalties and differences, agency commitments, resource availability, priorities and agreements. A significant amount of this effort is about relationship building and resulting conflicts.

Critical outcomes of these discussions are development of short and long-term blueprints for the overall program, projections of number of participants, and creation of a budget. In the current case, the program's success has exceeded expectations of the planners, thus straining resources. More assessment of interest and specification of the program at the outset might have avoided some of these issues.

Sources

Kelli Beavers, Teen Specialist, Office of Teenagers, Arlington County, VA Department of Parks, Recreation and Community Resources.

Beth Zeidman, Community Services Supervisor, Arlington County, VA Department of Parks, Recreation and Community Resources.

Designed & Printed by
Murray-McCaul
301-572-2512
nancy.e.murray@verizon.net